HUMAN RIGHTS IN THE WORLD

An introduction to the study of the international protection of human rights

Third edition

by

A. H. ROBERTSON
B.C.L., S.J.D.
former *Professeur Associé*, University of Paris I
former Simon Visiting Professor at the University of Manchester
former Director of Human Rights, Council of Europe

and

J. G. MERRILLS
B.C.L., M.A.
Professor of Public International Law
at the University of Sheffield

MANCHESTER UNIVERSITY PRESS
Manchester and New York
Distributed exclusively in the USA and Canada by St. Martin's Press

Published by
Manchester University Press
Oxford Road, Manchester M13 9PL, UK
and Room 400, 175 Fifth Avenue,
New York, NY 10010, USA

Distributed exclusively in the USA and Canada
by St. Martin's Press Inc., 175 Fifth Avenue,
New York, NY 10010, USA

Reprinted with minor revisions 1992

British Library cataloguing in publication data
Robertson, A. H. (Arthur Henry), 1913–1984
Human rights in the world: an introduction to the study of the international protection of human rights.—3rd ed.
1. Human rights. International legal aspects
I. Title II. Merrills, J. G. (John Graham), 1942–
341.4′81

Library of Congress cataloging in publication data
Robertson, A. H. (Arthur Henry), 1913–
Human rights in the world: an introduction to the study of the international protection of human rights / by A. H. Robertson and J. G. Merrills.—3rd ed.
p. cm.
Includes bibliographical references.
ISBN 0–7190–2278–9
1. Human rights. I. Merrills, J. G. II. Title.
K3240.4.R6 1989
341.4′81—dc20 89–36489

ISBN 0 7190 2278 9 *hardback*
ISBN 0 7190 3886 3 *paperback*

Typeset by J&L Composition Ltd, Filey, North Yorkshire

Printed in Great Britain by Biddles Ltd

Contents

Preface

Between the first edition of this book in 1972 and the second, ten years later, the importance of human rights in international affairs increased immeasurably. The United Nations Covenants of 1966 came into force; the Helsinki Agreement on Security and Co-operation in Europe was concluded; the American Court of Human Rights was set up and the case law of the European Commission and Court of Human Rights underwent a rapid and dramatic development. In the period since 1982 these advances have been consolidated and extended and progress has been made on a number of other fronts. The African Charter on Human and Peoples' Rights has come into force; States' obligations under the Covenants are now monitored by the Human Rights Committee, the Commission on Human Rights and the newly created Committee on Economic and Social Rights; the Helsinki process has received fresh impetus with the conclusion in January 1989 of the latest review conference; the American Court and Commission have both been active; the jurisprudence of the Strasbourg organs has continued to develop and several important treaties have been concluded, including three conventions on the subject of torture.

In this new edition I have attempted to describe and analyse these and other developments, while retaining the clear and concise outline of the legal background which was a feature of the late Dr Robertson's work. My revision is based on material which was available in December 1988, although it has been possible to refer to developments beyond that date in one or two cases. In the few places where I found that my views on a particular issue differed from those of Dr Robertson I have modified the earlier text to achieve consistency. A number of stylistic changes have been made for the same reason and the last chapter, which offers some general reflections on the state of human rights law, is entirely new.

Two points relating to what this book is and, no less important, what it is not, should perhaps also be mentioned. A reader who expects to find here an exhaustive account of every human rights treaty, a comprehensive list of every case decided by this or that tribunal, or a detailed analysis of every institution or procedure, will be disappointed. As its sub-title indicates, the book is an introduction and is intended to complement more specialised studies. Secondly, the book is an account of human rights law, not a study of the domestic practice of States. The difference between what governments say and what they do is, of course, particularly marked in the field of human rights and cannot be overlooked. We have taken account of this discrepancy, not by repeating the work of those who have already catalogued the many abuses of human rights in the world today, but by explaining how the formulation, the application and the enforcement of human rights law must be seen in a political, as well as a moral, context.

My thanks are due to the secretarial staff of the Law Faculty and particularly to Mrs Margaret Keys for preparing an immaculate manuscript and to my wife, whose advice on matters stylistic and pragmatic was, as always, invaluable.

J. G. Merrills
Sheffield
April 1989

CHAPTER 1

International concern with human rights

I. The idea of international human rights

One of the most striking developments in international law since the end of the Second World War has been a concern with the protection of human rights. This development is the reflection of a wider phenomenon: the increased concern of people all over the world with the treatment accorded to their fellow human beings in other countries, particularly when that treatment fails to come up to minimum standards of civilised behaviour. Legal rules are a reflection of social standards and the current interest in the international protection of human rights is the result of a profound change in individual and governmental attitudes. The first half of the nineteenth century saw a similar development when the abhorrence of slavery led to the acceptance of legal rules prohibiting the slave trade and then the institution of slavery itself. In the second half of the twentieth century we are witnessing the development of international legal rules prohibiting many other forms of cruel or oppressive behaviour. Genocide is a prominent example. Others are arbitrary arrest, detention without trial, political executions and torture. The fact that violations of human rights continue to occur does not mean that attempts to prevent them by international action are pointless – any more than the existence of crime at the national level disproves the value of criminal law. Widespread violations of human rights show that the attempts to provide international protection are not as effective as they ought to be and that a great deal remains to be done to improve the existing international procedures. But in order to improve them we need to know what they are and how they function. That is what this book is about.

The protection of human rights through international action is a revolutionary idea and traditional international law had no place for it at all. Thus Oppenheim, the leading authority on international law in the United Kingdom at the beginning of this century wrote that the 'so-called rights of man' not only do not but cannot enjoy any protection under international law, because that law is concerned solely with the relations between States and cannot confer rights on individuals.[1] It was therefore the accepted doctrine that relations between individuals and the States of which they were nationals were governed only by the national law of those States, as a matter exclusively within their domestic jurisdiction. To move from this attitude to a position in which the fundamental rights of the individual are a matter of international law, with international remedies available if those standards are not respected, is clearly a major step. It is not surprising if such a change takes time. We are at present in the middle of this process of transformation and, as we shall see, many governments seek to shelter behind the old view of international law and hide their actions behind the cloak of national sovereignty. But such regressive policies cannot alter the fact that today the protection of human rights has a place in international law which it never occupied in earlier times and there is widespread recognition of the need to render the system of international protection more effective.

A realistic view involves recognising that there are more countries in the world today where fundamental rights and civil liberties are regularly violated than countries where they are effectively protected. Amnesty International recently pointed out that more than eighty countries hold political prisoners and that the systematic use of torture and execution is also widespread.[2] In contrast, the principles of liberal democracy, with its respect for fundamental rights, are observed in fewer than thirty countries today. However, something is changing in the world: international opinion, as expressed in the United Nations and elsewhere; national opinion in many countries; and, for innumerable people throughout the world, individual opinion.

Non-governmental groups such as Amnesty International, the International Commission of Jurists, the International League for the Rights of Man and, in the educational field, the International Institute of Human Rights are tireless in their work and increasingly numerous and influential. All this has produced a new awareness of human rights. Not everywhere, to be sure, but certainly enough to put the matter firmly on the international agenda. So attitudes on this issue have changed in the last fifty years and will change further in the years to come. In the pages which follow we shall see how this concern for human rights is now being reflected in the institutions and principles of international law.

II. Different cultures and their approach to human rights

1. The liberal tradition of the Western democracies

When we consider the philosophical foundations of the concept of human rights, it is clear that the main stream has its origins in the liberal democratic tradition of Western Europe – a tradition which is itself the product of Greek philosophy, Roman law, the Judaeo–Christian tradition, the Humanism of the Reformation and the Age of Reason.[3] It is the parliamentary democracies of Western Europe which are the direct heirs of this tradition. Other countries which have inherited this political philosophy have carried the tradition to other parts of the world. Others in turn have absorbed some of it – but to varying degrees and incompletely.

A detailed formulation of that philosophy as applied to the specific problem of human rights may be found in the French Declaration of the Rights of Man and the Citizen of 1789 and particularly in its second article: 'The aim of all political association is the conservation of the natural and inalienable rights of man. These rights are: liberty, property, security and resistance to oppression.' The Declaration does not discuss why these rights are 'natural' and 'inalienable' (in French: '*imprescriptibles*'). No doubt its authors would have considered that to be self-evident. Many believed that they can be deduced from the nature of man as a sentient and intelligent being; others, following Aristotle, from his nature as a political animal; yet others, drawing inspiration from the Bible, from the nature of man created by the Almighty in his own image. The doctrine of natural law, holding that there are laws of nature or laws of God above and beyond positive law edicted by man, also contributed to this belief. It is interesting incidentally that this belief in natural law as the basis of certain rights and duties finds expression in the twentieth century in the Constitution of Ireland of 1937, which recognises the family as 'a moral institution possessing inalienable and imprescriptible rights, antecedent and superior to all positive law'. It also acknowledges that man 'has the natural right, antecedent to positive law, to the private ownership of external goods'.

The French Declaration proclaimed a number of entitlements which are now generally called civil and political rights: the basic principle that all men are born and remain free and equal in their rights; also particular rights, including equality before the law, freedom from arrest except in conformity with the law, the presumption of innocence, protection against retroactivity of the law, freedom of opinion, freedom of expression and the well known definition of liberty as freedom to do anything which is not harmful to others. The Declaration and the philosophy which it enshrined inspired liberals and romantics all over Europe and led the poet Wordsworth to write the famous lines:

> Bliss was it in that dawn to be alive,
> But to be young were very heaven.

Its political impact on the French nation and on other peoples struggling against authoritarian governments was such that Lord Acton, the historian, described it as 'a single confused page . . . that outweighed libraries and was stronger than all the armies of Napoleon'. Its perpetual resonance is indicated by the fact that one of the French political parties in 1977 reprinted the Declaration of 1789 and distributed it all over France.

But if the French Declaration of 1789 constituted the proclamation of rights which is the most widely known and the most far-reaching in its consequences on the continent of Europe, other historic texts fulfilled a similar role elsewhere. In England, Magna Carta of 1215 guaranteed to the citizen freedom from imprisonment or from dispossession of his property and freedom from prosecution or exile 'unless by the lawful judgment of his peers or by the law of the land'. It also included a primitive formulation of the right to a fair trial in the famous words 'To none will we sell, deny or delay right of justice'. These and other provisions of the charter were of such importance that it was confirmed and reissued no fewer than thirty-eight times by later sovereigns in succeeding centuries. The civil war and the peaceful revolution of the seventeenth century led to the Habeas Corpus Acts and the Bill of Rights of 1689 (just a century before the French Declaration) which assured the supremacy of Parliament, the right to free elections, freedom of speech, the right to bail, freedom from cruel and unusual punishments and the right to trial by jury. The independence of the judiciary and freedom of the press were established shortly thereafter; and the philosopher John Locke devised a seminal political theory to sustain constitutional arrangements which had developed in a pragmatic fashion. He held that sovereignty pertains not to the monarch but to the people as a whole, and that government is an instrument for securing the lives, the property and the well-being of the governed without enslaving them in any way. 'Government is not their master; it is created by the people voluntarily and maintained by them to secure their own good.' The individual conveys to society his own right to exercise certain functions; all other natural rights he retains. The theory of reserved natural rights is the basis of the maintenance of fundamental liberties; they belong to the individual by nature, have not been surrendered to the community and therefore cannot be limited or denied by the State.

This political philosophy was inherited by the colonists in North America. Their most eloquent spokesman was Thomas Jefferson, who had studied Locke and Montesquieu, and asserted that the Americans were a 'free people claiming their rights as derived from the laws of nature and not as the gift of their Chief Magistrate'. The first Continental Congress in its Declaration of Rights of 14 October 1774 considered 'the immutable laws of nature' as the principal source from which the colonies derived their rights. It is therefore not surprising that when Jefferson came to draft the Declaration of Independence in the summer of 1776 he referred to the necessity for a people 'to assume among the powers of the Earth the separate and equal station to which the Laws of Nature and of Nature's God entitled them'. This leads on directly to the belief in natural rights expressed in the second sentence: 'We hold these truths to be self-evident, that all men are created equal, that they are endowed by their Creator with certain unalienable rights, that among these are life, liberty and the pursuit of happiness.' This has much in common with the second article of the French Declaration quoted earlier, particularly the idea that the rights of man are 'natural and inalienable'. It will be observed, however, that Jefferson selects as the three cardinal rights life, liberty and the pursuit of happiness, whereas the French Declaration chooses liberty, property and security. However, 'resistance to oppression', which also comes in the second article of the French Declaration, follows in the next paragraph of the Declaration of Independence. Immediately after the reference to the three cardinal rights we read: 'that to secure these rights Governments are instituted among men, deriving their just powers from the consent of the governed; that whenever any form of government becomes destructive of these ends, it is the right of the people to alter or abolish it . . .'. The voice of Locke is thus unmistakable.

It is evident, then, that there is much in common between the two Declarations. Indeed, the demonstration could be carried further, because the American text refers to a number of other fundamental rights – not so much by proclaiming them as such as by complaining of their violation: independence of the judiciary, subordination of the military to the civil power, freedom of trade, freedom from taxation without consent, and the right to trial by jury. When to these are added equality before the law, and the rights to life, liberty and the pursuit of happiness, we have an extensive catalogue. But the Declaration, important as it was, did not form part of the positive law of the infant republic. It was not made part of the federal constitution drafted in 1787, and which was criticised for not including a statement of fundamental rights. Two years later, therefore, twelve amendments to the Constitution were drafted by the first Congress in New York and approved on 25 September 1789 – just a month after the French Declaration. When ten were ratified by the states, they entered into force in 1791. They are generally known as the Bill of Rights and include the more important civil and political rights.

The fact that there is much in common – as regards the content, though not the drafting – between the American texts and the French Declaration need not surprise us. On both sides of the Atlantic the objective was the same: to protect the citizen against arbitrary power and establish the rule of law. The French philosophers, including both Montesquieu and Rousseau, were studied in the Americas. Fifty years earlier Voltaire in his *Lettres philosophiques* had studied and described the English constitutional arrangements resulting from the peaceful revolution and the Act of Settlement. Lafayette was a member of the drafting committee of the Constituent Assembly which produced the French Declaration and submitted to it his own draft based on the

Declaration of Independence and the Virginia Bill of Rights. The *rapporteur* of the Constitutional Commission proposed 'transplanting to France the noble idea conceived in North America' and Jefferson himself was present in Paris in 1789, having succeeded Benjamin Franklin as American Minister to France.

We therefore find in 1789 two parallel and broadly similar currents, the American and the French – the former largely inspired by English doctrines on the liberty of the subject – which together go to make up the main stream of the philosophical and historical foundation for the modern idea of human rights, and there were, of course, similar developments in other European countries. And it is the same main stream which, after the horrors of the Second World War, found expression in the Universal Declaration of Human Rights of 1948. Appropriately, it may be thought, the chairman of the Human Rights Commission which drafted it was an American, Mrs Eleanor Roosevelt, while one of the principal authors was a Frenchman, M. René Cassin, and one of the most important documents considered by the Commission was the draft presented by the United Kingdom. Thus the Universal Declaration, accepted, as it was, without a dissentient vote, and with few abstentions, by all States members of the United Nations at that time, is a clear expression of the concept of human rights which evolved from the political and philsophical thinking outlined above. It is the human rights conception of one political culture, that of the parliamentary democracies.

2. *The universal tradition*

But there are other streams of thought and other cultures.

At the International Conference on Human Rights in Tehran, in 1968, the Shah of Iran noted in his opening address that the precursor of the celebrated documents recognising the rights of man was promulgated in his country by Cyrus the Great about 2,000 years earlier.[4] Christian Daubie has recounted the magnanimity and clemency of Cyrus to subject peoples – in marked contrast to the practice of earlier conquerors – and particularly his respect for their religion. The author deduced from the ' Charter of Cyrus' the recognition and protection of what we now call the rights to liberty and security, freedom of movement, the right of property, and even certain economic and social rights.[5]

Cyrus was not the only ruler to manifest such sentiments. Ambassador Polys Modinos in '*La Charte de la Liberté de l'Europe*' quotes one of the Pharoahs of ancient Egypt giving instructions to his Vizirs to the effect that 'When a petitioner arrives from Upper or Lower Egypt ... Make sure that all is done according to the law, that custom is observed and the right of each man respected'. He goes on to cite the Code of Hammourabi, King of Babylon 2,000 years before Christ, in which the monarch records his mission 'to make justice reign in the kingdom, to destroy the wicked and the violent, to prevent the strong from oppressing the weak ... to enlighten the country and promote the good of the people'.[6] Elsewhere the same author recalls that the essential problem of Sophocles' Antigone is the perennial conflict between the positive law of the sovereign maintaining order in his country and the unwritten law of the gods or of nature which commands respect for the dead and love of a brother.

The number of cultures which have made a contribution to the elaboration and dissemination of the rights of man is very large. In International Human Rights Year in 1968 UNESCO published a collection of texts gleaned from different cultural traditions and periods of history which tried to show the universality of the notion of individual rights or, as the title puts it, *The Birthright of Man*. Now there is a certain risk in removing texts from their cultural context. It is not just time which separates the outlook of a Pharaoh from that of a twentieth century democrat. But although it is necessary to guard against the shallow and unhistorical view that at root human societies have always subscribed to similar values, it is equally clear that the moral worth of the individual is an idea which no culture can claim as uniquely its own.

The idea of individual worth can be found in the work of sages, philosophers, prophets and poets from different countries and many faiths in all continents, including India, China, Japan, Persia, Russia, Turkey, Egypt, Israel, several countries of black Africa and the pre-Columbian civilisations of South America. It is apparent, therefore, that the premise for human rights has been cherished through the centuries in many lands. The struggle for human rights is as old as history itself, because it concerns the need to protect the individual against the abuse of power by the monarch, the tyrant or the State. If we have referred above to a mainstream manifested in the political traditions of the parliamentary democracies of Western

Europe, this is not because they have any monopoly of the subject, it is rather because they have produced its best-known formulations and instituted the most effective systems of implementation – both nationally and internationally.

This leads on naturally to a further question: Are human rights relevant only to a particular type of culture? This question concerns not the formulation of texts, but the more fundamental problem whether the need and the desire to protect such rights are more characteristic of certain political systems than of others. The question is worth considering because it is sometimes suggested that the rights proclaimed in the historic texts mentioned earlier, and the majority of the rights proclaimed in the Universal Declaration, are the product of a bourgeois or capitalist society with little or no applicability in socialist States based on Marxist principles. Alternatively, the argument is that rights which are considered important in industrially developed countries are relatively unimportant in developing countries or, if their value is admitted, that they are luxuries which the people of the Third World cannot afford.

3. The socialist concept

Some years ago Dr Imre Szabo and other members of the Hungarian Academy of Sciences explained the 'Socialist Concept of Human Rights'; other writers have done so more recently.[7] It is beyond the scope of this chapter to analyse this concept in any detail, but we must note that what these writers are describing is essentially a different culture with a fundamentally different approach to the philosophy of human rights. The point of departure is of course Marxist. Socialist theory 'rejects the natural-law origin of citizens' rights and is unwilling to deduce them from either the nature of man or from the human mind'. Equally, it rejects the idea that citizens' rights reflect the relationship between man and society or between an abstract 'man' and the State. The basis is rather society organised in a State; 'these rights should reflect the relationship between the state and its citizens'. This relationship in a socialist society is very different from that under bourgeois conditions and 'is tied up with the fact that the production and distribution process ... are owned by the state, and the socialist state is in charge of organising the national economy'.

'As national economy in a socialist economy becomes state-run, this creates the conditions for uniformly securing citizens' rights as state rights.' The State 'has to give expression to the class-will, the will of the working class, which will is ultimately determined by the socialist production relations'.

This emphasis on the primordial role of the State – which itself is seen as the guardian or incarnation of the interests of the workers – places human rights in an entirely different light from that in which they are perceived in the Western democracies. Since the State by definition represents the interests of the people, the citizens can have no rights against the State. At the same time, this emphasis on the role of the State as the source of citizens' rights leads to a belief in the absolute sovereignty of the State and a refusal to admit any form of international control over its actions. No conflict, it is said, can exist between individuals and the State, since the latter assures the economic well-being and the cultural development of the former. The individual must therefore behave as required by the State, because such behaviour corresponds to the interests of society as a whole. The socialist State expresses the will of the mass of the workers, and the individual owes it absolute obedience. At the international level, we are told that 'co-operation of states in the field of human rights must be combined with unfailing observance of the principles of sovereign equality of states and non-interference in the affairs which are essentially within their domestic jurisdiction'. The 'UN Charter, as well as the post-war agreements in the field of human rights, refer the direct provision and protection of human rights and freedoms exclusively to the domestic jurisdiction of the states'. Exceptions to this rule are admitted only in certain clearly defined circumstances: under the trusteeship system (Chapter VI of the UN Charter) and in colonial territories; when violations of human rights are perpetrated on a mass scale, which endangers international peace and security, and brings Chapter VII of the Charter into play and finally when UN organs decide to set up special bodies of investigation.[8] Even when there are systems of international control, as in the two UN Covenants of 1966, the organs of control, we are told, may only make 'general recommendations'. For the UN bodies:

> have no right to make concrete recommendations on specific measures to be taken to implement particular human rights and freedoms. The elaboration and implementation of such measures is the internal affair

of states. International control over the activity of states in securing human rights and freedoms must be exercised with strict observance of their sovereignty and non-interference in their internal affairs.

It is not the aim of this book to review the strengths and weaknesses of particular theories, but rather to acknowledge the varying conceptions of different cultures towards human rights. We see therefore in the socialist States a quite different approach to human rights from that of the liberal democracies, rejecting the view that they are 'natural' to human personality and 'inalienable', but asserting that they are the emanation of the State, which itself is the incarnation of the interests of the workers in a State-run national economy. The sovereignty of the State is pre-eminent and no limitation thereon may be accepted, either nationally or internationally.

This emphasis on the sovereignty and infallibility of the State is reminiscent of doctrines current in the West at an earlier period, and particularly those of Machiavelli and Hobbes. It also has something in common with the postulate of English law that 'the King can do no wrong' – a doctrine which has now been largely abandoned. The difficulty with the doctrine of infallibility of the State is plainly to be found in its consequences. In modern industrialised societies, whether capitalist or socialist, the State controls, directs or interferes with the daily lives of the citizens to a degree that would have been inconceivable 100 years ago. The practical problem which results from this concerns the relationship of the individual not with an abstract conception of the State but with the army of officials (including policemen and gaolers) who represent it and who purport to apply laws and regulations promulgated in the name of the State by imperfect human beings. Even if, in theory, the State can do no wrong, in practice wrongs ranging from the errors of a tax inspector to the abomination of the concentration camps can be committed in its name. Hence the need to protect the individual, which is what human rights are all about.

This applies both nationally and internationally and leads to the question whether a system of international control violates the principle of non-interference in matters which are within the domestic jurisdiction of States, which will be discussed later. It must suffice for the present to say that matters with regard to which States have accepted international obligations by treaty thereby become subject to rules of international law and are no longer exclusively within their domestic jurisdiction. Moreover, any system of international control becomes meaningless if the matters to be controlled continue to be treated as exclusively subject to the sovereign will of the States concerned. Acceptance of the United Nations Charter, of the Universal Declaration and of the United Nations Covenants therefore involves moving beyond nineteenth-century conceptions of national sovereignty and recognising a common set of basic values.

4. Developing countries and human rights

We must now consider briefly another problem which arises in relation to different cultures and their approach to human rights; is it true that the rights which are considered important in industrially developed countries are relatively unimportant in developing countries or, if their value is admitted, that they are luxuries which the people of the Third World cannot afford? This is a very large issue which involves consideration of the relationship between, and the comparative importance of, the two main categories of human rights; civil and political rights on the one hand, and economic, social and cultural rights, on the other.

We may start with three simple propositions. First, the traditional approach of the Western democracies has been principally (some would say excessively) concerned with civil and political rights with much less attention to economic, social and cultural rights. Secondly, there is now widespread recognition of the importance of the second category. As the Tehran Conference stated in its Resolution XXI: 'the problems of economic, social and cultural rights should receive due and increasing attention ... in view of the increasing importance of realising these rights in the modern world'. Thirdly, as we have already seen, the socialist countries attach much more importance to the second category than to the first, which, in contrast to some of the less attractive features of Marxism, enables them to act as advocates for human rights and champions of the underprivileged.

What is the relevance of all this to the Third World?

The General Assembly of the United Nations decided in 1952, reversing an earlier decision, that there should be two separate international covenants dealing with the two separate categories of rights. However, although two separate covenants were approved by the General Assembly in 1966, and entered into force ten years later, almost all States which have ratified one covenant have also ratified the other. In other words, the practice of States appears to support treating both categories on an equal footing.

What then of the argument that developing countries attach less importance to civil and political rights? As regards treaty commitments this argument cannot stand. By 1 January 1988 more than eighty States had ratified the two UN Covenants. Half of them were States from what is generally considered the Third World, and almost all of them had ratified both Covenants. It is true, nevertheless, that many developing countries are more concerned with economic and social rights than with their civil and political counterparts. This is not surprising, having regard to their political and economic situation; nor is it cause for regret, provided that one category of rights is not sacrificed to the other.

A leading authority on the attitude of African States to human rights is Keba M'Baye, President of the Supreme Court of Senegal and a former President of the UN Commission on Human Rights. In his writings he has examined the problem with which we are now concerned. He recognises that in many African countries governments struggling to combat famine, illness and ignorance tend to overlook the classic liberties of the Western world. They consider that in the fight against underdevelopment they are in a state of war or emergency which permits derogations to be made – a new, and it must be said questionable, application of a principle generally recognised in national constitutions and international texts. At the same time he looks forward to a future when economic and social developments will have been largely achieved and the general respect of the classic rights and liberties secured. He deduces a 'right to development' as a necessary corollary of the other fundamental rights recognised in international texts. In particular, he sees it as the natural consequence of the right of self-determination and the right of all peoples freely to dispose of their natural wealth and resources – rights which are proclaimed in both the UN Covenants.[9] It is now generally recognised that there is a crucial correlation between the enjoyment of human rights and economic development. Neither is possible without the other; rather there is an essential connection between them. Thus, the International Conference on Human Rights at Tehran in 1968 stated in its Resolution XVII: 'The enjoyment of economic and social rights is inherently linked with a meaningful enjoyment of civil and political rights, and . . . there is a profound interconnection between the realisation of human rights and economic development.'

This affords an appropriate conclusion to our brief review of the varying approaches of different cultures to human rights. There seems little point in trying to decide whether one category of rights is more important than the other, and it is equally vain to hurl opprobrium at those who adopt a different system of priorities. Instead, we should recognise that the different categories of rights – civil and political, economic, social and cultural – are interrelated and that all are desirable, and actually necessary, to the full realisation of the human personality.

III. The first international measures for the protection of human rights

1. The abolition of slavery

The first international texts relating to what we should now call a human rights problem were formulated at the beginning of the nineteenth century. The problem they related to was slavery. Shocking as it now seems, the institution of slavery was generally legal under national law at the end of the eighteenth century; it remained legal in the United States until 1863, in Brazil until 1880, and in some countries into the twentieth century. In England it was illegal according to the decision in *Somersett's case* in 1772,[10] and at the turn of the century a humanitarian movement, largely inspired by Wilberforce, sought to prohibit it internationally. Since it was not possible to secure the immediate liberation of slaves in legal servitude in other countries, the first step was to secure the abolition of the slave trade, so as to prevent any increase in the number of slaves. The slave trade was prohibited in the British colonies in 1807. The institution of slavery was also abolished in France, and by the Treaty of Paris of 1814 the British and French governments agreed to co-operate in the suppression of the traffic in slaves. This undertaking was generalised and accompanied by a solemn condemnation of the practice by the major European States at the Congress of Vienna in 1815.

More than fifty bilateral treaties on the subject were concluded between 1815 and 1880, and the Conference of Berlin on Central

Africa of 1885 was able to state in its General Act that 'trading in slaves is forbidden in conformity with the principles of international law as recognised by the signatory powers'. The powers concerned, which were fifteen in number, also agreed that the territories of the Congo basin should not serve as a market or means of transit for the trade in slaves and that they would employ all means at their disposal for putting an end to the trade and punishing those engaged in it.

Matters were taken a step further at the Brussels conference in 1890. An anti-slavery Act was signed, and later ratified by eighteen States, including the United States, Turkey and Zanzibar. It not only condemned slavery and the slave trade, but also drew up a list of agreed measures for their suppression both in Africa and on the high seas, including the right of visit and search, the confiscation of ships engaged in the trade and the punishment of their masters and crew. In addition, the Act provided for the establishment of a special office attached to the Belgian Foreign Ministry and for an International Maritime Office in Zanzibar to assist in implementing these provisions – one of the earliest examples of international measures of implementation.

The General Act of the Brussels conference was the most comprehensive instrument on the subject of slavery until the outbreak of the First World War. Thereafter, the mandate system established by Article 22 of the League Covenant declared that the well-being and development of the peoples in the mandated territories should form a 'sacred trust of civilization' and that the mandatory powers should administer the territories under conditions 'which will guarantee freedom of conscience and religion . . . and the prohibition of abuses such as the slave trade'. And both the Convention of St Germain-en-Laye of 1919 and the International Convention on the Abolition of Slavery and the Slave Trade, concluded under the auspices of the League of Nations in 1926, proclaimed as their object 'the complete suppression of slavery in all its forms and of the slave trade by land and sea'.

There were more developments after the Second World War. Article 4 of the Universal Declaration reads: 'No one shall be held in slavery or servitude; slavery and the slave trade shall be prohibited in all their forms.' The institutional arrangements of the 1926 Convention were brought up to date in 1953 by a Protocol amending the Convention, while a Supplementary Convention on the Abolition of Slavery, the Slave Trade and Institutions and Practices Similar to Slavery was concluded in 1956 and entered into force in the following year.[11] In 1958 the Geneva Convention on the High Seas laid down in Article 13 that the Contracting States must take steps to prevent and, where necessary, punish any transport of slaves in their vessels and that any slave taking refuge thereon shall be free. Article 99 of the 1982 Law of the Sea Convention is to the same effect.

Condemnation of slavery and associated practices is also to be found in the various general human rights treaties concluded in the modern period. Article 8 of the 1966 United Nations Covenant on Civil and Political Rights follows the corresponding provision of the Universal Declaration. Slavery, along with servitude and forced or compulsory labour, is prohibited by Article 4 of the 1950 European Convention on Human Rights. The American Convention on Human Rights, which was concluded in 1969, is in similar terms and deals with these matters in Article 6, while the latest regional instrument, the African Charter on Human and Peoples' Rights, which came into force in 1986, covers the issue in Article 5.

This evolution over a period of more than 150 years shows that the right to freedom of the person, and the concomitant prohibition of slavery and the slave trade are now the subject of established rules of international law. Indeed, such widespread and uniform State practice has unquestionably generated a rule of customary international law prohibiting slavery and the slave trade. The problem today – for unfortunately a problem still exists – is not agreeing the rules, but rather seeing that they are enforced. In other words, it is no longer a question of making the law, but by police action in the widest sense, of seeing that it is observed.

2. *Humanitarian Law*

The second development by which international law began to be concerned with human rights – or, as some would prefer to say, a closely related subject – was the evolution of humanitarian law. Though there have been notable exceptions through the ages, the vanquished in war was normally at the mercy of the victor, and frequently little mercy was shown. The atrocities which accompanied the Thirty Years' War, for example, were notorious. During the eighteenth century a more enlightened attitude appeared. After the battle of Fontenoy in 1745, Louis XV ordered that the enemy wounded were to be treated in the same way as his own soldiers 'because once they are wounded they are no longer our enemies'. The English General Amherst applied the same rule at the siege of Montreal in 1762. Vattel advocated similar principles, while Rousseau wrote in his *Contrat Social* in 1762:

> The object of war being the destruction of the enemy State, one has the right to kill its defenders only when they have weapons in their hands; but immediately they put them down and surrender, thus ceasing to be enemies or agents of the enemy, they once more become ordinary men and one no longer has any right to their life. Sometimes one can extinguish a State without killing a single member of it; moreover, war confers no right other than that which is necessary for its purpose. These principles are not those of Grotius; they are not founded on the authority of poets, but they flow from the nature of things and are founded upon reason.[12]

The transformation of these principles into positive law was due to the work of the nineteenth-century Swiss philanthropist Henry Dunant. In 1859, having gone to Castiglione to see the emperor Napoleon III, he witnessed the battle of Solferino. Appalled at the slaughter and the suffering of the wounded, he personally helped more than a thousand casualties and called on the local inhabitants to assist him in the work. Determined as a result of this experience to institute a permanent system for humanitarian relief, he founded with the Geneva lawyer Gustave Moynier and others the *Comité International et Permanent de Secours aux Blessés Militaires*. Later the same year (1863) he organised a conference at which sixteen States were represented, and the delegates agreed to set up in their own countries private societies to supplement the work of the national army medical corps. They chose as their emblem the Swiss flag in reverse, i.e. a red cross on a white background. Official recognition of these arrangements was accorded in the following year by the Geneva Convention of 1864, in which twelve States undertook to respect the immunity of military hospitals and their staff, to care for sick and wounded soldiers whatever their nationality, and to respect the emblem of the Red Cross. This Convention formed the basis of humanitarian activities during the Franco-Prussian War (1870), the Spanish-American War (1898) and the Russo-Japanese War (1904). It was revised and developed by a diplomatic conference in 1906, and further revised and improved in the light of the experience of the First World War, by the Geneva Convention of 1929.[13] The further development of humanitarian law during the last half century is summarised in Chapter 8.

It was, of course, necessary to extend a similar system of protection to the sick and wounded in naval warfare. This was achieved in a different framework, through the Hague Peace Conferences of 1899 and 1907. The Hague Convention No. III of 1899 extended the provisions of the original Geneva Convention to maritime warfare; when the latter was revised in 1906, its principles were extended to war at sea by the Hague Convention No. X of 1907. This remained in force for more than forty years, during both the First and the Second World Wars, and was not replaced until 1949.

Another branch of humanitarian law relates to a field of activity for which the Red Cross is particularly well known – the care of prisoners of war. This concerns in the first place their identification and the communication of information on their whereabouts and physical condition to their home countries; secondly, it involves arranging facilities for correspondence with their families and the despatch of parcels; thirdly, it covers visits to prisoner-of-war camps and the furnishing of medical supplies; and fourthly, it extends to the repatriation, usually on an exchange basis, of the seriously wounded.

The legal basis for this work was the Hague Convention No. IV of 1907, dealing with the Laws and Customs of War on Land. In accordance with its provisions during the First World War the International Committee of the Red Cross set up an International Agency for Prisoners of War in Geneva. This body established an index of over 5,000,000 cards, containing particulars of the identity and whereabouts of prisoners of war.

The humanitarian work of the Red Cross during the First World War was of such value for all the belligerents that the authors of the Covenant of the League of Nations included the following provision as Article 25:

> The Members of the League agree to encourage and promote the establishment and co-operation of duly authorized voluntary national Red Cross organizations having as purposes the improvement of health, the prevention of disease and the mitigation of suffering throughout the world.

It had thus become clearly established by a number of treaties, and finally by the explicit recognition of the Red Cross in the League Covenant, that the conditions of the sick and wounded and the care of prisoners of war had become matters of concern to international law. This laid the foundation for further legal developments in this field and also made a major contribution to the process whereby the protection of the individual became the concern of international law and respect for human rights in general an obligation on all members of the United Nations.[14]

3. The protection of minorities

The third development whereby international law came to be concerned with the rights of individuals relates to the protection of minorities. This was principally the result of the redrawing of frontiers which formed part of the peace settlement in 1919, though earlier in the Treaty of Berlin (1878) Bulgaria, Montenegro, Serbia, Romania and Turkey had all assumed obligations to grant religious freedom to their nationals. The political changes of 1919 and 1920, including the restoration of Poland and the creation of successor States after the dissolution of the Austro-Hungarian Empire, sought to respect the principle of nationality, but the populations in many areas were so mixed that, wherever the frontiers were drawn, it was impossible to avoid the existence of minorities on the other side of the line.

The arrangements for protecting the new minorities took three main forms. First, there were five special treaties on minorities with the allied or newly created States: with Poland (Versailles, 1919), with Czechoslovakia and Yugoslavia (St Germain-en-Laye, 1919), with Romania (Trianon, 1920), and with Greece (Sèvres, 1920). Secondly, chapters on the rights of the minorities within their borders were included in the peace treaties with the ex-enemy States: with Austria (St Germain-en-Laye, 1919), with Bulgaria (Neuilly, 1919), with Hungary (Trianon, 1920), and later with Turkey (Lausanne, 1923). Thirdly, certain States made declarations before the Council of the League of Nations as a condition of their admission to the League: Finland (1921, as regards the Åland Islands), Albania (1921), Lithuania (1922), Latvia (1923), Estonia (1923), and later Iraq (1932).

Generally speaking, the various arrangements for the protection of the rights of minorities provided for equality before the law in regard to civil and political rights, freedom of religion, the right of members of the minorities to use their own language, and the right to maintain their own religious and educational establishments. It was also usual to provide for teaching in the language of the minority in State schools in districts where the minority constituted a considerable proportion of the population. Moreover, it was recognised that these various provisions protecting the rights of minorities constituted 'obligations of international concern', which were placed under the guarantee of the League of Nations and could not be modified without the consent of the Council of the League.

When violation of a State's obligations was alleged, minority groups could bring their complaints before the League. The usual procedure was that if the Secretary-General considered the case admissible, the Council would appoint an *ad hoc* Minorities Committee to investigate the matter and try to reach a friendly settlement; if this failed, the complaint was referred to the full Council. The Council in turn could refer the matter to the Permanent Court of International Justice. Although such references were rare, one well known case in which this occurred was that of the *Minority Schools in Albania*,[15] in which the Court insisted on the need to maintain equality in fact as well as equality in law and held that the closing of the minority schools was incompatible with equality of treatment.

Of particular importance – both for its practical effect at the time and for the precedent it created for the future – was the 1922 German-Polish Convention on Upper Silesia, a region which was divided into two parts, one on each side of the frontier between Germany and Poland. This Convention not only contained guarantees for the protection of the minorities on both sides of the frontier, but also set up an elaborate system of measures of implementation: a Minorities Office in each part of Upper Silesia, a Mixed Commission and an Arbitral Tribunal. The commission and the tribunal each had an independent president appointed by the League Council. The Mixed Commission dealt with more than 2,000 cases during the fifteen years of its existence (1922–37), and was essentially concerned with conciliation. The Arbitral Tribunal, on the other hand, was a judicial body, with competence to hear claims by individuals and gave judgments which were binding on the courts and administrative authorities of the two countries. Either government could refer any difference of opinion relating to questions of law or fact to the Permanent Court of International Justice. One case so referred in 1928, after the failure of settlement before the Mixed Commission and the League Council, was that of the *Rights of Minorities in Upper Silesia*, in which the Court held that the question whether a person belonged to a racial, linguistic or religious minority, which was the criterion for admission to the German-speaking minority schools in Poland, 'is subject to no verification, dispute, pressure or hindrance whatever on the part of the authorities'.[16]

The arrangements for protecting national minorities worked better than might have been expected, but came under intolerable strain in the political turmoil of the 1930s. Even so, by the end of the interwar period it had been clearly established that with regard to several matters international law was concerned with the status or the treatment of the individual and not simply with relations between States. However, this was true only in relation to a limited number of topics – slavery, humanitarian questions, the rights of minorities – and it remained to generalise the field of application of this principle and extend it to all the basic rights of the individual. Moreover, it was only in the special situation regulated by the minority treaties that the individual had possessed a remedy which would permit him to take action on the international scene to protect his rights. The question of international enforcement measures had therefore barely been touched. International law was, however, ripe for development in both these respects. The cataclysm of the Second World War drove home the point and thus set the stage for the many developments which have occurred since 1945 and which are the subject of this book.

Notes

1 A. H. Robertson, *Human Rights in Europe*, second edition, Manchester University Press, 1977, p. 149, quoting a paragraph from the first edition of Oppenheim's *Treatise on International Law*, 1905. When Sir Hersch Lauterpacht prepared the eighth edition of Oppenheim in 1955 he modified this passage considerably.

2 See Amnesty's report for 1987. This also stated that 135 countries were guilty of human rights abuses in that year.

3 For a more detailed account of the liberal democratic tradition see E. Kamenka

and A. E.-S. Tay (eds), *Human Rights*, London, 1978, chapters 1 and 2; J. J. Shestack, 'The jurisprudence of human rights', in T. Meron (ed.), *Human Rights in International Law*, Oxford, 1984, pp. 69–113 and R. J. Vincent, *Human Rights in International Relations*, Cambridge University Press, 1986, chapter 2.

4 *The Final Act of the International Conference on Human Rights*, Tehran, 1968, is published in UN document A/Conf 32/41.

5 C. Daubie, 'Cyrus le Grand – un precurseur dans le domaine des Droits de l'homme', *Human Rights Journal*, V, 1972, p. 293.

6 P. Modinos, 'La Charte de la Liberté de l'Europe', *Human Rights Journal*, VIII, 1975, pp. 677–8.

7 I. Szabo *et. al.*, *The Socialist Concept of Human Rights*, Hungarian Academy of Sciences, Budapest, 1966, particularly pp. 53–81. See also V. Kartashkin, 'Human rights and peaceful coexistence', *Human Rights Journal*, IX, 1976, p. 5; F. Przetacnik, 'The socialist concept of human rights: its philosophical background and political justification', *Revue Belge de Droit International*, XIII, 1977, p. 238; A. E.-S. Tay, 'Marxism, socialism and human rights', in Kamenka and Tay, *Human Rights*, pp. 104–13 and R. N. Dean, 'Beyond Helsinki: the Soviet view of human rights in international law', *Virginia Journal of International Law*, XXI, 1980–81, p. 55.

8 For example, the *ad hoc* working groups concerned with southern Africa and Chile and the Special Committee concerned with human rights in the territories occupied by Israel. For discussion of these and similar special bodies see Chapter 3.

9 K. M'Baye, 'Les réalités du monde noir et les droits de l'homme', *Human Rights Journal*, II, 1969, p. 382 and 'Le droit au développement comme un droit de l'homme', *ibid*, V, 1972, p. 505. See also T. C. Van Boven, 'Some remarks on special problems relating to human rights in developing countries,' *Human Rights Journal*, III, 1970, p. 383 and Y. K. Tyagi, 'Third world response to human rights', *Indian Journal of International Law*, XXI, 1981, p. 119. For further discussion of the right to development and other suggestions for new human rights, see Chapter 7.

10 20 *State Trials*, p. 1.

11 By 1 January 1988 there were 102 parties to this treaty, see J.-B. Marie, 'International instruments relating to human rights', *Human Rights Law Journal*, IX 1988, p. 113.

12 Quoted by Draper, *op. cit.*, n. 13, p. 63.

13 For the history of the humanitarian conventions see H. Coursier, 'L'Evolution du droit international humanitaire', 99 *Hague Recueil des Cours*, 1960, p. 357 and G. I. A. D. Draper, 'The Geneva Conventions of 1949', *ibid.*, 1965, vol. 114, p. 63.

14 The relationship between humanitarian law and human rights law is discussed in Chapter 8 below.

15 P. C. I. J., Series A/B, No. 64.

16 P. C. I. J., Series A, No. 15, pp. 46–7.

CHAPTER 2

The United Nations and human rights I: the International Covenant on Civil and Political Rights

I. The Charter

As is well known, the Charter of the United Nations contains a number of references to the promotion of human rights. The first is in the Preamble, which reads:

> We the peoples of the United Nations, determined ... to reaffirm faith in fundamental human rights, in the dignity and worth of the human person, in the equal rights of men and women and of nations large and small ... have resolved to combine our efforts to accomplish these aims.

Then, among the purposes of the United Nations set out in Article 1, is 'to co-operate ... in promoting respect for human rights and fundamental freedoms for all'. The most important provisions are probably those contained in Articles 55 and 56 of the Charter. Article 55 provides that the United Nations shall promote 'universal respect for, and observance of, human rights and fundamental freedoms for all without distinction as to race, sex, language or religion'; while in Article 56 'all members pledge themselves to take joint and separate action in co-operation with the Organisation for the achievement of the purposes set forth in Article 55'. Other references in the Charter are in Article 13, which authorises the General Assembly to make studies and recommendations about human rights; Article 62, which contains a somewhat similar provision relating to the Economic and Social Council; Article 68, which requires the Council to set up Commissions in the economic and social fields and for the promotion of human rights; and Article 76, which makes the promotion of human rights and fundamental freedoms for all one of the basic objectives of the trusteeship system.

Less well known is the fact that the Charter very nearly gave to human rights only a passing reference. The Dumbarton Oaks proposals for the United Nations, prepared in 1944 by the four great powers, contained only one general provision about human rights. However, the delegations of several smaller countries and the representatives of a number of non-governmental organisations who attended the San Francisco conference as consultants to the United States delegation were able, by energetic lobbying, to secure the inclusion in the Charter of the much more positive provisions summarised above.[1] The obligation now contained in Article 56 was at one stage actually intended to be stronger. The first draft would have required member States 'to take separate and joint action and to co-operate with the Organisation for the promotion of human rights', which clearly implied an obligation for them to act individually, irrespective of the action, or failure to act, of other States. But this formulation was not approved, and the undertaking finally accepted was to 'take joint and separate action in co-operation with the Organisation'.

It is also worth pointing out that certain delegations at San Francisco considered that the phrase 'promoting respect for human rights' was too weak and so various suggestions were made to substitute the words 'assuring' or 'protecting' for 'promoting', and to require the 'observance' of human rights rather than merely 'respect' for them.[2] These proposals were not accepted. However, in view of the fact that a number of delegations and influential non-governmental organisations considered that the human rights provisions of the Charter, though markedly stronger than the original Dumbarton Oaks proposals, were still too weak, it was agreed that a Bill of Rights should be drawn up separately and as soon as possible. There had, indeed, been suggestions, notably by Panama, for the incorporation of a Bill of Rights in the Charter itself. Although this proved impossible, partly for lack of sufficient support and partly for reasons of time, President Truman, in his closing speech to the conference, stated that:

> We have good reason to expect the framing of an international bill of rights, acceptable to all the nations involved. That bill of rights will be as much a part of international life as our own Bill of Rights is a part of our Constitution. The Charter is dedicated to the achievement and

observance of human rights and fundamental freedoms. Unless we can attain those objectives for all men and women everywhere – without regard to race, language or religion – we cannot have permanent peace and security.[3]

II. The Universal Declaration

No time was lost in acting on the proposal for a more detailed document. The Charter was signed in June 1945 and entered into force in October of the same year. In the autumn of 1945 the Preparatory Commission recommended that the Economic and Social Council should immediately establish a Commission on Human Rights and direct it to prepare an international Bill of Rights. The General Assembly approved this recommendation on 12 February 1946 and the Economic and Social Council acted on it four days later. The Commission on Human Rights was constituted within a matter of months, first with a nucleus of nine members. In May 1946 it recommended by majority vote that, since the Council consisted of representatives of governments, the members of the Commission should be elected by the Council from a list of nominees submitted by governments, but serve in an individual capacity. The USSR, however, opposed this proposal, and ECOSOC decided that the Commission should consist of eighteen members, appointed by the governments which were selected by the Council. Later in the same year the Council decided to leave it to the governments concerned to decide whether to appoint government officials or independent persons. It is, therefore, governments which are members of the Commission, and its members in fact attend as representatives of governments. In 1962 the membership was increased to twenty-one; in 1966 to thirty-two; and in 1980 to forty-three.

The first regular session of the Commission opened in January 1947, and its first task was the drafting of the International Bill of Rights. It decided later in the year that this should have three parts: a Declaration; a Convention containing legal obligations; and 'measures of implementation', that is to say, a system of international supervision or control. Work started immediately on the Declaration, for which purpose a drafting committee of eight members was appointed: the representatives of Australia, Chile, China, France, Lebanon, the United Kingdom, the United States and the USSR. The chairman of the Commission and of the drafting committee was Mrs Eleanor Roosevelt. The full Commission examined and revised the draft Declaration thus prepared, and submitted it through the Economic and Social Council to the General Assembly in 1948. At the same time it submitted a draft Covenant which the drafting committee had also prepared. However, the Assembly, at its third session, held in Paris in the autumn of 1948, decided to consider only the draft Declaration. The Third Committee devoted eighty-one meetings to examination of this text and to the 168 amendments which were tabled. In due course it submitted a revised version to the General Assembly. After a Soviet proposal to postpone further consideration of the matter until the following year had been defeated, the Declaration was adopted on 10 December 1948, with forty-eight votes in favour, none against and eight abstentions.[4]

The Universal Declaration was adopted by Resolution 217 (III) of the General Assembly. It was not intended to impose legal obligations on States, but rather to establish goals for States to work towards. Thus, the operative part of the Resolution reads as follows:

> Now, therefore, the General Assembly proclaims this Universal Declaration of Human Rights as a common standard of achievement for all peoples and all nations, to the end that every individual and every organ of society, keeping this Declaration constantly in mind, shall strive by teaching and education to promote respect for these rights and freedoms and by progressive measures, national and international, to secure their universal and effective recognition and observance, both among the peoples of Member States themselves and among the peoples of territories under their jurisdiction.

Mrs Roosevelt stated in the General Assembly that the Declaration was 'first and foremost a declaration of the basic principles to serve as a common standard for all nations. It might well become the Magna Carta of all mankind.' She considered that its proclamation by the General Assembly 'would be of importance comparable to the 1789 proclamation of the Declaration of the Rights of Man, the proclamation of the rights of man in the Declaration of Independence of the United States of America, and similar declarations made in other countries'.[5] A leading commentator has observed that:

> There seems to be an agreement that the Declaration is a statement of general principles spelling out in considerable detail the meaning of the phrase 'human rights and fundamental freedoms' in the Charter of the United Nations. As the Declaration was adopted unanimously, without a dissenting vote, it can be considered as an authoritative interpretation of the Charter of the highest order. While the Declaration is not directly binding on United Nations Members, it strengthens their obligations under the Charter by making them more precise.[6]

Since 1948, the Universal Declaration has acquired a greatly reinforced status, not only as 'a common standard of achievement for all peoples and all nations' but also as a statement of principles which all States should observe. It has been reaffirmed by the General Assembly on a number of occasions, of which the most striking were perhaps the adoption of the Declaration on Colonialism in 1960,[7] which provided 'All States shall observe faithfully and strictly the provisions of the Charter of the United Nations, the Universal Declaration of Human Rights and the present Declaration . . .'; and the unanimous adoption in 1963 of the Declaration on the Elimination of Racial Discrimination,[8] which contained a similar provision.

In the world outside the United Nations the influence of the Universal Declaration has been no less profound. It has inspired more than forty State constitutions, together with the regional human rights treaties of Europe, Africa and the Americas, and examples of legislation quoting or reproducing provisions of the Declaration can be found in all continents. Thus, the impact of the Universal Declaration has probably exceeded its authors' most sanguine expectations, while its constant and widespread recognition means that many of its principles can now be regarded as part of customary law.

III. The International Covenant on Civil and Political Rights

Resolution 217 (III) of 10 December 1948 not only approved the text of the Universal Declaration, it also decided that work should go ahead on the other two parts of the Bill of Rights: a Covenant containing legal obligations to be assumed by States, and measures of implementation. The Commission had indeed already prepared and submitted a preliminary draft for the Covenant, but it was not yet ready for adoption and was referred back by the General Assembly.

There then began a period of discussion, drafting and negotiation which lasted for eighteen years. The initial work of the Commission resulted in a text devoted to the classic civil and political rights, but when the General Assembly was consulted in 1950 for guidance on certain issues of policy, it decided that economic, social and cultural rights should also be included.[9] The Commission implemented this directive, but when the Security Council considered the results, and particularly the differences in the two categories of rights, it recommended that the General Assembly should reconsider its decision. As a result, the Assembly, after a long debate, decided in 1952 that there should be two separate Covenants, with as many similar provisions as possible, and that both should include an article on 'the right of all peoples and nations to self-determination'.[10]

The articles on measures of implementation gave the Commission much more trouble than the normative provisions, largely because the views of its members were sharply divided on the basic question of how far governments could be expected to accept a system of international control. A number of far-reaching proposals were considered, including an Australian suggestion for an International Court of Human Rights, a proposal by Uruguay for the establishment of an office of a United Nations High Commissioner for Human Rights, and a French proposal for an International Investigation Commission, coupled with the appointment of an Attorney-General of the Commission. India proposed that the Security Council should be apprised of alleged violations, investigate them and enforce redress, while Israel suggested the creation of a new Specialised Agency for the implementation of the Covenants.[11] The attitude of the United Kingdom and the United States was more cautious; they proposed that Human Rights Committees should be set up on an *ad hoc* basis, but only for inter-State disputes. The Soviet Union was consistently opposed to all arrangements of this sort on the ground that they would interfere in the internal affairs of States, contrary to Article 2(7) of the Charter, and would undermine their sovereignty and independence.[12] The Commission finally decided by seven votes to six, with one abstention, in favour of the establishment of a permanent Human Rights Committee to consider complaints of violations of human rights on an inter-State basis. However, it rejected by larger majorities the possibility of considering complaints by non-governmental organisations or petitions by individuals.[13]

Since there will be many references in this book to the problem of the meaning and effect of Article 2(7) of the Charter, it is worth examining this question more closely. Different governments have taken different positions at different times, according to the political context. Not the least remarkable feat of UN diplomacy is the facility with which some delegates argue that it is outside the competence of the UN to discuss human rights situations on their own territory or on that of their allies, but quite proper to discuss alleged violations by their political opponents. Among the attitudes and statements which it is instructive to recall are those of Mr Vyshinsky (USSR) in 1946 that Article 2(7) did not prevent the UN from discussing the situation of Indians in South Africa; and of Mr Santa Cruz (Chile) in 1949 that 'abuse of Article 2(7) of the Charter might paralyse the action of the United Nations' and in 1952 that 'the international law created by conventions and agreements among countries removes a number of questions from the exclusive competence of States ... since the adoption of the Charter, all fundamental human rights have formed part of international law since they are included in that multilateral treaty, the Charter'. Among the texts of major importance is the Report of the UN Commission on the Racial Situation in South Africa of October 1953. This discusses at length the meaning of Article 2(7) of the Charter, citing the views of such eminent jurists as Lauterpacht, Cassin and Kelsen, and contains the following statement:

> ... The United Nations is unquestionably justified in deciding that a matter is outside the essentially domestic jurisdiction of a State when it involves systematic violation of the Charter's principles concerning human rights, and more especially that of non-discrimination, above all when such actions affect millions of human beings, and have provoked grave international alarm, and when the State concerned clearly displays an intention to aggravate the position.

When this report was discussed in the General Assembly in 1953, South Africa introduced a draft resolution rejecting its conclusions and maintaining that the matters dealt with therein – principally racial policies in the Union – were 'matters essentially within the domestic jurisdiction of a Member State' and therefore outside the competence of the United Nations. This draft was rejected by an overwhelming majority of forty-two votes to seven, with seven abstentions – an event which deserves to be remembered. This result has, of course, been repeated on many subsequent occasions, as is illustrated by the Second Report on the Racial Situation in South Africa, and discussions in the Security Council in 1960 on the request of twenty-nine States that the Council should consider the Sharpeville massacre, and the discussions in the Security Council in 1963–64 on the report of the Special Committee on the Policies of Apartheid and in 1970 on the question of the arms embargo against South Africa. Here, for example is a statement of the American position by Mr Cabot Lodge in March 1960:

> We all recognise that every nation has a right to regulate its own internal affairs. This is a right acknowledged by Article 2, paragraph 7, of the Charter. At the same time, we must recognise the right – and the obligation – of the United Nations to be concerned with national policies in so far as they affect the world community. This is particularly so in cases where international obligations embodied in the Charter are concerned.

Until 1945 the manner in which a State treated its own nationals was, apart from the limited circumstances in which humanitarian intervention was permissible, a question within its own jurisdiction and competence with which other States had no right to concern themselves. Since then, however, the legal position has changed. Human rights, or any other matters with regard to which States have accepted international obligations, cease to be issues solely within their domestic jurisdiction. Other States have a legitimate interest in seeing that these undertakings are respected. The fact that the undertakings in question concern a State's duty to respect the rights of its own citizens in no way qualifies the fundamental principle that a State must perform its international obligations and cannot invoke national sovereignty as a pretext for failing to do so.

The Commission on Human Rights completed its work on the draft Covenants in 1954, and submitted its texts to ECOSOC and the General Assembly.[14] In the following year the Secretary-General prepared an analysis of the texts and of the issues which had been discussed during their preparation, which is a valuable additional source for understanding their provisions.[15]

When the draft Covenants prepared by the Commission on Human Rights were reviewed by the General Assembly's Third

Committee, substantive issues naturally attracted the largest share of its attention. There was much discussion of the right of all peoples to self-determination, which resulted in Article 1, common to both Covenants. During the years 1956–58 the articles relating to economic and social rights were approved with a good deal of detailed revision but with little major amendment. From 1958 to 1961 the same was done for the civil and political rights. In 1962 and 1963 discussion centred mainly on the introductory articles, i.e. the obligations of States to respect the rights set out, with particular reference to the question whether the obligation is of immediate or progressive effect – a question to which we will return later. In 1964 and 1965 comparatively little attention was devoted to the Covenants, as the Third Committee was principally concerned with the Convention on the Elimination of All Forms of Racial Discrimination. In 1966, however, a determined and successful attempt was made to finish the work on the Covenants and so it turned finally to the measures of implementation.

Here the Third Committee made substantial changes to the proposals of the Commission. It agreed to the establishment of a Human Rights Committee, but increased the number of its members from nine to eighteen. It also decided that the members should be elected by the States parties, instead of by the International Court of Justice, as had been proposed by the Commission. As regards the Covenant on Economic, Social and Cultural Rights, the Committee retained the system of reports to the Economic and Social Council, on the basis of which the Council may adopt recommendations 'of a general nature', that is, not referring to particular situations or even to particular States. This is a subject we will return to in Chapter 7.

As regards the Covenant on Civil and Political Rights, the Committee decided in favour of a double system of implementation, that is to say, a compulsory system of reporting to the new Human Rights Committee to be established under the terms of the Covenant and an optional system of fact-finding and conciliation, which would apply only in relation to States which had expressly agreed to this procedure. This was supplemented by a provision for *ad hoc* Conciliation Commissions, if the parties to a dispute agreed. The Netherlands proposed a further optional clause providing for the possibility of individual petitions, which appeared to have more chance of success in 1966 than in previous years, since a comparable provision had been inserted in the Racial Discrimination Convention the year before. The attempt, however, was unsuccessful and the Third Committee decided by a very narrow majority that a text permitting individual petitions or communications to the Human Rights Committee should be incorporated in a separate 'Optional Protocol' to the Covenant, and thus apply only to States which, by a separate act, ratified the Protocol.[16]

The Covenants, as revised by the Third Committee, were finally approved unanimously by the General Assembly in December 1966 with more than 100 votes in favour.[17] They required thirty-five ratifications and entered into force in 1976. The Optional Protocol was approved by majority vote (sixty-six to two, with thirty-eight abstentions) and required ten ratifications; it entered into force at the same time as the Covenant on Civil and Political Rights. At the present time ninety-one countries have ratified the Covenant on Economic, Social and Cultural Rights, and eighty-seven the Covenant on Civil and Political Rights, while thirty-nine have ratified the Optional Protocol.[18]

This culmination of eighteen years' work in the unanimous approval of the Covenants by over a hundred States was in itself a remarkable achievement. Even the long time taken over the negotiations had one important advantage. Whereas about fifty States participated in the initial discussions, this number had more than doubled by the time the texts were completed, with the result that the treaties which finally emerged can be regarded, not as the work of a particular group of States, but as truly reflecting the views of the modern international community.

The contents of the two Covenants have already been the subject of much comment.[19] The Covenant on Economic, Social and Cultural Rights will be discussed in Chapter 7, and the Covenant on Civil and Political Rights in the remainder of this chapter.

2. *The general provisions of the Covenant*

In accordance with the decision of the General Assembly taken in 1952, both Covenants begin in identical terms, with an article on the right of self-determination. This right is stated as one which exists and is of immediate application ('All peoples *have* the right of self-determination') and which results in peoples' right freely to determine their political status. It is then elaborated in subsequent paragraphs which establish the right of peoples to dispose of their natural resources, and the obligation of States to 'promote the realisation of the right of self-determination'.

This article of both Covenants is, of course, in accordance with the political philosophy of the General Assembly. However, using such a philosophy to ground a legal obligation produces something of a problem. The Universal Declaration was an instrument for proclaiming rights in general terms and the Covenants, as we have seen, are intended to make respect for human rights a legal duty. 'Rights' in this context are normally taken to mean the rights of individuals as human beings. The difficulty with the right of self-determination is twofold. First, it is a collective right and not an individual right, and so some would question whether it is appropriate in the present context – especially as it was proclaimed elsewhere in the Declaration on the Granting of Independence to Colonial Countries and Peoples of 1960.[20] Secondly, the right is stated as belonging to 'all peoples'. But what constitutes a 'people'? Without going outside Western Europe, one may ask, does the right of self-determination belong to the Scots and the Welsh, the Bretons, the Corsicans and the Alsatians, the Basques and the Catalans? The same question can be put in relation to many other parts of the world. At the political level the issue can be treated as one of policy or of expediency. The difficulty stems from the attempt to transform a political principle into an enforceable right and means that the inclusion of the articles on the right of self-determination in the two Covenants could well give rise to problems.[21]

Articles 2–5 of both Covenants constitute Part II. They contain in each case an undertaking to respect, or to take steps to secure progressively, the substantive rights which follow in Part III, together with certain other provisions of a general nature.

In the Covenant on Civil and Political Rights, Article 2 provides that each State party 'undertakes to respect and to ensure to all individuals within its territory and subject to its jurisdiction the rights recognised in the present Covenant . . .'. Does this impose on States an obligation of immediate implementation, or only an obligation to do something in the future? From the words just quoted, which are from the first paragraph of Article 2, one would conclude that the obligation is immediate. This would, indeed, appear to have been the intention as regards civil and political rights. At the same time it seems clear that some States cannot immediately accept all the obligations resulting from the Covenant, because the list of rights secured is, as we shall see shortly, very extensive. To encourage the largest possible number of ratifications Paragraph 2 of Article 2 therefore creates an obligation to take 'the necessary steps ... to adopt such legislative or other measures as may be necessary to give effect to the rights recognised in the present Covenant', in cases where they are not already provided for in the national law. It thus appears that while the first principle is one of immediate obligation, the possibility of progressive application is also recognised. Moreover, it is significant that a proposal to set a time limit for taking 'the necessary steps', which was made during the negotiations, was not accepted. The immediate nature of the obligation is therefore somewhat weakened.

The first paragraph of Article 2 of the Covenant on Civil and Political Rights also contains a non-discrimination clause in what may now be considered the standard form, and the third paragraph an undertaking to make available an effective remedy to anyone whose rights set out in the Covenant are violated. The non-discrimination clause is amplified by Article 3, which contains an undertaking to respect the principle of equality of men and women in the enjoyment of the rights secured. Article 4 provides for the possibility of derogation 'in times of public emergency which threatens the life of the nation and the existence of which is officially proclaimed'; while Article 5 contains two separate provisions. The first is designed to prevent abuse of the rights and freedoms set out and is based on Article 30 of the Universal Declaration; and the second is a general saving clause which states that nothing in the Covenant may be interpreted as limiting the rights and freedoms already existing or recognised under national law or under other conventions.

3. *The rights protected*

Part III of the Covenant on Civil and Political Rights sets out the rights which the Covenant is designed to protect. They are as follows:

Article 6 The right to life.
7 Freedom from torture and inhuman treatment.
8 Freedom from slavery and forced labour.

Article 9 The right to liberty and security.
10 The right of detained persons to be treated with humanity.
11 Freedom from imprisonment for debt.
12 Freedom of movement and of choice of residence.
13 Freedom of aliens from arbitrary expulsion.
14 The right to a fair trial.
15 Protection against retroactivity of the criminal law.
16 The right to recognition as a person before the law.
17 The right to privacy.
18 Freedom of thought, conscience and religion.
19 Freedom of opinion and of expression.
20 Prohibition of propaganda for war and of incitement to national, racial or religious hatred.
21 The right of assembly.
22 Freedom of association.
23 The right to marry and found a family.
24 The rights of the child.
25 Political rights.
26 Equality before the law.
27 The rights of minorities.

This is an extensive list. The number of rights included is greater than in the Universal Declaration or the European Convention. A detailed comparison with the latter is contained in Chapter 4. As regards the Universal Declaration, it may be observed that the rights set out in the Covenant are generally defined in greater detail and include the following, which were not contained in the Declaration:

10 The right of detained persons to be treated with humanity.
11 Freedom from imprisonment for debt.
20 Prohibition of propaganda for war and of incitement to hatred.
24 The rights of the child.
27 The rights of minorities.

On the other hand, the right of property, which was included in Article 17 of the Universal Declaration, is not included in either Covenant. This was because it proved impossible to reach agreement between countries of widely different political philosophies on a definition of this right.

The way the Covenant defines the various civil and political rights has been the subject of extensive commentary and analysis and need not be considered in detail here. However, two general points should be made.

First, not only is the number of rights protected in the Covenant greater than in comparable instruments, but also the definitions given are frequently broader and more enterprising. For example, Article 6 on the right to life does not actually prohibit the death penalty, but is clearly drafted with the intention of indicating that it should be abolished. It refers to countries which have not abolished the death penalty as if this is a temporary state of affairs which should be remedied, and states specifically that nothing in the article shall be invoked to prevent or delay the abolition of capital punishment. Similarly, Article 10 provides that all detained persons shall be treated humanely and with respect for the inherent dignity of the human person. This is a positive obligation going well beyond the mere prohibition of inhuman treatment found in other texts. Moreover, Article 10 continues by laying down separate standards for accused persons and juveniles, who shall be separated from convicted persons; while paragraph 3 of this article provides that the aim of the penitentiary system shall be the reformation and social rehabilitation of prisoners.

Another example may be seen in Article 25, which sets out certain political rights. This appears to apply not only to the right to vote in national elections, but also to the same right in local elections and to the right to take part in the government of one's country and in the public service. A further illustration is Article 27, which protects the rights of minorities 'to enjoy their own culture, to profess and practise their own religion, and to use their own language'.

Article 14 on the right to a fair trial is a provision of particular importance and wide scope. In addition to the usual guarantees of an independent and impartial tribunal, public hearings, the presumption of innocence and the rights of the defence, it also provides for protection against self-incrimination, the right of appeal, and compensation for miscarriage of justice, and lays down the principle that no one may be tried twice for the same offence.

A second general comment is that if the list of rights enumerated in the Covenant is extensive, and if the definitions given are often more far-reaching than in earlier texts, some of them are so general or imprecise that they appear to be more statements of political principle or policy than of legally enforceable rights. This point has already been made in relation to 'the right of self-determination of all peoples'. It could also be made as regards several other provisions, notably those relating to the aim of the penitentiary system (Article 10(3)), the right to recognition as a person before the law (Article 16), the prohibition of propaganda for war (Article 20) and the right to take part in the conduct of public affairs (Article 25(a)). Some of these points will be examined further in Chapter 4.

In the last analysis, however, the effectiveness of the Covenant depends less on the definition of the rights to be protected, than on its arrangements to ensure that governments respect the obligations they have assumed. The measures of implementation of the Covenant on Civil and Political Rights will now therefore be examined in a little more detail.

4. *The Human Rights Committee*

Article 28 of the Covenant provides for the establishment of the Human Rights Committee, which thus becomes the principal organ of implementation of the Covenant on Civil and Political Rights. This contrasts with the Covenant on Economic, Social and Cultural Rights, where no new body is created and implementation is the responsibility of the existing Economic and Social Council.

As already noted, the Third Committee doubled the number of members of the Human Rights Committee from the figure of nine, which had been proposed in the 1954 draft, to eighteen. This was eminently reasonable, having regard to the fact that the number of members of the United Nations had doubled by 1966.[22] As regards the qualifications of members of the Committee, in the first place they must be nationals of States which are parties to the Covenant; secondly, they must be 'persons of high moral character and recognised competence in the field of human rights'; and, thirdly, consideration shall be given 'to the usefulness of the participation of some persons having legal experience'. In 1954 the Commission had proposed 'some persons having a judicial or legal experience', but the Third Committee decided to delete the reference to judicial qualifications. The change in fact makes little difference, since consideration of persons with legal experience clearly does not exclude judges, and, in any event, the requirement is not mandatory.

Under Articles 29 and 30 of the Covenant the members of the Committee are elected by secret ballot by the States parties at a special meeting convened for the purpose by the Secretary-General of the United Nations. Each party may nominate no more than two candidates, who must be nationals of that State. The detailed procedure for the election is set out in Article 30. The following article provides that the Committee may not include more than one national of any State and that consideration shall be given to the principle of equitable geographical distribution and to representation of the different forms of civilisation and the principal legal systems.[23] The term of office is four years, though that of nine members elected at the first election was only two years, in order to avoid a complete change of membership at any one time (Article 32). Members of the Committee are eligible for re-election (Article 29). Articles 33 and 34 deal with the possibilities of incapacity and casual vacancies, while the following article provides that the members of the Committee shall receive emoluments from United Nations resources, reinforcing the principle already stated in Article 28 that they 'shall serve in their personal capacity', that is, not as representatives of their governments. This principle is further emphasised in Article 38, which requires each member of the Committee to make a solemn declaration that he will perform his functions impartially and conscientiously.[24] Article 36 then provides that the Secretary-General of the United Nations shall provide the necessary staff and facilities for the functioning of the Committee.

The Covenant on Civil and Political Rights and the Optional Protocol entered into force in March 1976, and the meeting of the States parties to elect the members of the Committee took place in September of the same year. By that time there were forty-four parties to the Covenant and sixteen to the Protocol. The principles of equitable geographical distribution and representation of the principal legal systems were respected, as may be seen from the following indications of the nationality of the members of the Committee: there were five from Western Europe: four from Eastern Europe; two from Asia; three from Africa; one from North America; and three from Latin America. The five Western Europeans were all from States which are parties to the European Convention, one of them being also a member of the European Commission of Human Rights.[25] The three Latin Americans were nationals of States parties to the American Convention on Human Rights. However, only seven members of the Human Rights Committee were nationals of States which had ratified the Optional Protocol providing for the right of individual petition.

The election of officers at the first session of the Committee in 1977 likewise respected the principle of geographical distribution: the Cypriot member was elected chairman; the three vice-chairmen were from Bulgaria, Mauritius and Norway; and the rapporteur from Colombia.

The first two meetings of the Human Rights Committee were held in March and August 1977. The Committee was then principally concerned with organisational matters and, in accordance with Article 39 of the Covenant, with settling its rules of procedure, though at the second session it also considered the first periodic reports and individual petitions, to which we will return later.

As regards the rules of procedure, the two most interesting points concerned the publication of the proceedings and the method of voting. It was agreed that reports, formal decisions and all other official documents of the Committee and its subsidiary bodies should be documents of general distribution, i.e. public, unless the Committee should decide otherwise in any particular case. Also, periodic reports by States parties and additional information submitted by them should be public documents. On the other hand, documents and decisions relating to inter-State complaints under Articles 41 and 42 of the Covenant and to individual communications under the Optional Protocol should have only restricted distribution, that is to say that they should remain confidential.[26]

The Covenant itself contains a provision dealing with voting arrangements. Although Article 39 provides that the Committee shall establish its own rules of procedure, paragraph 2 stipulates that these shall provide (a) that twelve members shall constitute a quorum; and (b) that decisions shall be made by a majority vote of the members present. During the drafting of the rules of procedure, some members of the Committee drew attention to the fact that in the United Nations and elsewhere there has been a tendency in recent years for legal bodies to adopt decisions on the basis of consensus. They urged that the Human Rights Committee should follow this method and thus 'underscore the resolve of members to work harmoniously and in a spirit of co-operation'. Other members maintained that while consensus was desirable if possible, to establish a rule to this effect 'might considerably restrict the Committee's power of decision-making' and would be inconsistent with Article 39, paragraph 2(b) of the Covenant, referred to above.

Finally, it was agreed to incorporate in Rule 51 the method of decision by a simple majority, but to add a footnote indicating that there was general agreement that the 'method of work normally should allow for attempts to reach decisions by consensus before voting ...'.[27] In practice the Committee has adopted consensus as the basis of its decision-making. Thus, the qualification to Rule 51 has become extremely important. It should be noted, however, that in the procedures for the consideration of communications under the Optional Protocol, provision is made in Rule 94 for a summary of any individual opinion to be appended to the collective view of the Committee.

In 1979, after the tenth State had made a declaration under Article 41, bringing the inter-State complaints procedure into force, the Committee put into effect Rules 72–7 of its rules of procedure to govern such complaints. In general, these follow the provisions of Article 41, and lay down that the Committee will consider communications only if both States have made declarations under Article 41 and all domestic remedies have been exhausted. Rule 75 provides that the Committee shall examine communications under Article 41 at closed meetings, but the Committee may, after consultation with the States parties concerned, issue communiqués through the Secretary-General, for the use of the media and the public. Through the Secretary-General the Committee may also request from either of the parties concerned additional information or observations in oral or written form and set a time limit for their submission. Under Rule 77 the parties have a right to be represented when the matter is considered by the Committee and to make submissions orally and/or in writing. The Committee shall adopt a report, in accordance with Article 41(1)(h), within twelve months of the notice bringing the matter to its attention, but the parties do not have a right to be present during the Committee's deliberations concerning the adoption of the report. If the matter is not resolved to the satisfaction of the parties, the Committee may, with their prior consent, proceed to the conciliation procedure prescribed in Article 42.

These rules are sound and their preparation was not hindered by efforts to limit the Committee's powers. Doubtless they were helped by the fact that most of the members of the Committee were nationals of countries that had not submitted to this regime, and their governments were not threatened by it. The few members of the Committee from countries that had accepted the system were eager to see it work, and their governments, having submitted to it voluntarily, were not disposed to try to weaken or frustrate it.

5. Reporting procedures

The draft Covenant prepared by the Commission on Human Rights envisaged as the principal measure of implementation a procedure of inter-State complaints before the Human Rights Committee. A reporting procedure was added only at the end of the relevant chapter, and it is clear from the context that it was considered a less important and subordinate measure. In the final text of the Covenant, however, the position was reversed. The reporting procedure emerged as the principal measure of implementation while the inter-State procedure is optional. Potentially, therefore, the submission of reports by States and their examination by the Human Rights Committee is of cardinal importance in the implementation of the Covenant on Civil and Political Rights, and so the practical and theoretical merits of such a system deserve careful study.

Considerable doubt is felt in some quarters about the value of reports by States dealing with the way in which they have performed their international obligations. Such reports are, of course, compiled by national officials who naturally try to give the best account they can of the situation in their country. Accordingly, it is unlikely that they will draw the attention of an international body to any shortcomings or failures in their national record, or confess to violations of human rights. Is there, then, any value in a reporting system?

There is certainly substance in this criticism. National reports in themselves do not constitute an effective measure of control. What matters is how they are dealt with after they have been received. That is to say, whether there is an opportunity for critical examination, for drawing attention to gaps or inaccuracies in the information provided, and for comparing official statements with other sources of information on the same subject. In short, whether the system is such that a judicious appraisal of the reports is possible.

Several elements are necessary to make a reporting system work: (1) the co-operation of governments in providing full information;

(2) the possibility of obtaining further (and perhaps less flattering) information from other responsible sources; (3) the examination of the information obtained by independent persons who are not government officials; and (4) the right of some organ or body taking part in the procedure to make suitable recommendations with a view to improvements in the law or practice of the country concerned.

This emphasis on the need for independent scrutiny and the power to recommend improvements is not dictated by prejudice or hostility towards particular governments. It arises from the complex nature of modern society, the vast range of subjects with regard to which government action affects the lives of citizens, beneficially or otherwise, and the huge apparatus of public administration. The greater the centralisation of power in the hands of governments, the greater is the need for effective safeguards to protect the rights of the individual citizen. In how many countries are there laws and even constitutional provisions which are beyond reproach, but administrative action which fails to correspond? It is against this general background that we need to look at the reporting system established by the Covenant on Civil and Political Rights.

The reporting system provided for in the Covenant is limited in many ways. Even so, it was scarcely greeted with general enthusiasm. When such procedures were first discussed in the Commission on Human Rights, the objection was made that 'any such procedure was contrary to the United Nations Charter, in particular to Article 2 paragraph 7, and constituted a violation of national sovereignty'.[28] This extreme and illogical view, however, was fortunately not repeated in the Third Committee. Indeed, in 1963 the Eastern European representatives indicated that they were prepared to accept a reporting system, so reversing their earlier position. A point of more substance, made both in the Commission and in the Third Committee, was that the requirement that States should report 'on the measures they have adopted which give effect to the rights recognised herein and on the progress made in the enjoyment of those rights' would seem to imply that the rights and freedoms set out in the Covenant are to be the object of progressive implementation by the contracting parties. Now it is agreed that the economic, social and cultural rights set out in the other Covenant are to be implemented progressively. Indeed, it would obviously be impossible for a number of them – the right to work, for example – to be implemented immediately and completely anywhere. Civil and political rights, on the other hand, are as a general rule capable of immediate application, and a State should put its laws and administrative practice in compliance with the Covenant before ratifying it. Consequently, an article which speaks of 'the progress made in the enjoyment of those rights' seems to derogate from or diminish the immediate obligation to secure respect for civil and political rights.[29]

While there is logic in this argument, it is not altogether realistic. Certainly the civil and political rights are intended to be of immediate application and should, so far as possible, be ensured at the time of ratification. But there may be certain legislative or administrative measures which require adjustment or amendment, and Article 2, paragraph 2, of the Covenant expressly recognises this possibility. Moreover, it would be foolish to pretend that no further progress can be made in the enjoyment of human rights after a State has ratified the Covenant. It is therefore reasonable and sensible to ask States to report on the progress which they have been able to make subsequent to the deposit of their instrument of ratification.

The obligation on States to report relates to 'the measures they have adopted' to give effect to the rights set out in the Covenant, to 'the progress made in the enjoyment of those rights', and also, under paragraph 2 of Article 40, to 'the factors and difficulties, if any, affecting the implementation of the present Covenant'. The United States proposed an amendment to the effect that the reports should relate to 'the legislative, judicial or other action taken ...', but certain countries opposed this on the ground that it was more restrictive than 'measures' without qualification, and the amendment was not adopted.[30] The reports are to be presented within one year of the entry into force of the Covenant for the States parties concerned, and thereafter when the Committee so requests (Article 40, paragraph 1). This means that for the thirty-five States which first ratified the Covenant, as the result of which it entered into force in March 1976, the first reports were due to be deposited by March 1977, which was also when the Human Rights Committee held its first session.

Of the four conditions enumerated above for an effective reporting system, we can see that the first is encouraged by the provisions of the Covenant, that is to say the co-operation of governments in providing full information. The Human Rights Committee quickly established its intention of following the practice of the Committee on the Elimination of Racial Discrimination in requesting additional information from governments when required and in inviting governments to send representatives to discuss their reports with the Committee and answer questions. Of course, common sense requires such action and it may be thought superfluous to draw attention to the development of this procedure. However, some governments are extraordinarily sensitive about anything in the nature of international examination of their human rights record, invoking arguments about national sovereignty and Article 2(7) of the Charter, and it is therefore a distinct achievement to get them to accept even the modest measures just described. One member of the Human Rights Committee argued that States had agreed to accept 'a reporting procedure, not an investigatory procedure' and that once they have submitted a report they have no further obligation to co-operate with the Committee.[31] The argument has even been put forward that Article 40 of the Covenant does not contain an express provision like that in Article 9 of the Racial Discrimination Convention authorising the Committee to 'request further information from the States Parties', and that the Committee should therefore not make such requests. It is consequently a cause for satisfaction that these negative attitudes have not prevailed.

As a result of these and other discussions, Rule 66 of the rules of procedure contains the general provisions about the submission of reports, including one which says that the Committee may inform States of its wishes as regards the form and contents of their reports. Rule 68 provides that representatives of the States parties may be present when their reports are examined and that any such representative 'should be able to answer questions which may be put to him by the Committee and make statements on reports already submitted by his State, and may also submit additional information from his State'. It is clear, then, that both the rules of procedure and the initial practice of the Human Rights Committee are conceived in that spirit of 'constructive dialogue' which is so clearly necessary.

At its second session in August 1977 the Committee formulated general guidelines about the form and contents of reports, asking that they should be in two parts. The first should briefly describe the general legal framework within which civil and political rights are protected, including information as to whether they are protected in the constitution or by a separate 'Bill of Rights'; whether the provisions of the Covenant are directly enforceable in internal law, and what remedies are available to an individual who thinks that his rights have been violated. The second part should deal with the legislative, administrative or other measures in force in regard to each right and include information about restrictions or limitations on their exercise.

The object of the 1977 guidelines was to provide governments with an indication of what should be included in their initial reports. By 1981 when many of these had been submitted and the Committee was well into its work, new guidelines were issued to assist the preparation of subsequent reports. Both sets of guidelines were designed to elicit information about the law of the reporting State and also its practice, which the Committee rightly sees as no less important. In accordance with the Committee's intention to keep itself up to date, it has also requested governments to provide information on significant new developments at any time.

Experience to date indicates that as far as the reporting obligation is concerned, most governments have at least fulfilled their formal obligations. In a few cases, however, the practice of certain parties has proved unsatisfactory. Some failed to submit an initial report; others did so, but then failed to provide additional information promised to the Committee during its consideration of their report. In 1979 the Committee took the bold step of rejecting one report as inadequate and has also occasionally criticised some reports as too brief. It would therefore be wrong to suggest that this is a matter on which there is no room for improvement. On the other hand, a student of the system has noted that 'Even the most sceptical observers have been impressed by the apparent seriousness that many states from different parts of the world, with diverse political systems, have taken toward their reporting obligations, as reflected by the quality of the reports and the calibre of the representatives, as well as their willingness to answer questions.'[32] The general picture, then, is reasonably encouraging. We may now therefore turn to consider how far the other three conditions have been met.

The second element in an effective reporting system, as already noted, is the possibility of obtaining further, and perhaps more critical, information from responsible sources other than governments. This is provided for in the systems established by the ILO for its international labour conventions and by the Council of Europe for the European Social Charter. The Covenant on Civil and Political Rights, however, does not contain any similar arrangements.

The nearest it comes to doing so is the provision in paragraph 3 of Article 40, which was introduced as an amendment by the United Kingdom in the Third Committee,[33] and which authorises the Secretary-General of the United Nations, after consultation with the Committee, to 'transmit to the Specialised Agencies concerned, copies of such parts of the reports as fall within their field of competence'. Both the ILO and UNESCO have expressed their willingness to co-operate with the Human Rights Committee in this respect, and appropriate provision has been made in the rules of procedure. The Committee has also decided that information concerning the Specialised Agencies' interpretation and practice with regard to the corresponding provisions of their instruments should be made available to the Committee. This is a constructive step. But although the ILO in particular has made use of this opportunity, too much should not be expected of such arrangements because comparatively few of the rights protected by the Covenant on Civil and Political Rights relate to matters within the competence of the ILO and UNESCO. Moreover, the Specialised Agencies do not possess a right to comment on States' reports and may do so only if specifically requested by the Committee.[34] The ILO, UNESCO, FAO and WHO have, however, been invited to send representatives to attend the public sessions of the Committee.

From what other responsible sources could the Committee obtain information to supplement, or possibly criticise, the information furnished by governments? The answer which springs most readily to mind is the non-governmental organisations (NGOs) having consultative status with the Economic and Social Council. Unfortunately, they have not been granted any rights to lay information before the Human Rights Committee when it is considering the reports of governments. This is a real defect in the system. However, it does not prevent the NGOs from supplying information to members of the Committee in their individual capacity, and the influence of evidence supplied by Amnesty International and other NGOs is often evident in the questions put to State representatives. This behind the scenes influence is, however, clearly different from the right to present information officially.

As regards the possibility of obtaining independent information, the conclusion must therefore be that the situation is not satisfactory. One way of improving it would be for the Committee to invite comments from individuals with expert knowledge of a particular country. There are still obstacles to such a development, but it is to be hoped that this, along with an enhancement of the role of the Specialised Agencies and NGOs, may one day be considered.

The third requirement which we have suggested is necessary in an effective reporting system is the independence of the persons who examine the reports. As we have seen in the previous section, the text of the Covenant is satisfactory in this respect. Article 28, paragraph 3, states that the members of the Committee 'shall be elected and shall serve in their personal capacity'. What is perhaps more important is the provision in Article 38 requiring each member to make 'a solemn declaration in open committee that he will perform his functions impartially and conscientiously'; and that in Article 35 that the members of the Committee 'shall ... receive emoluments from United Nations resources ...'. Furthermore, Rule 16 of the rules of procedure reiterates the requirement of a solemn declaration of impartiality; while Rule 13 requires that in the event of a member of the Committee resigning, this must be notified by the member concerned to the Chairman or the Secretary-General, so guarding against the possibility that a government may decide to remove a member of the Committee and simply notify the Chairman or the Secretary-General of its decision.

The record to date indicates that the aim of ensuring that the Committee is in a position to discharge its functions competently and free from undue governmental pressure, has been achieved. Not only are the individual members of the Committee usually well qualified, many being lawyers with expertise in human rights, but in scrutinising national reports and questioning State representatives they demonstrate an independence and objectivity which ensures that no government is safe from criticism. The individuals who make up the Committee do not agree on all matters relating to the application of the Covenant. There is, as we have seen, more than one way of approaching the issue of human rights, while the function and authority of the Committee, which lie at the heart of the Covenant system, are also controversial. These differences are naturally reflected in disagreements within the Committee. Such disagreements are, however, inevitable at this stage in the development of international human rights law. Much more important is the fact that, despite these differences, the quality and independence of the Committee's members has generated mutual respect and an *esprit de corps* which augur well for the future.[35]

The fourth requirement of an effective reporting system is the power to make recommendations about necessary improvements in the law or practice of the country concerned. In this respect the Covenant on Civil and Political Rights is sadly deficient. To understand why we must look more closely at the powers and procedure of the Committee when it has received the reports of States parties. The relevant text is paragraph 4 of Article 40 which requires the Committee to study those reports and provides that it 'shall transmit its reports, and such general comments as it may consider appropriate, to the State Parties'. When the Committee considered the scope of its powers under this provision in 1980 two radically different schools of thought emerged.[36]

According to one view the Committee's task is to study the national reports to satisfy itself that the reporting obligation has been fulfilled and, more importantly, to determine whether the reporting State has fulfilled its obligations. It follows that the Committee should prepare a report on each national report, thus monitoring each party's compliance and making appropriate recommendations to the State concerned. The other view is that the 'reports' referred to in Article 40 are simply the annual report which the Committee is required to supply to the General Assembly under Article 45. On this interpretation the Committee's function is to assist States in promoting human rights, but not to pass judgement on them. Hence the Committee is not permitted to make an assessment of, or report on, each State's conduct.

The reference to 'general comments' in Article 40 is similarly subject to differing interpretations. To those who support the Committee's right to issue individual reports the reference means that it can make comments on an individual State, provided such comments are 'general' in character, that is do not relate to named individuals. To those who view the issue more narrowly, however, 'general comments' are recommendations directed to all States, as opposed to particular parties, a condition which is seen as confirming the limited interpretation of the Commmittee's powers.

Faced with these very different views of its functions, and committed to decision-making by consensus, the Committee has so far been unable to issue reports on individual States, although this view of the Committee's powers has majority support. Instead, in accordance with the minority view firmly supported by a number of members, the Committee issues only annual reports containing general comments and does not assess the conduct of individual States. Thus, the narrower view of the Committee's competence has prevailed. It does not make recommendations to individual States, with the result that the Covenant system lacks one of the essential requirements of an effective reporting procedure.

Despite the shortcomings of Article 40, the arrangements provided for in the Covenant, as implemented in the practice of the Human Rights Committee, should not be thought of as wholly ineffective. As we have seen, members of the Committee can question representatives of the reporting State, and since these exchanges are recorded in the Summary Records and in the Committee's annual reports to the General Assembly, they provide some indication of how a national report was received. This is clearly less useful than the detailed review of individual reports which many members of the Committee would prefer, but as a way of demonstrating satisfaction or disapproval it is significant. Moreover, although confined to making general comments, the Committee has been able to use the opportunity provided by its own reports to encourage implementation of the Covenant. In its early reports the Committee concentrated on procedural aspects of reporting, emphasising, for example, the importance of punctuality and completeness. Recently, however, the Committee's comments have begun to address substantive issues. The latter, inevitably, are more contentious, but the Committee has at least begun the task of using its own reports to spell out to States, albeit in a general way, the meaning and implications of the Covenant.

Under paragraph 5 of Article 40 States may respond to any comments the Committee has made by submitting observations to it. Since the Committee does not comment on individual reports, this provision is less important than it might appear. There is, in any case, nothing in the Covenant which makes compliance with such comments obligatory and so even if the Committee were to change its practice and review reports individually, States would remain free to reject its recommendations. This does not mean they would always do so, of course. Under the present arrangements States have been known to revise national laws as a result of the Committee's questioning.[37] It does, however, further emphasise the point that Article 40 of the Covenant cannot be regarded as an effective procedure for implementation.

In summary, then, the provisions of the Covenant dealing with States' obligations to report are as they should be, and in practice it has proved possible to establish a constructive dialogue with governmental representatives and obtain additional information from them. Secondly, the opportunities for obtaining independent information are clearly inadequate, and this presents a particular problem for NGOs and imposes an additional burden on members of the Committee. Thirdly, the provisions of the Covenant and rules of procedure concerning the independence of members of the Committee are adequate, though vigilance will always be necessary to ensure that governments respect them scrupulously. Fourthly, the Covenant is clearly defective as regards the possibility of recommending remedial action where national measures are insufficient to give effect to the rights which the Covenant is designed to secure.

It is not really surprising that there are weaknesses and deficiencies in the reporting system instituted by the Covenant on Civil and Political Rights. It is, after all, the product of a heterogeneous United Nations community, some of whose members were in complete disagreement on the fundamental question of setting up any system of international control at all. Seen in this perspective, the reporting system is a compromise conditioned, like all arrangements based on international agreement, by the background and circumstances of its conclusion. Like other procedures we shall consider, it should also be seen as an arangement with the capacity to evolve, and in certain respects it has already developed beyond what might have been anticipated. Since there is a genuine place for reporting procedures in the machinery of human rights protection, it is important that the Human Rights Committee maintains this progress in the future.

6. *Proceedings between States parties*

As already noted, a great variety of proposals for implementation of the Covenants was put forward in the Commission on Human Rights when it was engaged in preparing its drafts between 1947 and 1954. These included suggestions for the establishment of an International Court of Human Rights, an International Investigation Commission, a High Commissioner for Human Rights, a new Specialised Agency for the implementation of the Covenants, and the creation of a panel of independent experts from whom an *ad hoc* Human Rights Committee could be selected when required. These proposals were launched during the period of enthusiasm for a new world order following the shattering experience of the Second World War. Before long, however, the traditional methods of diplomacy and notions of sovereignty reasserted themselves and these ambitious new ideas failed to attract the necessary support. By 1950 the Commission had decided that there should be a permanent body of independent persons to examine alleged violations of human rights, but that it should be accessible only to States and not to individuals or non-governmental organisations. This position remained unchanged when the Commission finished its work on the draft Covenants in 1954.

The Third Committee of the General Assembly, instead of strengthening the powers of the Human Rights Committee in relation to inter-State disputes, did just the opposite. The most important change which it made was to render the competence of the Committee to examine inter-State complaints an optional procedure, instead of one applying automatically to all States parties, as the Commission had recommended. Thus, Article 41 of the Covenant, which sets out in detail the procedure for considering inter-State 'communications', starts off with the words: 'A State Party ... may at any time declare ... that it recognises the competence of the Committee to receive and consider communications to the effect that a State Party claims that another State Party is not fulfilling its obligations under the present Covenant.' A separate declaration recognising this competence, in addition to the act of ratification, is therefore required. Moreover, it is not enough for the State alleged to be responsible for a violation to have made such a declaration. Communications can be considered by the Committee only if the complaining State has also done so. Thus, it is only States which have agreed to expose themselves to this procedure which have the right to use it against another party. Furthermore, under paragraph 2 of Article 41, the procedure would come into force only when ten States had made the necessary declarations. This number was achieved in 1979.[38] It is clear, nevertheless, that this procedure is not the principal means of implementation provided for in the Covenant.

It is interesting to compare the various human rights treaties from the point of view of the obligatory or optional nature of the systems of international control. To take them in chronological order, the European Convention on Human Rights makes the procedure for inter-State complaints obligatory for all contracting parties and the procedure of individual petition optional. The UN Covenant, as we have seen, makes both procedures optional. The American Convention on Human Rights makes the procedure of individual petition obligatory for all contracting parties and the procedure of inter-State complaints optional, while the African Charter on Human and Peoples' Rights adopts exactly the opposite approach to that of the United Nations Covenant and makes both the inter-State and individual complaints procedures compulsory.

Another way in which the Third Committee diluted the Commission's proposals is that the Human Rights Committee no longer has the right to express an opinion on the question of violation. The procedure set out in Article 41 of the Covenant envisages, in the first place, bilateral negotiations between the two States concerned. Secondly, if the matter is not settled, either State may refer it to the Human Rights Committee, which must examine the question in closed meetings, provided that domestic remedies have been exhausted. The Committee may call for all relevant information and the States parties may be represented and make oral and written submissions. Thirdly, the Committee is to make available its good offices with a view to a friendly settlement of the matter based on respect for human rights. Fourthly, and finally, if a friendly settlement is not achieved, the Committee is required to submit a report which is to be confined to a brief statement of the facts, with the written and oral submissions of the States parties attached. It is apparent, therefore, that the functions of the Committee in relation to inter-State disputes are limited to establishing the facts, proposing its good offices and exercising them if the offer is accepted. As certain representatives stated in the Third Committee, the Human Rights Committee is 'no longer the same as the quasi-judicial body originally proposed by the Commission on Human Rights' but 'more in the nature of a functional organ'.[39]

There is, however, another procedural possibility offered by Article 42 of the Covenant. This provides that if a matter referred to the Committee under Article 41 is not resolved to the satisfaction of the States concerned, the Committee may, if those States consent, appoint an *ad hoc* Conciliation Commission. This will in turn make available its good offices 'with a view to an amicable solution of the matter on the basis of respect for the present Covenant'. The Commission is to consist of five members who are nationals of States which have accepted the Article 41 procedure, but not nationals of the States parties to the dispute. Article 42 deals in some detail with the composition, method of election and procedure of the Conciliation Commission. In particular, it provides that the information obtained by the Human Rights Committee shall be made available to the Commission, which may also call on the States concerned for further information.

When it has completed its work, and in any event within a year of being apprised of the matter, the Conciliation Commission is to draw up its report. If an amicable solution has been reached, the report will contain a brief statement of the facts and the solution reached. If an amicable solution has not been reached, the report will contain a full statement of the facts and the Commission's views on 'the possibilities of an amicable solution of the matter'. Within three months of the receipt of the report, the States parties must indicate whether or not they accept the contents of the Commission's report.

The procedure laid down in Articles 41 and 42 of the Covenant has been aptly described as 'complex, delicate and long-winded'.[40] It can be summarised by saying that in inter-State disputes the function of the Human Rights Committee is one of good offices, while that of the Conciliation Commission is good offices and conciliation. However, neither function can be exercised except in relation to States both of which have made an express declaration accepting the competence of the Committee to exercise this function and, as regards the Conciliation Commission, consented to its appointment. To date only twenty-one States have made such a declaration and, having regard to this, it is likely to be some considerable time before the Human Rights Committee has any significant part to play in inter-State disputes. This conclusion is strengthened by the fact that twelve of the States to accept the Committee's competence are parties to the European Convention on Human Rights[41] and, as we shall see in Chapter 4, will not normally refer to the United Nations matters which can be considered by the European Commission. Furthermore, a number of States have made it clear that they will not accept this optional procedure, as they are opposed to the basic principle on which it rests. Indeed, it is hard to believe that many governments, other than those of democracies with genuine guarantees of freedom of expression and association, free elections, protection against arbitrary arrest and due process of law, will be willing to expose themselves to the possibility of complaints by other States that they are violating civil and political rights. As we have seen, the number of such States is not large. Twenty-one of them are members of the Council of Europe and parties to the European Convention and will therefore use the Strasbourg procedures in preference to those of Articles 41 and 42 of the UN Covenant. The prospects of extensive use of the latter, therefore, are not substantial.[42]

IV. Individual communications: the Optional Protocol

1. Background

The real test of the effectiveness of an international system for the protection of human rights is whether it permits an individual who believes that his rights have been violated to seek a remedy from an international institution. According to the classic conception, as we have seen, international law is the law which governs relations between States and the individual has no place. His interests are supposed to be protected by the State of which he is a national, and he has no *locus standi* before international tribunals or international organisations. However, there is no doubt that in the second half of the twentieth century certain inroads upon, or exceptions to, this classic doctrine have been established. The question which the modern international lawyer has to face is whether these inroads and exceptions are to be encouraged and further developed, or resisted and restricted. Opinion among international lawyers has been divided on this issue for forty years, and the debate will no doubt continue for at least another generation. There is an immense literature on the subject, and there have been and will continue to be innumerable speeches about it in the United Nations and elsewhere.[43]

To move from the general to the particular, there are two practical arguments which in our view are decisive. One is that the classic doctrine of international law simply does not work in the context of the protection of human rights. If an individual's rights are violated, in the great majority of cases it will be the result of acts by organs or agencies of the State of which he is a national. It is therefore absurd to pretend that his rights will be championed by the State of which he is a national when that State is *ex hypothesi* the offender. The other argument is that, as is well known, the United Nations receives thousands of communications each year complaining of violations of human rights throughout the world. Article 1 of the Charter states that one of the purposes of the United Nations is 'to achieve international co-operation ... in promoting and encouraging respect for human rights and fundamental freedoms for all ...', and there are seven other references in the Charter to the functions of the United Nations and its organs in relation to human rights. If, as was once the case, the organisation takes no action with regard to the communications it receives, it is failing to fulfil one of its principal functions. Considerations both of common sense and of the job of the United Nations under the Charter therefore make it necessary to adopt a constructive and positive attitude to the question of the individual's access to international remedies.

Such considerations produced discussions which lasted for many years in different UN organs about whether the Commission on Human Rights could take any action about human rights complaints from individuals and non-governmental organisations. In 1970 these finally led the Economic and Social Council to adopt its Resolution 1503, which authorises the Commission to examine 'communications, together with replies of governments, if any, which appear to reveal a consistent pattern of gross violations of human rights'. The procedure is rather complicated and will be discussed in the next chapter. Its existence has been mentioned at this stage because it was really the first recognition of the fact that the United Nations can and should respond to individual complaints of violation of human rights.

There is also a third important argument for allowing individuals who believe that their rights have been violated to appeal to an international organ of control. Once it is admitted that an international organ can be seized of inter-State complaints, then if no right of individual petition exists the only remedy available is the inter-State procedure. This means that aggrieved individuals will be tempted to look for another government that will champion their cause by bringing a case against the government of which they are nationals. Thus, Greek citizens whose rights were violated by the military regime in their country in 1967 were led to appeal to the Scandinavian governments for help. It is obviously in the interests of peaceful relations between States that what is essentially an individual or national problem should be dealt with as such and should not be transformed into an international dispute between States, with all the consequences which that entails.

When the Covenant on Civil and Political Rights was being drafted, it became necessary to face squarely the question whether the measures of implementation should include the right of individual petition to the Human Rights Committee. The Third Committee discussed the matter at length.[44] After it had approved the two articles on inter-State procedures, it considered an amendment by the Netherlands proposing the addition of a new article providing for the competence of the Human Rights Committee to receive and consider individual petitions on an optional basis – a text which was largely inspired by the corresponding provisions of the European Convention. Jamaica and France tabled further amendments, the French proposal being aimed at limiting the functions of the Committee to the simple receipt and transmission of communications. There followed a ten-power revised amendment, which followed the general lines of the earlier proposal of the Netherlands, but set out the procedure in greater detail. This would have authorised the Committee, when examining individual communications, to 'forward its suggestions, if any, to the State Party concerned and to the individual'.

During the discussion in the Third Committee all the old arguments for and against the right of individual petition were raised. Finally the debate turned on the question whether such a procedure should be included in the Covenant itself, on an optional basis, or in a separate protocol, which would also be optional. The representative of Lebanon made a formal proposal in the latter sense, which was adopted in a roll call vote by forty-one votes to thirty-nine, with sixteen abstentions. It was thus decided by a very narrow majority to incorporate the right of individual petition in a separate legal text.[45]

In one way it is a pity that such an important measure of implementation had to be omitted from the Covenant itself. On the other hand, this was probably a wise decision, because its inclusion would no doubt have discouraged ratification by countries suspicious of these arrangements. There is also perhaps a certain psychological advantage in the fact that the measure is included in a separate Optional Protocol, because this serves to emphasise the existence of the procedure of individual petition more than if it were set out in Article 43. The Protocol is now included separately in the list of United Nations treaties and ratifications are published and to some extent publicised. It is thus an object of greater attention than the optional procedure in Article 41 of the Covenant. The importance of this point should not be exaggerated, but given that the procedure could not be made compulsory, nothing seems to be lost and probably something is gained by the fact that the Optional Protocol exists as a separate legal text.

The Optional Protocol provides that any State party to the Covenant which ratifies the Protocol thereby 'recognises the competence of the Committee to receive and consider communications from individuals subject to its jurisdiction who claim to be victims of a violation by that State Party of any of the rights set forth in the Covenant'.[46] Articles 2 and 3 of the Protocol introduce the rule of exhaustion of domestic remedies and provide that communications shall be considered inadmissible if they are anonymous, abusive or incompatible with the provisions of the Covenant. Article 5, paragraph 2, introduces a further condition of admissibility, excluding communications which relate to a matter which is being examined under another procedure of international investigation or settlement. In itself this rule is entirely reasonable. It is curious, however, that it appears to burden the Committee with the positive obligation of ascertaining that the matter is not being examined under another international procedure, whereas it would seem more logical to provide that the Committee will examine a communication unless it can be shown that the matter is in fact being examined under another international procedure. The relationship between the procedures of the UN Committee and those of the European Commission of Human Rights will be examined in Chapter 4.

Paragraph 2 of Article 5 also repeats the rule of exhaustion of domestic remedies, adding that the rule shall not apply if the domestic remedies are unreasonably prolonged.

Article 4 and the remaining paragraphs of Article 5 deal with the procedure of the Committee when dealing with individual communications. They must be communicated to the State party concerned, which shall within six months 'submit to the Committee written explanations or statements clarifying the matter and the remedy, if any, that may have been taken by that State'. Nothing is said about oral hearings of the case, and Article 5, paragraph 2 makes it clear that the proceedings shall be based on 'all written information made available ... by the individual and the State Party concerned', which would seem to exclude oral hearings and information from other sources. Communications are to be examined at closed meetings and, under Article 5, paragraph 4, 'The Committee shall forward its views to the State Party concerned and to the individual'. At the present time thirty-nine States have ratified the Optional Protocol.[47]

2. *The work of the Committee*

Since the Human Rights Committee began its work under the Optional Protocol it has considered on average between twenty and twenty-five communications from individuals each year.[48] Of the cases referred to the Committee about half have been concluded without any decision on the merits, either because they here held to be inadmissible, or because they were discontinued, suspended, or withdrawn. The remainder, apart from some cases held over, have been decided on the merits.

The Committee's first reports to the General Assembly on its activities recorded the appointment of various working groups to consider the admissibility of individual communications, but since the proceedings are confidential, information was not published about the identity of the applicants, about the nature of the alleged violations or about the States against which the complaints were lodged. The Committee's early reports tell only the results of the procedural steps taken: decisions of inadmissibility; decisions to transmit communications to governments for their observations on admissibility; requests to applicants for further information, including steps to exhaust domestic remedies; and so on. The reports also give indications of the Committee's thinking on four topics: the standing of the author, the examination of complaints *ratione temporis*, the exhaustion of domestic remedies, and the problem of determining whether a matter is being examined under another international procedure of investigation or settlement.

In 1979 the Committee for the first time 'forwarded its views to the State Party concerned and to the individual' (Article 5(4)) and made public what was, in effect, its first 'decision' on a private communication under the Protocol. The Committee had received a 'communication' from a Uruguayan citizen alleging mistreatment of herself and three members of her family. Each had been charged with 'subversive association' or 'assistance to subversive association', and was allegedly detained without trial, held incommunicado and tortured. The Committee brought the communication to the attention of the government of Uruguay (Article 4(1)). The government of Uruguay objected to the admissibility of the claim on the grounds that domestic remedies had not been exhausted, and that the alleged violations against the principal complainant had occurred before the Covenant entered into force for Uruguay. The Committee agreed that acts occurring before the Covenant's entry into force were outside its jurisdiction. As regards violations alleged to have occurred after that date, however, the Committee found that no further domestic remedy was available. It decided also that the 'close family connection' permitted the author of the communication to act on behalf of herself and the other victims. When, after six months (Article 4(2)), the government of Uruguay failed to give a satisfactory explanation of its actions, the Committee formulated its views on the basis of the facts as alleged. It expressed the view that the facts disclosed several violations of the Covenant, including: torture and detention in unhealthy conditions, contrary to Articles 7 and 10(1); imprisonment after a release order, contrary to Article 9(1); failure to inform the prisoners of the charges against them, contrary to Article 9(2); denial of a prompt and fair trial, contrary to Articles 9(3) and 14; inadequate possibilities of appeal, contrary to Article 9(4); imprisonment incommunicado, contrary to Article 10(1); and denial of political rights, contrary to Article 25. The Committee expressed the view that the government of Uruguay was obliged to 'take immediate steps to ensure strict observance of the provisions of the Covenant and to provide effective remedies to the victims'.[49]

This first case is typical of many which the Committee has considered in recent years. Indeed, of the first sixty-four cases in which the Committee gave a decision on the merits, no less than forty-one, or sixty-four per cent, related to Uruguay and involved violations of the Covenant's most basic provisions. In the *Cubas Simones case*,[50] for example, a thirty-seven year old Uruguayan woman complained that she was arrested without a warrant at her family's home, held incommunicado at an unknown place for three months, then charged before a military court with subversion and aiding a conspiracy to violate the law. She was tried *in camera* without being present, given a defence counsel whom she could not consult, and the court's judgement was then not given in public. The Committee found her communication admissible in 1981 and in its decision on the merits a year later found that there had been violations of Article 10(1) (the right to be treated with humanity), Article 14(1) (the right to a fair and public hearing), Article 14(3)(b) (the right to an adequate defence) and Article 14(3)(d) (the right to be tried in one's presence).

The *Conteris case*[51] in 1985 was even worse. The victim here was a former Methodist pastor, journalist and university professor, who was arrested by the security police on account of previous connections with the Tupamaros movement. He was held incommunicado for three months in various military establishments where he was hung by the wrists, burned and subject to other forms of torture too horrible to describe. After signing a confession he was sentenced by a military court to fifteen years in prison, but following a change of government in Uruguay was subsequently released.

The communication in this case was submitted by the victim's sister and declared admissible in 1984. In the course of its study of this case the Committee emphasised the State's duty under Article 4(2) of the Optional Protocol to investigate alleged violations of the Covenant and to provide the Committee with any information in its possession. Finding, however, that the Government had failed to shed any light on the matter, the Committee did what it normally does in such situations and based its views on the evidence submitted by the author. Not surprisingly, the Committee concluded that the treatment endured by Mr Conteris involved violations of many articles of the Covenant including Article 7 (prohibition of torture), Articles 9(1) (prohibition of arbitrary arrest), 9(2) (right to be informed promptly of reasons for arrest), 9(3) (right to be brought promptly before a judge), 9(4) (habeas corpus), and Articles 10(1), 14(1) and 14(3), which have already been mentioned. While severely critical of the conduct of the Uruguayan authorities in this case, the Committee also expressed its satisfaction with the measures of the new government, especially the release of political prisoners.

Not all the cases involving flagrant violations of the Covenant have involved Uruguay. In 1985, for example, the Committee decided the *Wight case*[52] which involved Madagascar. The victim was a South African pilot, en route for Mauritius, who made an emergency landing in Madgascar. He was sentenced to five years' imprisonment for overflying the country without authority and when he escaped and was recaptured, sentenced to a further two years. After his recapture he was kept incommunicado and in solitary confinement for a period of three and a half months, during which he was chained to the floor with little food or clothing. He was then moved to a tiny basement where he spent a further month, after which he served the remainder of his sentence in a normal prison. As in the *Conteris case*, the Committee had no difficulty in deciding that the facts indicated violations of Articles 7, 10 and 14 of the Covenant. Counsel for Mr Wight also tried to show that the reason for his treatment was his South African nationality. However, although there was some evidence to support this, the Committee observed that the information available was not sufficient to prove discriminatory treatment.

Earlier, in 1982, the Committee decided an unusual case involving Colombia. The *Suarez de Guerrero case*[53] concerned the application of a law providing members of the police force with a defence to certain criminal charges. A police patrol was ordered to raid a house which it was believed was being used by kidnappers. Nothing was found, but the police decided to hide and await the suspects' arrival. Seven people subsequently came to the house and as each person arrived he or she was shot dead, at point blank range and often in the back. Criminal proceedings were begun against the policemen involved, but all were acquitted because the law provided a defence where the act which was the subject of a criminal charge was committed in the course of operations to prevent kidnapping.

The author of the communication in this case, who was acting on behalf of the husband of one of the victims, alleged that the application of this law violated the right to life which is guaranteed by Article 6(1) of the Covenant. The Committee agreed. Pointing out that the facts were not in dispute and that the emergency which, according to the government, had made special measures necessary could not justify a derogation from the right to life, the Committee ruled that the Covenant had been violated and that Colombia should take measures to compensate the victim's husband and amend the law in question.

Although a large part of the Committee's work has been taken up with consideration of serious abuses of one sort or another, these types of cases are by no means the whole of its work. In addition to cases involving torture, arbitrary detention and the grosser violations of human rights, the Committee is sometimes called upon to consider issues similar to those which arise under the European Convention. We shall see in Chapter 4 that almost all the cases which come to the European Commission of Human Rights concern either maladministration or the kinds of conflicts of interests which are features of any complex society. Cases of this type demonstrate that human rights are not just an issue in undemocratic societies and therefore from time to time also come to the Human Rights Committee. Indeed, because many of the world's democratic States have accepted the Optional Protocol, whereas most undemocratic States have not, such cases are more prominent than might be expected.

Typical of the cases in this second group is the *Hartikainen case*,[54] which concerned the State's obligation under Article 18(4) of the Covenant 'to have respect for the liberty of parents ... to ensure the religious and moral education of their children in conformity with their own convictions'. The author of the communication, who was a school teacher in Finland, complained that children who did not receive formal religious instruction were required to enrol in a course on the history of religions and ethics. The latter, according to the complaint, was biased towards Christianity and as such violated the rights of parents under the Covenant. An obvious objection to the communication was that as the author was a teacher, not a parent, he lacked standing to bring the complaint. However, since Finland had not sought to argue that the communication was inadmissible, the Committee reviewed the case on the merits.

The Committee decided that the law requiring the alternative course was not itself incompatible with the Covenant, provided 'such alternative course of instruction is given in a neutral and objective way and respects the convictions of parents and guardians who do not believe in any religion'. Noting that even the alternative course was not obligatory in all circumstances, and that the State was taking steps to deal with difficulties which had arisen over its implementation, the Committee decided that in all the circumstances there was nothing here incompatible with Article 18(4).

The issue in this case was rather similar to that considered in 1976 by the European Court in the *Danish Sex Education case*[55] and the Committee's reasoning is virtually identical. This shows the way in which, when similar issues arise, decisions under one human rights instrument can be influential elsewhere. In 1983, moreover, the Finnish government informed the Committee that it had amended its legislation and taken steps to monitor the teaching of the course complained of, so demonstrating that even a complaint which is formally unsuccessful, may nevertheless be effective.

Another case of the same type is the *Aumeeruddy-Cziffra case*, which was brought by a number of Mauritian women, some of whom had married foreigners and who now complained that their husbands' rights to residency and citizenship were subject to review. Since the same measures of control were not applicable to foreign wives, they complained of interference with the family contrary to Article 17(1) of the Covenant, and discrimination on grounds of sex, contrary to Articles 2(1), 3 and 26. Finding that the grounds for discriminatory treatment, which related to national security, were inadequate, the Committee upheld the complaint of the married petitioners on all counts.[56]

The *Aumeeruddy-Cziffra case* was decided in 1981 and two years later Mauritius informed the Committee that, in the light of its decision, the legislation in question had been amended so as to remove the element of sex discrimination. Again it is interesting to note that a case raising rather similar issues has been considered by the European Court,[57] which also found the element of discrimination objectionable.

When dealing with the question of the protection of the family under the Covenant, the Committee observed that 'the legal protection or measures a society or a State can afford to the family may vary from country to country and depend on different social, economic, political and cultural conditions and traditions.' This point, that there is often room for different ways of applying international obligations, is one of general importance in human rights law.

Another case in which this was emphasised was the *Hertzberg case*,[58] where the complaint related to the censorship of broadcasting in Finland. The author of the communication complained that programmes dealing with homosexuality were censored by the State broadcasting authorities and alleged that this violated the right to freedom of expression which is protected by Article 19(2) of the Covenant. The Committee, however, rejected the complaint. Explaining that as 'public morals differ widely ... a certain margin of discretion must be accorded to the responsible national authorities', the Committee held that the measures in question could not be regarded as contrary to the Covenant. We shall see in Chapter 4 that on numerous occasions the European Court has employed the concept of a 'margin of appreciation' as a way of accommodating national differences. Since the Human Rights Committee is dealing not with a single region, but with States from all over the world, it is not surprising that in its work also the concept of a national margin of discretion has proved extremely useful.

Not all the cases which the Committee decides concern rights which are also protected by other instruments. One of the Committee's most interesting cases, the *Lovelace case*,[59] raised an issue under Article 27 of the Covenant which concerns the protection of minorities and which, as we have seen, is unique to the Covenant. The petitioner in this case was an Indian woman who married a non-Indian and thereby lost her status under Canadian law. When her marriage broke up she returned to the Indian reserve, but found that she was not accepted. Since Indian men do not lose status if they marry non-Indian women, she complained that this treatment violated the Covenant.

The Committee decided that although the Covenant obviously does not guarantee the right to live on an Indian reserve, it does guarantee the members of a minority access to native culture and language, which in the circumstances of this case had been unjustly denied. Following the Committee's decision, the Canadian government amended the legislation so as to restore the petitioner's status. It is interesting to note, however, that this change was opposed by some Indian leaders on the ground that the right to preserve their culture, which is guaranteed by Canadian law, includes the right to maintain a social structure of which sex-based discrimination is, in their view, an essential part.[60] Although this claim has not yet been raised before the Human Rights Committee, it is a striking demonstration of the complexity of these issues and the adjudicator's dilemma when incompatible claims come into collision.

3. *Appraisal*

An evaluation of what has been achieved under the Optional Protocol and how the work of the Human Rights Committee may develop in the future calls for consideration of several aspects of its record to date.

First, there is the scale of this dimension of the Committee's activity. Between five and ten decisions on the merits each year is a respectable number by international standards, but seems insignificant when set against the deplorable state of human rights in many parts of the world. When it is also recalled that more than half of the early decisions relate to a single State, the selective nature of the Committee's work, and hence the limited contribution of the Protocol to the protection of human rights, is further emphasised.

The factors which shape the Committee's case-load are not difficult to identify. The majority of members of the United Nations have not accepted the Optional Protocol. Indeed, less than half the parties to the Covenant have done so. In addition, the States which have not accepted the right of individual petition include many of those with the worst record on human rights. This situation, which is, of course, not accidental means that many of the most serious cases lie outside the Committee's jurisdiction. Since it is unlikely that the range of the Committee's competence will be enlarged much in the foreseeable future, the fact that so many States cannot be the object of petitions seems bound to remain a major limitation.

When the States which have accepted the Protocol are considered, other factors became apparent. Many of the States which have accepted the Committee's jurisdiction have an excellent record on human rights and already provide domestic means of dealing with complaints. While this does not make international procedures irrelevant, it does reduce the number of complaints which reach the international level. The fact that the Committee is never going to have a large number of complaints against, say, Canada or Norway, is therefore another influence on the nature of its work.

It is also necessary to remember that many of the States with good human rights records, and some whose records are less good, are already parties to regional treaties on human rights. These may provide an alternative forum for consideration of individual complaints. The participation of a State in a regional system does not in itself prevent an individual from referring a case to the Human Rights Committee if the State concerned has also accepted the Optional Protocol. However, as we shall see later, it is not usually possible to have a complaint considered in both systems. Consequently, the number of cases referred under the Optional Protocol is to some extent a reflection of the vigour and attractiveness of regional systems. Since the European and Inter-American systems are conspicuously active, and have now been joined by an African system, the relation between the Committee's work and regional systems is another factor of continuing importance.

The second element to be considered in assessing the Optional Protocol is how the Committee has discharged the task of deciding the cases which have been referred to it and the contribution its decisions have made to the law. No organ of the type represented by the Human Rights Committee can be counted as successful unless it deals competently with matters which fall within its jurisdiction. A body which is incompetent will not only antagonise States, which is particularly damaging for an organ which lacks compulsory jurisdiction and depends on co-operation, but will also lose the confidence of individuals on whose communications its work depends. The importance of such confidence should not be overlooked. After all, the Covenant is not the only human rights treaty, and, as we have mentioned, individuals who consider that their rights have been violated may have avenues of complaint available elsewhere. If, therefore, the Human Rights Committee is to be regarded as an effective forum for ventilating complaints, it is essential that it should be proficient.

Judged by the criterion of competence, the Human Rights Committee can certainly be rated a success. It is true that about half the communications to the Committee are rejected on grounds of admissibility, but this is not unusual for a body dealing with human rights complaints, and is actually low by international standards.[61]

The Committee's decisions on admissibility are now published and, since they are fully reasoned, already constitute a body of case-law providing a useful indication of the scope of the Committee's powers. Analysis of this record suggests that the Committee has interpreted its jurisdiction quite broadly and has certainly adopted a less restrictive approach to admissibility than the European Commission of Human Rights in its early years.[62] The latter often used to reject claims at the stage of admissibility on grounds which it would have been more appropriate to consider as part of the merits. Although a similar tendency has been detected in certain recent decisions of the Human Rights Committee,[63] its handling of issues of admissibility in general has been satisfactory.

Cases which proceed to the merits call for the Committee to attempt to establish the facts, and here, as we have seen, it has sometimes encountered problems. When governments co-operate, as they generally do in cases involving the less serious type of complaint, there is no difficulty. In the many cases involving allegations of flagrant violations of human rights, on the other hand, the governments concerned are often much less helpful, with the result that the Committee can face formidable evidentiary problems. In such situations, as we have seen, the Committee has taken the view that the test is not whether a complaint has been proved beyond all reasonable doubt, a test which would frequently be impossible to satisfy, but rather whether a complaint which is consistent with the evidence available to the Committee has been successfully refuted by the State. If it has not, the Committee will regard the facts as proved, and the absence of an adequate explanation as indicative. As regards the facts, then, the Committee does its best but, using an approach which has also been adopted by the American Commission of Human Rights for such situations,[64] will not allow non co-operation to prevent a decision.

As regards its approach to the law, the Committee again emerges with credit. Although it is important to remember that the Committee is not an international court, but rather a quasi-judicial body, its decisions demonstrate the advantages of entrusting the interpretation and application of the Covenant to a body of independent experts rather than to government representatives. Because its decisions are reasoned, the Committee's work constitutes an important body of case-law in which, as noted above, fundamental issues of life and liberty and philosophically interesting problems of human rights have all been considered.[65] In dealing with these questions the Committee has made little reference to the wider body of human rights law, but its decisions, as might be expected, are none the less a reflection of that tradition. It is true also that some of the most controversial issues in human rights law have still to be considered under the Protocol and that when they are, differences of opinion among the members of the Committee are likely to be reflected in its decisions. This, however, is inevitable. While matters would be simpler if everyone saw the Covenant in the same way, as this is not the case, another of the Committee's functions will be to provide a forum where differences can be articulated and the possibility of a common understanding explored.

The third and final factor to be considered in assessing the work of the Human Rights Committee under the Optional Protocol is the effect of its decisions on States which are found to be in breach of their obligations. From our review of a representative sample of the Committee's case-law it will be obvious that the reception of decisions is something which can vary widely. Governments which co-operate with the Committee at the stage of investigation are normally those involved in the less serious cases and, as a rule, are anxious to take whatever steps are needed to correct any deficiency which the Committee has identified. Thus, as we have seen, Canada amended its legislation following the decision in the *Lovelace case*, Mauritius changed its law in response to the *Aumeeruddy-Cziffra case*, while Finland changed its law in the light of the *Hartikainen* decision, even though no violation of the Covenant had been found. These cases show that use of the Optional Protocol can have a direct effect on the protection of rights within a State and demonstrate a point which we shall find confirmed in Chapter 4, that governments which have the least to be ashamed of are usually also the first to correct their mistakes.

When we turn from these cases to those in which the allegation is of gross violations of human rights, the record is much less satisfactory. Steps may be taken to deal with a problem identified by the Committee, as in the *Suarez de Guerrero case*, but compliance with the letter, and more important, the spirit of the Committee's decision certainly cannot be guaranteed. Just as governments which routinely abuse rights will do their best to obstruct investigation of their practices, so when an international decision is handed down, it is unlikely that much will be done in the way of either compensating the victim, or dealing with the general problem. If the parallel with the first type of case is the ready compliance of States with decisions under the European Convention on Human Rights, the parallel with the second is the experience of the Inter-American Commission which, as we shall see in Chapter 5, has the thankless task of supervising a very different regional system.

The contrast between the effectiveness of some of the Committee's decisions and the apparent ineffectiveness of others is a reminder of the single most important factor about the Optional Protocol, that the Human Rights Committee is not like a domestic court, issuing judgements and equipped with the power to enforce them, but a body which 'forwards its views' to the individual and government concerned and reports to the General Assembly through the Economic and Social Council, which is the organ with political responsibility for supervising the Covenant.

In relation to States with a poor record on human rights the significance of the Optional Protocol is that, where it has been accepted, it provides a way of publicising abuses and putting pressure on the State to improve in much the same way as the compulsory reporting procedure. As a way of ensuring that States respect the rights of the individual, this is indirect, not always visible and, of course, may not be effective. However, since political pressure is sometimes the best, and often the only way of encouraging governments to improve their practice, the procedure under the Optional Protocol has a value which should be recognised.

If we think of the Human Rights Committee as a sort of Supreme Court of Human Rights, we shall inevitably be disappointed by the scale and effect of its activity. If, on the other hand, we see the Committee for what it is, as one of several bodies charged with responsibility for human rights, then the procedure under the Optional Protocol appears in its true light – as just one of a number of ways in which States can be encouraged to respect their obligations. The Committee, then, is significant and certainly to be encouraged, but it is not alone. Procedures which need to be taken into account if the role of the Committee is to be seen in perspective, will therefore now be considered.

Notes

1 The leading work on the provisions of the Charter relating to human rights is Sir H. Lauterpacht, *International Law and Human Rights*, London, 1950. Part III contains the author's own proposals for an International Bill of Human Rights.
2 L. B. Sohn, 'A short history of United Nations documents on human rights', in *The United Nations and Human Rights*, eighteenth report of the Commission to Study the Organisation of Peace, New York, 1968, pp. 51–2.
3 Quoted by Sohn, *ibid*, p. 55.
4 The eight abstentions were from the Soviet bloc, South Africa and Saudi Arabia. For the history of the Universal Declaration see Lauterpacht, *Human Rights*.
5 Quoted in Sohn, 'A short history', p. 70.
6 *Ibid.*, p. 71.
7 Resolution 1514 (XV), which was passed with ninety votes in favour, none against and nine abstentions.
8 Resolution 1904 (XVIII).
9 Resolution 421 (V) of 4 December 1950.
10 Resolutions 543 (VI) and 545 (VI) of 5 February 1952.
11 Sohn, 'A short history', pp. 103, 105, 125, 132, 137.
12 *Ibid.*, pp. 127, 132, 154, 163.
13 *Ibid.*, pp. 143–4, 161.
14 *Report of the tenth session of the Commission*, doc. E/2573, pp. 62–72.
15 Document A/2929 of 1 July 1955.
16 The decision of the Third Committee on this issue was taken by a majority of forty-one votes to thirty-nine with sixteen abstentions.
17 Resolution 2200 of 16 December 1966.
18 As of 1 January 1988. See J. B. Marie, 'International instruments relating to human rights', *Human Rights Law Journal*, IX, 1988, p. 113.
19 The following works and articles on the Covenants are particularly recommended: C. M. Eichelberger (ed.), *The United Nations and Human Rights*, New York, 1968; E. Schwelb, 'Civil and political rights: the international measures of implementation', *American Journal of International Law*, LXII, 1968, p. 827 and A. G. Mower, 'The implementation of the UN Covenant on Civil and Political Rights', *Human Rights Journal*, X, 1977, p. 271. Further references relating to the Covenant on Economic, Social and Cultural Rights will be found in Chapter 7.
20 Resolution 1514 (XV) of 14 December 1960.
21 For an attempt to rely on the right to self-determination in proceedings before the Human Rights Committee see the *Mikmaq case*, Communication No. R. 19/78. Text of the decision of the Human Rights Committee in *Human Rights Law Journal*, V, 1984, p. 194.
22 It is interesting to compare the different approaches to this issue by the regional organisations. The European Commission of Human Rights, established under the European Convention, consists of a number of members equal to the number of contracting parties, currently twenty-one. By contrast, the Inter-American Commission of Human Rights, whose composition is now defined by the American Convention on Human Rights, consists of only seven members. The

African Commission, on the other hand, now formed in accordance with the African Charter on Human and Peoples' Rights, has eleven members.

23 Compare Article 9 of the Statute of the International Court of Justice which requires that 'the representation of the main forms of civilisation and of the principal legal systems of the world should be assured'.

24 The same principle is to be found in Article 23 of the European Convention, Article 36 of the American Convention, and Article 38 of the African Charter.

25 Mr T. Opsahl of Norway. In 1980 the British member of the UN Committee, Sir Vincent Evans, was elected a judge of the European Court of Human Rights, while the Austrian member of the European Commission was elected to the UN Committee.

26 *First Annual Report of the Human Rights Committee to the General Assembly*, doc. A/32/44 (1977), paras 46–7. As noted below, however, decisions in relation to individual communications are now published.

27 *Ibid.*, paras 28–32.

28 UN doc. A/2929, Chapter VII, para. 161.

29 *Ibid.*, paras 162–6; UN doc. A/6546, para. 382.

30 UN doc. A/6546, para. 384.

31 I.C.J. *Review*, No. 20, 1978, p. 25.

32 See D. D. Fischer, 'Reporting under the Covenant on Civil and Political Rights: the first five years of the Human Rights Committee', *American Journal of International Law*, LXXVI, 1982, pp. 142, 145.

33 UN doc. A/6546, 1966, paras 378 and 385.

34 Rule 67, para. 2 states that the Committee 'may invite the Specialised Agencies ... to submit comments on those parts ...'. In other words, they may do so only on request.

35 See Fischer, 'Reporting under the Covenant', p. 144.

36 See T. Meron, *Human Rights Law Making in the United Nations*, Oxford, 1986, pp. 124–5.

37 See Fischer, 'Reporting under the Covenant', pp. 151–3.

38 By 1 January 1988 such declarations had been made by twenty-one States. See Marie, 'International instruments'.

39 UN doc. A/6546 (1966), para. 308.

40 P. R. Ghandi, 'The Human Rights Committee and the right of individual communication', *British Year Book of International Law*, LVII, 1986, pp. 201, 203.

41 The States concerned are: Austria, Belgium, Denmark, German Federal Republic, Iceland, Italy, Luxembourg, Netherlands, Norway, Spain, Sweden, and the United Kingdom.

42 At the time of writing the inter-State procedure has still be be used.

43 See, for example, F. Ermacora, 'Human rights and domestic jurisdiction', 124, *Hague Recueil des Cours*, 1968, p. 371 and the works cited in Council of Europe, *Bibliography on the European Convention on Human Rights*, third edition, 1978, pp. 42–6.

44 *Report of the Third Committee*, doc. A/6546 (1966), paras 474–85.

45 *Ibid.*, para 485. Most of the Soviet bloc, and the Asian and African States voted in favour. Most of the Western group and the Latin American States voted against. Among the abstentions were: Brazil, China, Cyprus, Greece, Israel and

Turkey. When it came to the vote in the General Assembly on 16 December 1966, the Optional Protocol was approved by sixty-six votes to two, with thirty-eight abstentions.

46 The Protocol was in part inspired by Article 14 of the Convention on the Elimination of All Forms of Discrimination, of 21 December 1965.

47 As of 1 January 1988. See Marie, 'International instruments'.

48 For an outline of the procedure under the Optional Protocol see H. Hannum (ed.), *Guide to International Human Rights Practice*, London, 1984, pp. 67–72. For a useful summary of the work of the Human Rights Committee see the periodic surveys of the Committee's decisions by M. Nowak in the *Human Rights Law Journal*, I, 1980, p. 136; II, 1981, p. 168; III, 1982, p. 207; V, 1984, p. 199; and VII, 1986, p. 287.

49 *Report of the Human Rights Committee*, doc. A/34/40 (1979), Annex VII.

50 Comm. No. R. 17/70 of 3 May 1980. Decision of 1 April 1982. See M. Nowak, *Human Rights Law Journal*, III, 1982, p. 214.

51 Comm. No. R. 139/1983. Decision of 17 July 1985. See M. Nowak, *Human Rights Law Journal*, VII, 1986, p. 295.

52 Comm. No. 115/1982, Decision of 1 April 1985. See M. Nowak, *ibid.*, p. 294.

53 Comm. No. R. 11/45, Decision of 31 March 1982. Text in *Human Rights Law Journal*, III, 1982, p. 168.

54 Comm. No. R. 9/40, Decision of 9 April 1981. Text in *Human Rights Law Journal*, II, 1981, p. 133.

55 Series A, No. 23.

56 Comm. No. R. 9/35, Decision of 9 April 1981. Text in *Human Rights Law Journal*, II, 1981, p. 139. The complaints of the unmarried petitioners, however, were rejected on the ground that their rights had not been interfered with.

57 See *Abdulaziz, Cabales and Balkandali* case, Series A, No. 94.

58 Comm. No. R. 14/61, Decision of 2 April 1982. Text in *Human Rights Law Journal*, III, 1982, p. 174.

59 Comm. No. R. 6/24, Decision of 30 July 1981. Text in *Human Rights Law Journal*, II, 1981, p. 158. For discussion see A. F. Bayefsky, 'The Human Rights Committee and the Case of Sandra Lovelace', *Canadian Yearbook of International Law*, XX, 1982, p. 244.

60 See H. M. Kindred and others, *International Law Chiefly as Interpreted and Applied in Canada*, fourth edition, Canada, 1987, p. 671.

61 It should be noted, however, that communications relating to States which are not parties to the Optional Protocol are not passed to the Human Rights Committee by the Secretariat. This obviously reduces the number of cases which are ruled inadmissible. See Hannum, *Guide*, p. 68.

62 For an excellent review of the Committee's treatment of admissibility see P. R. Ghandi, 'The Human Rights Committee'.

63 See M. Nowak, 'UN – Human Rights Committee. Survey of decisions given up to July 1986', *Human Rights Law Journal*, VII, 1986, p. 287 at p. 303.

64 See Chapter 5.

65 For discussion of the significance of the Committee's early decisions, see B. C. Ramcharan, 'The emerging jurisprudence of the Human Rights Committee', *Dalhousie Law Journal*, VI, 1980–81, p. 7.

CHAPTER 3

The United Nations and human rights II: other instruments and procedures

1. Standard Setting

There are many other United Nations texts and procedures which concern human rights in addition to the Universal Declaration and the two Covenants, but space does not permit consideration of them in detail. We must, however, mention the more important Conventions, whose character is evident from their titles. They include the Convention on the Prevention and Punishment of the Crime of Genocide of 1948; the Supplementary Convention on the Abolition of Slavery and the Slave Trade of 1956; three Conventions on Nationality and Statelessness, which deal with the Nationality of Married Women (1957), the Reduction of Statelessness (1961) and the Status of Stateless Persons (1954); the Convention on the Status of Refugees (1951) and its Protocol (1966); the Convention on the Political Rights of Women (1952); the Convention on the Non-applicability of Statutory Limitations to War Crimes and Crimes against Humanity (1968); and the Convention against Torture (1984).[1]

As is well known, the United Nations has been particularly concerned with the prevention of discrimination. This concern is reflected in the 1965 International Convention on the Elimination of All Forms of Discrimination and the 1979 Convention on the Elimination of All Forms of Discrimination against Women, which are discussed below, the International Convention on the Suppression and Punishment of the Crime of Apartheid of 1973, and the 1981 Declaration on the Elimination of All Forms of Intolerance and Discrimination based on Religion or Belief. The Specialised Agencies, for their part, have produced conventions for the elimination of discrimination in employment (ILO) and in education (UNESCO) which we will examine in Chapter 7.

This considerable volume of international legislation is the product of what may be called the promotional or standard-setting function of the United Nations, that is to say the creation of rules of international law which lay down the standards of human rights which States must observe. This was the main activity of the organisation in relation to human rights until 1966, when the Covenants were adopted, and, as the list above indicates, the Commission on Human Rights has continued to produce texts on a variety of important issues. There has, however, now been something of a change of emphasis and more attention has been given in recent years to the protection of human rights, that is to the prevention or remedying of violations which occur. Certain procedures designed to afford a remedy for violations were included in the Covenants and have already been described. Other procedures of this nature form the subject of the rest of this chapter.

2. The Resolution 1503 procedure

From the time the United Nations was first established the Secretary-General has received thousands of communications annually from individuals or non-governmental organisations, complaining of violations of human rights. For many years, however, the Commission on Human Rights considered that it had 'no power to take any action in regard to any complaints concerning human rights'. This attitude was approved by the Economic and Social Council in 1947 and reaffirmed by the Council in 1959.[2] Various attempts to adopt a more positive approach were made, but were regularly countered by the argument, from the Soviet Union and others, that consideration of individual complaints would constitute 'intervention in matters which are essentially within the domestic jurisdiction of States', in violation of Article 2(7) of the Charter.

After 1965, however, the situation changed. The principal reason was the large increase in Afro-Asian members of the United Nations and the increase in the membership of the Commission on Human Rights. The enlargement of the Commission was intended to encourage the participation of new members who were particularly concerned with such problems as racial discrimination and apartheid, colonialism and underdevelopment.

The new orientation of the Commission, and the organisation as a whole, produced a refreshing change of attitude towards the role of the United Nations with regard to human rights. In 1966 the General Assembly, in Resolution 2144 (xx), invited the Economic and Social Council and the Commission 'to give urgent consideration to ways and means of improving the capacity of the United Nations to put a stop to violations of human rights wherever they might occur'. One of the consequences was a proposal by the Commission that it should be permitted to examine 'communications, together with replies of governments, if any, which appear to reveal a consistent pattern of gross violations of human rights'. In 1970 this step was approved by the Economic and Social Council in its Resolution 1503, which authorised the Commission to perform this function. The system is therefore known as 'the Resolution 1503 procedure'.

Following the Council's authorisation, the Commission set up an elaborate procedure for processing communications involving a body called the Sub-Commission on the Prevention of Discrimination and Protection of Minorities,[3] to consider communications and, where appropriate, pass them on to the Commission. If a communication reaches the Commission, it can decide to reject it, pass it on to the Economic and Social Council, or keep it under review. Up to this point the whole procedure is confidential, but when a communication reaches ECOSOC the proceedings become public. It is rare, however, for matters to reach that stage. This happened in 1979 in relation to communications concerning Equatorial Guinea and again in 1985 with regard to Argentina and Uruguay. In the latter cases, however, the reference to the Council was at the request of the two governments.

Although the Resolution 1503 procedure is confidential, in 1978 the Chairman of the Commission began the practice of announcing which countries had been the subject of consideration. We therefore know that in the next seven years complaints relating to twenty-nine countries were dealt with under the confidential procedure.[4] Since 1984 the Chairman has also announced when countries are no longer under review. When a country is removed from the list it is not usually difficult to see why. In 1984, for example, Afghanistan was removed, following the Commission's decision to appoint a special rapporteur to conduct an investigation there. In 1985, on the other hand, Uruguay, which had been on the list since 1980, was removed following a change of government.

When the Resolution 1503 procedure was set up many saw it as an important breakthrough and a move away from a neglect of human rights which had been described by the Secretary-General as 'bound to lower the prestige and authority not only of the Commission on Human Rights but of the United Nations in the opinion of the general public'.[5] How far have the expectations invested in this procedure been realised?

Criticism of the procedure has tended to focus on two of its prominent features: its confidential nature and its apparent lack of effectiveness. Critics of the confidentiality of the procedure seem to assume that the best way to change behaviour is by confrontation, but in international affairs, as in personal relations, this is not the case. Significantly, confidentiality is a feature of the initial stage of proceedings under the European Convention on Human Rights and, as we shall see shortly, the United Nations Commission has a public procedure available in situations where this is appropriate. Moreover, although the procedure under Resolution 1503 is confidential, it is certainly not secret. Every communication is seen in summary by the forty-three government representatives on the Commission. Since the Commission is also informed of the government's response at each stage, it has been pointed out that 'all decision-makers in the United Nations in the field of human rights are aware of the available information on the human rights situation in the country concerned.'[6] A procedure which was both confidential and secret would clearly be open to objection on the ground that governments would have no compelling reason to improve their practices. Under the Resolution 1503 procedure, however, there is a sufficient degree of openness for the desire to avoid embarrassment to be significant.

This brings us to the second point, which concerns the effectiveness of the system. Here the criticism is that the procedure is cumbersome and slow and that this, together with the fact that the whole procedure is confidential, means that for long periods of time nothing appears to be happening. Is this then a system which achieves results, or is it one which promises more than it can deliver?

Any procedure for protecting human rights must ultimately be judged by its results, and it is right that Resolution 1503 should be assessed from this point of view. Before rejecting the confidential procedure as ineffective, however, we should be clear about what this kind of arrangement is meant to achieve. The objective is not, as is sometimes assumed, to register convictions against a State and then pass the decision elsewhere for enforcement. If this were so, criticism of the slowness and complexity of the procedure would certainly be justified. But this is not the aim. Rather the aim is to establish a dialogue with the government concerned and to make it clear, on the one hand, that if there is no improvement consideration of the case will continue, and on the other that co-operation will be rewarded.

Since the object of the procedure is not to produce a judgement, but to maintain discreet political pressure, the complexity of the procedure is actually an advantage, for as a member of the Sub-Commission has observed:

> Everything which induces a government to co-operate is particularly important because the efficacity of United Nations procedures in the field of human rights depends to a large extent, on the measure of dialogue which can be established between the United Nations and the government of the country concerned. The procedure is useful as long as it is a means of exercising pressure on the country concerned. By expressing regrets when communications are kept pending ... instead of being forwarded to the superior organ, human rights friends overlook the point that there is no real solution to the problem at the end of the procedure. The succession of steps composing the procedure is more influential than the actual step itself.[7]

Because the procedure is confidential it is, of course, difficult to know precisely what effect it has on governments' behaviour. As we pointed out earlier, however, governments are sensitive to criticism on human rights matters. As a result, procedures which have the effect of drawing attention to their shortcomings, whether publicly, as with the decisions of the Human Rights Committee, or in the more limited forum of the Commission on Human Rights, can all be regarded as useful.

Although it would be wrong to exaggerate the significance of the Resolution 1503 procedure, we can conclude that it fulfils a modest but constructive role. Specifically, three advantages of dealing with human rights complaints through this procedure may be identified.

First, it provides a way of bringing abuses of human rights to the attention of international bodies in circumstances where this might not otherwise occur. Governments, as we have seen, are often reluctant to take up human rights cases and the procedure under the Optional Protocol to the Covenant on Civil and Political Rights, which allows individuals to initiate proceedings, is binding on only a limited number of States. Anyone, however, can write to the United Nations and ask to have his case considered. There is naturally no guarantee that a complaint will be taken up, but the evidence suggests that complaints which are numerous and serious are unlikely to be ignored, which was certainly not the position before the confidential procedure became available.

The second advantage of the Resolution 1503 procedure is that once a human rights issue is on the international agenda, the government concerned may be persusaded to do something about it. As we saw in Chapter 2, this is true of human rights procedures generally, but the distinctive features of the confidential procedure are that, being confidential, it may sometimes be more effective than more dramatic methods and that, because it is so elaborate, it provides a way of maintaining pressure on a government almost indefinitely.

The third advantage is that dealing with the human rights situation in a country through the confidential procedure may make it easier for the Commission to take the next step and deal with it through its public procedure. As we shall see shortly, most of the Commission's public investigations of the situation of human rights in a particular country have been preceded by consideration of communications under the confidential procedure. Although, therefore, the Resolution 1503 procedure may not in itself bring about a change of practice, it can sometimes prepare the way for the use of other procedures which may have the desired effect.

3. *Investigation of particular countries*

In June 1967 the Economic and Social Council adopted Resolution 1235 in which it approved the Commission's decision to give annual consideration to an item entitled 'Questions of the violation of human rights and fundamental freedoms, including policies of racial discrimination and segregation and of apartheid, in all countries, with particular reference to colonial and other dependent countries and territories.' Like Resolution 1503, this was the result of the renewed interest in human rights shown by General Assembly Resolution 2144 and, as with the confidential procedure, has been extensively used.

The Resolution 1235 procedure, which is public, can be initiated by a member State, or group of States, or by the Sub-Commission on the Prevention of Discrimination and the Protection of Minorities. The Commission itself decides whether or not to act on any proposal that is made, and its decision, as might be expected, is generally influenced by political considerations. If the Commission decides to make a thorough study of a particular situation, it may appoint a working group or a special rapporteur to study and report, or ask the Secretary-General to do so. It may also adopt a resolution condemning a situation and notify the government concerned. In all cases it will report, through the Council, to the General Assembly.

The precedent for the public investigation of the situation in a particular country was the appointment of the Ad Hoc Working Group of Experts on the situation of human rights in Southern Africa. This was established by the Commission in March 1967,[8] originally to investigate and report on the torture and ill-treatment of prisoners and persons arrested by the police in South Africa. Its mandate has been periodically renewed and was enlarged so as to extend to other countries in Africa: Namibia and, until they obtained their independence, the Portuguese colonies of Angola, Mozambique and Guinea Bissau, and also Southern Rhodesia (now Zimbabwe). This Ad Hoc Group of Experts was unable to visit the countries concerned, because permission was refused, but did visit neighbouring countries, where they heard witnesses and considered communications from interested parties. In 1974, for example, they heard over 100 witnesses on the situation in the territories concerned, and on the basis of this evidence drew up reports for the Commission and the Economic and Social Council. The resolutions and recommendations of these bodies are communicated to all organs of the United Nations concerned with the situation in southern Africa and given wide publicity.

The next group to be established was the Special Committee to investigate Israeli practices in the Occupied Territories, that is the territories occupied by Israel as a result of the war of 1967. This special committee was created by the General Assembly in December 1968, after earlier discussions in the Security Council and at the International Conference on Human Rights in Tehran. The government of Israel proposed that the terms of reference of the special committee should be extended to cover the treatment of Jewish minorities in Arab countries, and when this request was refused and after difficulties over the appointment of the members of the special committee, Israel refused to co-operate with it or to admit its members to the territories concerned.

The special committee obtained whatever information it could from various sources, including investigations in neighbouring countries, and has produced reports which have been considered by the General Assembly and by the Commission on Human Rights, which has kept this question on its agenda.

The third investigation of this kind was carried out by the Ad Hoc Working Group on the situation of human rights in Chile. After the *coup d'état* in September 1973, the situation there was discussed at the session of the Commission on Human Rights in February 1974 and a telegram was sent to the Chilean government expressing concern at the numerous reports of flagrant and massive violations of human rights. In the summer of that year the Sub-Commission requested the Commission to study the situation in detail at its next session and invited both governmental and non-governmental organisations with information about torture and inhuman treatment in Chile to submit it to the Commission. In the autumn of 1974 the General Assembly supported this request and asked the Commission to undertake an investigation. At its session in February 1975 the Commission decided to do so, and appointed an Ad Hoc Working Group of five members, asking the Chilean government to grant to it all necessary facilities. At first the government promised to do so, and arrangements were made for the group to visit Chile in July of that year. But when its members met in Lima on the way to Santiago, they learned that authorisation for their visit had been cancelled. They were therefore forced to use different and less satisfactory methods, such as collecting information from other sources and hearing witnesses outside the country. On this basis the Working Group, whose mandate was renewed annually, submitted several reports to the General Assembly and the Commission in which they concluded that flagrant violations of human rights continued to take place in Chile. The Assembly and the Commission therefore renewed their appeals to the Chilean government.

In 1978 the Chilean government finally agreed to a two-week visit by the Ad Hoc Working Group, during the course of which it had meetings with government officials and judges, and representatives of the Churches and private organisations. It also visited detention centres and interviewed prisoners. In its reports to the General Assembly and the Commission it stated that the human rights situation had improved to a certain extent, but that there were still frequent and serious violations.[9]

In 1979 the Commission once more demanded that the Chilean government should take a series of measures to restore human rights in Chile. It decided to continue to follow the situation in that country and appointed a special rapporteur for the purpose.[10] This put an end to the mission of the Ad Hoc Working Group itself, but not to the interest of the United Nations, for successive rapporteurs continued to report annually to the Commission and the General Assembly. Though the proceedings of the Working Group had been slow and fraught with difficulties, it was the first case of a United Nations mission of enquiry carried out on the territory of a member State and, as such, was to prove an important precedent.[11]

The appointment of a special rapporteur to examine the situation of human rights in a particular country was next used in the case of Equatorial Guinea.[12] Originally the examination of complaints against the Macias dictatorship in that country was undertaken as a confidential procedure under Resolution 1503. But in 1979 the Commission decided to make a public enquiry under Resolution 1235 and appointed a special rapporteur for the purpose. In August 1979 Macias was overthrown by a *coup d'état*, following which the special rapporteur was able to visit the country and investigate the situation. The Commission considered his report in 1980. It indicated a considerable improvement as regards respect for human rights, and appealed to the Commission to provide Equatorial Guinea with assistance which the new government wished to receive in order to restore human rights on its territory. In 1981 the Commission requested the Secretary-General to draw up a draft plan of action. This was done, and in 1984 the Commission asked the Secretary-General to appoint an expert to advise on its implementation. The expert, who was in fact the former rapporteur, visited the country again and reported that although progress had been made, other measures, including modifications in the constitution, were needed. The Commission took note of this and requested the Secretary-General to appoint a further expert to assist the government in implementing the plan of action.

The investigations undertaken by the Commission during the same period in Bolivia, El Salvador and Guatemala followed a broadly similar pattern.[13] In each case study of the situation was begun under the Resolution 1503 procedure and subsequently broadened. In each case also, the Commission was assisted by information obtained through visits to the territory. The Special Envoy to Bolivia, who was appointed in 1981, visited the country three times, the Special Rapporteur for Guatemala paid four visits between 1983 and 1985, while the Special Representative to El Salvador visited the country annually after his appointment in 1981 and reported each year to the General Assembly and the Commission.

In the cases just mentioned, as in the Equatorial Guinea case, the Commission benefited from co-operation from the government, with the result that the procedure lost its adversarial character and became more of a consultative exercise. Other cases, however, have underlined the lessons of the Commission's earlier experience with Chile, that governments are not usually anxious to have their record on human rights investigated, and so the Commission's representatives may find themselves working under severe handicaps.

In 1984, for example, following earlier expressions of concern, the Commission requested the appointment of a special representative to investigate the situation in Iran.[14] The representative was duly appointed and in the following year presented a report, though without having obtained any co-operation from the government.

An attempt by the Commission to investigate the situation in Afghanistan met with an equally unhelpful response.[15] In February 1980 the Commission condemned the Soviet invasion of Afghanistan which had taken place two months earlier and began to review the situation there under the confidential procedure. In 1984, as we have mentioned, this review was discontinued when the Commission decided to appoint a special rapporteur.

Professor F. Ermacora of Austria was appointed special rapporteur for Afghanistan by the Chairman of the Commission in August 1984. He received no co-operation from the authorities in Afghanistan, but, after visiting Pakistan, reported back to the Commission in February 1985. In a long and detailed report,[16] running to nearly 200 paragraphs, the rapporteur examined the political and historical background to the situation, the impact of recent events on civil and political rights, economic and social rights and self-determination, and considered the state of human rights in the armed conflict which was in progress. The report recommended, inter alia, that the government of Afghanistan should respect its international obligations and stop torturing its political opponents; that all the parties to the conflict should meet with a view to restoring normality; that all parties to the conflict should also respect their obligations under humanitarian law and accept the supervision of an organisation such as the Red Cross; and finally, that the rights of the 4,000,000 Afghan refugees to return to their homes should be recognised and that a general amnesty should be declared for everyone, regardless of their political opinions.

In spite of his inability to visit Afghanistan, the special rapporteur succeeded in producing a remarkably comprehensive report which contributed to the pressure on the Soviet Union, as the key protagonist, in the Commission on Human Rights and elsewhere. The part which this pressure played in the eventual Soviet decision to withdraw from Afghanistan can only be a matter of speculation. It is a cause for satisfaction, however, that in a situation in which the co-operation of the State under review was non-existent, it was nevertheless possible to carry out an investigation which shed valuable light on the situation and may have influenced subsequent events.

Lack of co-operation from the government whose activities are under investigation is one obstacle to the Commission's work. Another, which has already been mentioned, is the intrusion of political considerations into the Commission's decisions. The essential point here is that it is only when a majority in the General Assembly or the Commission on Human Rights is prepared to offend a given State that action will be taken. Thus, States such as Chile, Israel and South Africa are vulnerable, whereas proposals to investigate human rights in the Soviet Union, or the Uganda of Idi Amin have been rejected for reasons which have nothing to do with the country's human rights record, but simply reflect the voting strength of the different regional groups in the United Nations.

The significance of political circumstances is naturally most evident when the prospect of United Nations action is first mooted. Such considerations can, however, be no less important at a later stage. In 1982, for example, following the military take-over by General Jaruzelski, the Commission requested the Secretary-General, or a person appointed by him, to undertake a study of the human rights situation in Poland.[17] The Secretary-General's representative reported to the Commission but was unable to secure the co-operation of the Polish authorities. Following a fresh request from the Secretary-General in 1983, another representative was appointed and he also reported to the Commission. In 1984, however, the Commission voted by a narrow majority to accept a proposal from Cuba to defer consideration of a draft resolution concerning the human rights situation in Poland. Then, at its next session, the Commission did not take any decision concerning Poland with the result that the procedure, which in this case had proved inconclusive, came to an end in 1985.

The fate of the Polish initiative is a demonstration of how maintaining the momentum when a human rights issue is before the United Nations is a matter of retaining and consolidating political support. If this can be done, as in many of the cases mentioned, the effect of the Commission's activity will depend on a government's concern for its reputation. An intransigent government will at least be inconvenienced, while a co-operative government can seek and be provided with assistance. In either case, a public investigation, like the confidential procedure which it often follows, can provide governments with an incentive to improve.

4. *Investigation of particular issues*

The last type of United Nations procedure which needs to be considered is the appointment of special working groups, or individual rapporteurs, to examine a particular type of human rights issue.[18]

In 1980 the Commission on Human Rights established a Working Group on Enforced and Involuntary Disappearances to deal with a problem which, as we shall see in Chapter 5, has also exercised the Inter-American Commission. The Working Group, which consists of five persons acting in an individual capacity, can receive information from governments, inter-governmental and non-governmental organisations, and individuals. Its chairman may transmit reports of enforced or involuntary disappearances which are received between sessions of the group and which call for urgent action, directly to the government concerned, accompanied by a request for information.

In each report of the Working Group reference is made to disappearances in specific, named countries. The first five reports of the Working Group referred to disappearances in a total of thirty-six countries. When it is recalled that this is more than one–fifth of the membership of the United Nations, the scale and importance of this problem can be appreciated. The Working Group was established for an initial period of one year, but in recognition of the seriousness of the issue of enforced and involuntary disappearances, has regularly had its mandate extended.

As with the investigation of particular countries, the Commission sometimes prefers to appoint a special rapporteur instead of a working group. This happened in 1981 when the Commission decided to study the issue of mass exoduses. This phenomenon, the large scale displacement of populations fleeing from war or persecution, was not unknown in earlier periods of history, but in our own age has occurred on a scale and with a frequency which the United Nations could not ignore. In 1980, after an earlier Canadian attempt to raise the issue which was unsuccessful, the Commission requested the Secretary-General to contact the relevant governments and report on the matter. In March 1981, when the Secretary-General reported, the Commission requested the appointment of a special rapporteur and in the following month Prince Sadruddin Aga Khan was appointed to the post. The Prince, who had been UN High Commissioner for Refugees, was an excellent choice and soon produced a comprehensive report. Accompanying it were three annexes in which the special rapporteur supplemented his findings with a great deal of evidence. One annex illustrated the problem by reference to mass exoduses involving about twenty countries or regions over the previous ten years; another set out detailed studies of the representative cases of Afghanistan, Ethiopia, Indochina and Mexico; while a third contained a survey of the whole issue in order to demonstrate the scale and variety of the problems.

The Commission considered the report in March 1982 and decided to transmit it to the General Assembly. The latter had encouraged the Commission throughout and in 1981 had established its own group of governmental experts, with the aim of improving co-operation and averting new flows of refugees.[19] The question remained on the Commission's agenda, but no further action was taken.

The Commission has also used the services of a special rapporteur to investigate the issue of summary executions. Here its action was prompted partly by the Sub-Commission, which in 1981 expressed its concern over the scale of politically motivated executions and imprisonment across the world, and partly by the General Assembly, which took up the issue at about the same time.

In March 1982 the Commission requested its Chairman to appoint a special rapporteur on summary and arbitrary executions. Soon afterwards Mr Amos Wako of Kenya was appointed and submitted his first report in 1983. In it he assembled data extending back over the previous twenty years and used this as the basis for both a general analysis of the phenomenon and a more detailed study of its recent manifestations. The special rapporteur's mandate was then extended and in subsequent reports he dealt with contemporaneous developments. In the course of his work he also sent urgent appeals to a number of governments and in 1984 visited Surinam to investigate allegations of arbitrary executions at first hand.

One of the Commission's most recent investigations has concerned another elementary issue of human rights, the practice of torture. In December 1975 the General Assembly took the initiative on this question by adopting a Declaration on the Protection of All Persons from Being Subjected to Torture and Other Cruel, Inhuman or Degrading Treatment or Punishment.[20] Two years later it took a further step by adopting a model unilateral declaration by which governments could declare their intention to comply with the Declaration and to implement it by legislation and other measures.[21] At the same time the Assembly requested the Commission to produce a draft convention against torture. This was done, and in 1984 the Convention against Torture and Other Cruel, Inhuman or Degrading Treatment or Punishment was adopted by the General Assembly.

The Convention, which will be described later, established a special procedure for investigating complaints of torture, but required twenty ratifications to bring it into force. In 1985, therefore, shortly after the Convention was opened for signature, the Commission decided to expedite matters and undertake its own investigation. It asked its Chairman to appoint a special rapporteur whose function would be to respond to allegations of torture and to investigate how and where it occurs. In May 1985 the Chairman of the Commission appointed Professor P. Kooijmans of the Netherlands as its special rapporteur.

Studies of particular issues of human rights have also been undertaken by the Sub-Commission on the Prevention of Discrimination and Protection of Minorities. In 1981, at about the same time as the Commission was appointing its special rapporteur on mass exoduses, the Sub-Commission set up a Working Group on Indigenous Populations. The Group, which held its first meeting in August 1982, has the task of identifying and developing standards relating to the rights of indigenous peoples, which includes finding a way of defining the relevant populations and protecting them from physical destruction and threats to their culture. The Working Group holds annual sessions which may be attended by non-governmental organisations with consultative status and the representatives of indigenous groups. Although the Working Group does not consider individual complaints, it accepts oral and written information from those attending and has indicated that it will give 'special attention to gross and persistent violations of human rights'.[22]

The Sub-Commission has also established a Working Group on Slavery. This is concerned with a practice which, as we have seen, has been the subject of international attention since the nineteenth century, but which unfortunately is still prevalent in some parts of the world. Like the Working Group on Indigenous Populations, the Group can receive information from non-governmental organisations with consultative status which may also attend its meetings and assist its work.

The question of religious intolerance and discrimination has the distinction of being the subject of investigations by both the Sub-Commission and the Commission. In 1981, as we have mentioned, the General Assembly adopted its Declaration on the Elimination of All Forms of Intolerance and of Discrimination based on Religion or Belief. This established certain standards, but contains no implementation provisions; consequently, in 1986 the Commission appointed a special rapporteur to examine incidents of religious intolerance and discrimination, to report on compliance with the Declaration, and to recommend remedial measures. In his first report in 1987 the rapporteur noted widespread violations of religious freedom and his mandate was extended. His second report, in 1988, concentrated on the role of governments and further emphasised the seriousness of this problem.

The Sub-Commission's involvement was somewhat earlier, for in 1983 it had appointed a special rapporteur with a very similar mandate. Indeed, when the issue subsequently came before the Commission, some members opposed the appointment of a rapporteur on the ground that the matter was already being dealt with. It is interesting to note that one of the points made by both rapporteurs was that consideration should be given to producing a convention on the subject of discrimination to consolidate the principles set out in the Declaration. An earlier attempt to draft a convention had to be abandoned in the face of problems which seemed insuperable. It will be interesting to see whether, as a consequence of these latest studies, further work on this project will be more successful.[23]

Although there is an obvious difference between investigating the state of human rights in a particular country and undertaking a study of an issue such as torture or slavery, the purpose of the two types of procedure is essentially the same. Both are concerned with the collecting of information, not as an end itself, but as a means of keeping questions of human rights on the international agenda and enabling pressure to be put on governments to change their practices. Since the aim is to change governmental behaviour, the country type of investigation, with its sharper focus, may seem superior to the thematic approach we have been describing. In fact this is not so, and the thematic approach has several advantages which account for its increasing popularity.

First, and most obviously, there is the point that thematic surveys can cover a much larger number of countries than could ever be dealt with in country type investigations. Since the United Nations is concerned with the protection of human rights everywhere, it is clearly important to have the geographical net spread as widely as possible, and this is something only thematic investigations can do.

The point about geographical spread is reinforced by a second consideration which is political. There is, as we have seen, an unwillingness on the part of the Commission to investigate certain countries. If, then, human rights practices in these places are to be investigated at all, it has to be by means of the thematic approach. Naturally, political considerations can come into play here also, but the nature of the exercise means that they have much less scope. The fact that in many cases the thematic type of investigation and the country type of investigation are not true alternatives therefore constitutes another advantage of the thematic approach.

Finally, there is the point that for some human rights issues the thematic approach is essential if the issue is to be properly understood. Mass exoduses, for example, which involve a world-wide movement of populations, can only be dealt with rationally by considering the problem as a whole. The same may be said of slavery, which can also involve the crossing of frontiers, and the rights of indigenous peoples, where comparative study is particularly instructive. Even issues such as torture or arbitrary executions, which can be exposed by a country-oriented investigation (if it is permitted), can be illuminated by the thematic approach.

While there are, therefore, circumstances in which the country type of investigation is undoubtedly useful, the thematic approach offers a way of investigating specific issues which already has been used quite extensively, and which students of the United Nations are likely to see a great deal more of in the future.

5. The implementation provisions of particular treaties

(a) The Convention on the Elimination of All Forms of Racial Discrimination This Convention, which was adopted by the General Assembly in December 1965, restates in a precise and more developed form the principles set out in the Declaration on the Elimination of All Forms of Racial Discrimination approved by the General Assembly in 1963.[24] In particular, it provides that the contracting parties will make it an offence to disseminate ideas based on racial superiority or hatred and to incite racial discrimination; also, that they will declare illegal and prohibit organisations which engage in such activities. Moreover, the Convention contains elaborate measures of implementation which many have thought could provide a model for other UN instruments on human rights.

The Convention entered into force on 4 January 1969 and has now been ratified by 124 States, making it the most widely ratified of all UN Conventions.[25] Article 8 of the Convention provides for the establishment of a Committee on the Elimination of Racial Discrimination (CERD) of eighteen independent experts, while Article 9 contains an undertaking by the parties to submit reports 'on the legislative, judicial, administrative or other measures which they have adopted and which give effect to the provisions of the Convention . . .'. The reports are to be submitted within one year of the entry into force of the Convention and thereafter every two years or on request. Article 9 also provides: 'The Committee may request further information from the States Parties.' It is clear that there is here a close, though not complete, parallel between Article 9 and Article 40 of the Covenant on Civil and Political Rights, and the experience gained in the implementation of the former, as already noted, has influenced the practice and procedure of the Human Rights Committee.

The Committee on the Elimination of Racial Discrimination has taken its task seriously and has succeeded in imposing its authority. It has indicated to States parties the form and character which their reports should take and has refused to accept very brief reports merely stating that there is no racial discrimination in the country in question. It has also required the production of demographic information about the existence of minorities and has made it very clear that, in its view, racial discrimination is not practised only by whites against blacks. It requires specific information on the way in which States have complied with their obligation under Article 4 to prohibit propaganda in support of racial discrimination and similar activities, and organisations which engage in it. It requests supplementary information when necessary and, if the State concerned fails to supply it, reports this to the General Assembly. More important, since 1972, and with the approval of the General Assembly, the Committee has adopted the practice of inviting States which have submitted reports to send a representative to take part in the Committee's proceedings when the report is under examination. Almost all States have accepted these invitations, and in this way a constructive dialogue has developed between the Committee and the governmental representatives, who answer questions, give explanations and provide additional information. A further advantage is that this procedure permits the Committee to indicate that a government is not fully complying with its obligations, without the need for a formal decision to that effect. The Committee appears to have established a basis of mutual confidence with governments, or at least with the majority, which is an encouraging sign for its future work.[26]

Apart from the reporting procedure, there is provision in

Article 11 for any State party to bring an alleged violation of the Convention by another party to the attention of the Committee. The allegation is communicated to the State concerned, which then has three months to provide the Committee with a written explanation or statement clarifying the matter. If the matter is not resolved to the satisfaction of both parties, either State has the right to refer it to the Committee again, and the chairman must then appoint an *ad hoc* conciliation commission.

Article 14 of the Convention contains an optional provision for individual complaints. A State party may at any time declare that it recognises the competence of the Committee on Racial Discrimination to consider communications from an individual or a group of individuals within its jurisdiction who claim to be the victim of a violation by that State of any of the provisions of the Convention. The procedure for dealing with such petitions is somewhat complicated. It involves investigation by the Committee, subject to certain safeguards, including the exhaustion of domestic remedies, and permits the Committee to make suggestions and recommendations. The procedure, which seems to have been partly inspired by the way the European Convention on Human Rights deals with the right of individual petition, required acceptance by ten States to bring it into force. This was achieved in December 1982 and at the present time twelve States have made the necessary declarations.[27]

(b) The Convention on the Elimination of All Forms of Discrimination against Women This Convention was adopted by the General Assembly in December 1979. Although it is not the first convention to deal with women's rights, it is the first universal instrument to address the issue of discrimination, and this, together with the fact that it contains arrangements for monitoring compliance, make it of special interest in the present context.[28]

The substantive provisions of the Convention cover a wide area of State conduct but, as they have been reviewed elsewhere,[29] need not be examined in detail here. Article 1 defines discrimination against women as:

> ... any distinction, exclusion or restriction made on the basis of sex which has the effect or purpose of impairing or nullifying the recognition, enjoyment or exercise by women, irrespective of their marital status, on a basis of equality of men and women, of human

> rights and fundamental freedoms in the political, social, cultural, civil or any other field.

This follows the approach of the Convention on the Elimination of All Forms of Racial Discrimination and, as in the earlier instrument, States undertake to adopt measures to promote the principle. Activities of this kind which are specifically mentioned include measures to suppress the exploitation of prostitution (Article 6); measures to eliminate sex discrimination in political and public life (Article 7); and equal rights in relation to nationality (Article 9), education (Article 10), employment (Article 11), and health care (Article 12). The Convention also provides for equality of the sexes with regard to marriage and family relations (Article 16), while recognising the legitimacy of 'special measures ... aimed at protecting maternity'.

The Convention deals with an issue of human rights of fundamental importance, and the decision to supplement the very general provisions on discrimination to be found in such instruments as the Covenant on Civil and Political Rights is clearly a positive step. Before moving on, however, we must mention that both the application and the interpretation of the Convention present certain difficulties. The fact that, in some form or other, sex discrimination is to be found in almost every country in the world makes this a vitally important issue, but means that persuading governments to implement their obligations fully will be a long and difficult task. That is the problem of application. The problem of interpretation involves deciding how the rights created by the Convention relate to different and apparently conflicting rights under other human rights treaties. Article 5, for example, requires States to take 'all appropriate measures':

> (a) To modify the social and cultural patterns of conduct of men and women, with a view to achieving the elimination of prejudices and customary and all other practices which are based on the idea of the inferiority or the superiority of either of the sexes or on stereotyped roles for men and women.

It has been perceptively noted that this:

> might permit States to curtail to an undefined extent privacy and associational interests and the freedom of opinion and expression. Moreover since social and cultural behaviour may be patterned according to factors such as ethnicity or religion, state action ... which

> is directed towards modifying the way in which a particular ethnic or religious group treats women may conflict with the principles forbidding discrimination on the basis of race or religion.[30]

While it is true that both the application and the interpretation of other treaties can give rise to similar problems, the subject matter of the present Convention is such as to pose them in a particularly acute form.

The Convention came into force on 3 September 1981 and has already been accepted by ninety-four States.[31] Supervision is the responsibility of the Committee on the Elimination of Discrimination against Women. This consists of twenty-three experts elected by the parties and, like their counterparts on the Committee on the Elimination of Racial Discrimination, they sit in an independent capacity, not as representatives of their nominating States. The main functions of the Committee are set out in Articles 18 and 21 of the Convention. Under Article 18 the parties are to submit reports on the measures they have adopted to give effect to the provisions of the Convention. As in the Convention on Racial Discrimination, the first report must be submitted one year after the entry into force of the Convention for the State concerned, but then subsequently at four year, rather than two year, intervals. Article 21 authorises the Committee to make 'suggestions and general recommendations based on the examination of reports and information from the States parties'.

The Committee was convened for the first time soon after the Convention came into force and, though hampered by the fact that it normally meets for no more than two weeks annually, began its work of reviewing State reports. The control machinery provided in the Convention has been described as 'modest'[32] and, though it is certainly better than nothing, experience has shown that the use of a reporting procedure to monitor States' compliance with their obligations is a form of supervision which leaves a good deal to be desired. It is, of course, excellent that supervision is carried out by a group of independent experts. However, it is a matter for regret that there is no provision authorising the Committee to deal with complaints by States, nor any procedure to enable it to deal with communications from individuals.

The limited powers which the Committee has under Article 21 clearly prevent it from determining that a particular State has violated the Convention. While this is also a limitation to be found in reporting procedures elsewhere, its effect is that the Committee cannot use its review of a State's report to compensate for its other deficiencies. It is interesting to note, however, that the Committee recently decided that the 'suggestions and recommendations' which it is authorised to make under Article 21 can 'in an appropriate case' be 'based on the examination of a report and information received from a State party'.[33] This decision, which was controversial, is to be welcomed as an indication that, in exercising its functions under the Convention, the Committee on the Elimination of Discrimination against Women intends to make the most of its limited powers.

(c) **The Convention against Torture and Other Cruel, Inhuman or Degrading Treatment or Punishment** This Convention was adopted by the General Assembly in December 1984 and provides a more detailed treatment of a subject which was first addressed in the Declaration on the Protection of All Persons from being subjected to Torture and Other Cruel, Inhuman or Degrading Treatment or Punishment, adopted by the General Assembly in 1975.[34] Following the adoption of the Declaration, the General Assembly requested the Commission on Human Rights to draw up a draft convention in the light of its principles. In 1983 the Assembly urged the Commission to complete this work as a matter of urgency and added that it should include provisions for its effective implementation. This was carried out by a Working Group of the Commission and the final text, which the General Assembly called upon all governments to consider signing and ratifying 'as a matter of priority', was opened for signature in the following year.

The first part of the Convention, which consists of Articles 1 to 16, establishes the scope of the Convention and the nature of the parties' obligations.[35] Article 1 defines torture in a way which follows the earlier Declaration and rectifies an omission in the Covenant on Civil and Political Rights and other human rights agreements. The obligations which the Convention creates are quite extensive and include a duty on the part of each State to take measures to prevent acts of torture in any territory under its jurisdiction; a duty not to return a person to a country where he may be subjected to torture; a duty to make torture a criminal offence and establish jurisdiction over it; a duty to prosecute or, where relevant, extradite persons charged with torture; a duty to co-operate with other States and ensure appropriate education and training for its own personnel; a duty to exclude evidence obtained by torture; and a duty to provide a remedy for those who allege they have been tortured. Many of the above obligations also extend to 'other acts of cruel, inhuman or degrading treatment or punishment' (Article 16), although these concepts, understandably, are not defined.

Articles 17 to 24, which make up the second part of the Convention, provide for the creation of a Committee against Torture to supervise its implementation. Like the committees already considered, this new Committee is to consist of independent experts elected by the parties and for a term of four years. The Committee, which is ten in number, is intended to perform three main functions. Under Article 19 it will receive and consider reports from the parties as to the measures they have taken to give effect to their undertaking under the Convention. Under Article 21 a State may complain to the Committee that another State is not fulfilling its obligations. And under Article 22 the Committee is empowered to consider complaints from individuals. However, both the inter-State procedure and the power of the Committee to receive individual complaints require a declaration from the State or States concerned that they recognise the Committee's competence in this area.

Article 20 of the Convention provides that if the Committee receives 'reliable information' that torture is being systematically practised in the territory of a party, it may invite the State to co-operate in examining the information and, whether co-operation is forthcoming or not, initiate a confidential enquiry. This procedure, unlike those laid down in Articles 21 and 22, is not subject to specific acceptance from the State concerned. It therefore provides the Committee with a further power which could be useful. It should be noted, however, that if a State has not accepted the competence of the Committee to receive individual applications, the Convention provides that no such communication 'shall be received' by the Committee. There could therefore sometimes be difficulty in obtaining the 'reliable information' which activation of Article 20 requires.

The Convention came into force in June 1987, when it had been ratified by twenty States, and there are currently twenty-eight parties.[36] The arrangements for inter-State complaints and individual communications required acceptance by five States and came into force at the same time as the Convention. Currently ten States have accepted these provisions.[37] The Committee against Torture was established in November 1987.[38] In view of the fact that the supervisory provisions of the Convention on Torture are modelled on those of the Covenant on Civil and Political Rights, it is reasonable to assume that, with the Convention now in force, the Committee's handling of the reporting system under Article 19 will be the first test of its effectiveness.

6. *Appraisal*

This summary account of developments in the United Nations aimed at securing a more effective respect for human rights throughout the world suggests a number of general conclusions.

First of all, it is useful to bear in mind that the Charter itself does not, as is sometimes supposed, demand observance of human rights from all members of the organisation. It requires them 'to co-operate ... in promoting respect for human rights' (Article 1) and 'to take joint and separate action ... for the achievement of the purpose' of promoting 'universal respect for, and observance of, human rights and fundamental freedoms for all ...' (Articles 55 and 56). In other words, respect for human rights is an aim for which the member States are pledged to work. It is not set out in the Charter as a condition of membership. Indeed, this could not be otherwise in what was envisaged as a universal organisation which now has more than 150 members, less than half of which observe the rule of law and the fundamental principles of democracy.

Secondly, the Universal Declaration of 1948, by reason of its constant reaffirmation by the General Assembly and in numerous other texts, both international and national, can now, more than forty years on, be taken as a statement of customary international law, establishing standards which all States should respect. But the Declaration, as we have seen, lacks measures of implementation. In other words, it sets standards but does not establish machinery for their enforcement.

Thirdly, it is the two Covenants of 1966 which reaffirm, and further elaborate, those standards, adding measures of implementation. In the case of civil and political rights these involve the procedures of the Human Rights Committee which we examined in the previous chapter. However, those procedures are applicable only to the States which have ratified the Covenants, and the measures which apply automatically to all contracting States – that is, the reporting system – are of only limited effect. The more effective optional provisions, on the other hand, including the Optional Protocol, have been accepted by a significantly smaller number of States.

As regards the Charter, the Declaration and the Covenants, therefore, it appears that the United Nations has done much in the realm of promotion and standard-setting but less as regards actual protection and measures of implementation. This conclusion is reinforced when we consider the other activities of the organisation in the human rights field. Much has been done in standard-setting by the conclusion of other Conventions relating to genocide, war crimes, discrimination, apartheid and so on, but these instruments contain relatively weak provisions for their implementation, if they contain any at all, and other procedures for the protection of human rights, notably those under Resolutions 1235 and 1503, have had rather mixed results.

All this is not to deny the great and genuine efforts made by a number of governments, by many delegates at UN meetings, by Secretariat officials, and by non-governmental organisations working for the protection of human rights. The political reality, however, is that an international organisation cannot do more than its member governments are prepared to accept, and the majority of members of the United Nations are not willing to accept a strong system of international control over actions which may affect the human rights of their citizens. Though the progress made has been remarkable as regards standard-setting, it has been modest as regards measures of implementation, and governments' unwillingness to accept more effective measures is the explanation.

Many people, and some governments, are aware of these shortcomings, and many attempts have been made to improve the effectiveness of the UN procedures. One difficulty in doing so stems from different political ideologies about the comparative importance of different categories of human rights. In 1977 the General Assembly tried to put an end to this dispute by affirming that all human rights and fundamental freedoms are indivisible and interdependent and that equal attention should be given to the implementation, promotion and protection of both civil and political, and economic, social and cultural rights.[39]

A proposal which has been made from time to time in an effort to reinforce the effectiveness of the United Nations in this field is the appointment of a United Nations High Commissioner for Human Rights.[40] As an independent and high-level personality, comparable in some respects to the UN High Commissioner for Refugees, he would have the primary function of investigating alleged violations of human rights. Proposals on these lines have been made on various occasions, starting with Uruguay and Costa Rica in earlier years and subsequently by President Carter in 1977. At one stage the Commission, by a very narrow majority, decided to recommend the creation of such a post, but the Economic and Social Council has not yet agreed to do so. In 1977 the General Assembly requested the Commission to undertake an overall analysis of ways and means within the United Nations system for improving the effective enjoyment of human rights and fundamental freedoms and in the following year asked it to include in its study a re-examination of the proposal for a High Commissioner, in the light of the views expressed by governments.[41] At its session in 1979, however, the Commission had to admit that it could not reach agreement. This was evidently because many governments were unwilling to submit their human rights record to international scrutiny.

We may therefore conclude that the United Nations has achieved a great deal in developing the international law of human rights, particularly as regards international standards which are increasingly significant as conventional or customary rules of law. If it has been less successful in securing the 'universal and effective recognition of those standards', as the Universal Declaration puts it, that is because the organisation cannot exercise greater powers than its member States are prepared to give it, and to change the practice of governments in almost every part of the world is a monumental task. Many governments are prepared to vote for idealistic texts in New York or Geneva, yet ignore these ideals in their daily conduct of affairs. Despite the difficulties, however, procedures for exposing hypocrisy and defending human rights have evolved and are being used. As we said in Chapter 1, although international law is not yet capable of preventing violations of human rights, it can be made more effective, and both inside the United Nations and outside it many are working with that aim.

Notes

1 The texts of most of these conventions can be found in I. Brownlie, *Basic Documents on Human Rights*, second edition, Oxford University Press, 1981.
2 See Resolutions 75(v) and 728(f). An excellent account of the history and development of the treatment of human rights petitions can be found in T. J. M. Zuijdwijk, *Petitioning the United Nations*, New York, 1982.
3 The Sub-Commission on the Prevention of Discrimination and Protection of Minorities consists of twenty-six independent experts, elected by the Commission to assist it in its work. In 1986, however, the activities of the Sub-Commission, together with certain activities of the Commission, were curtailed as a way of reducing expenditure. For criticism of these restrictions see *Recommendations and Conclusions of the NGO Seminar on Human Rights in the United Nations, Geneva, 8–10 September 1986*, in Council of Europe *Human Rights Information Sheet* No. 20, Strasbourg, 1987, p. 111.
4 See M. J. Bossuyt, 'The development of special procedures of the United Nations Commission on Human Rights', *Human Rights Law Journal*, VI, 1985, pp. 179, 182.
5 *Report on Communications concerning Human Rights*, doc. E/CN.4/165 of 2 May 1949.
6 Bossuyt, 'Development of special procedures', p. 184.
7 *Ibid*, pp. 183–4.
8 Resolution 2 (XXIII). For description of an earlier mission to Viet-Nam see Bossuyt, 'Development of special procedures', p. 185.
9 Documents A/33/331 (1978) and E/CN.4/1310 (1979).
10 *Report of the thirty-fifth session of the Commission*, doc. E/1979/36, p. 124.
11 See General Assembly Resolution 33/176 of 20 December 1978 on the importance of the experience of the Special Working Group.
12 See Bossuyt, 'Development of special procedures', pp. 188–9.
13 *Ibid.*, pp. 189–191.
14 *Ibid.*, pp. 192–3.
15 *Ibid.*, p. 193.
16 *Report on the situation of Human Rights in Afghanistan*, doc. E/CN.4/1985/21 of 19 February 1985. Text in *Human Rights Law Journal*, VI, 1985 p. 29.
17 See Bossuyt, 'Development of special procedures', pp. 191–2.
18 See Bossuyt, *ibid.*, pp. 194–9; T. C. Van Boven, 'Protection of human rights through the United Nations System', in H. Hannum (ed.) *Guide to International Human Rights Practice*, London, 1984, p. 46. and D. Weissbrodt, 'The three "theme" Special Rapporteurs of the UN Commission on Human Rights', *American Journal of International Law*, LXXX, 1986, p. 685.
19 See L. T. Lee 'The U.N. Group of Governmental Experts on International Cooperation to Avert New Flows of Refugees', *American Journal of International Law*, LXXVIII, 1984 p. 480.
20 Resolution 3452 (XXX) of 9 December 1975.
21 Resolution 32/64 of 8 December 1977.
22 Van Boven, 'Protection of human rights', p. 53. See also R. L. Barsh, 'Indigenous peoples: an emerging object of international law', *American Journal of International Law*, LXXX, 1986, p. 369.

23 For discussion of this issue and the developments described in the text, see D. J. Sullivan, 'Advancing freedom of religion or belief through the UN Declaration on the Elimination of Religious Intolerance and Discrimination', *American Journal of International Law*, LXXXII, 1988, p. 487.

24 For the text of this Convention, see Brownlie, *Basic Documents*, p. 150. For analysis and discussion of its provisions see T. Buergenthal, 'Operating the U.N. Racial Convention', *Texas International Law Journal*, XII, 1977 p. 187; K. J. Partsh, 'Elimination of racial discrimination in the enjoyment of civil and political rights', *ibid.*, XIV, 1979 p. 193; T. Meron, 'The meaning and reach of the International Convention on the Elimination of All Forms of Racial Discrimination', *American Journal of International Law*, LXXIX, 1985 p. 283, and *idem*, *Human Rights Law-Making in the United Nations*, Oxford, 1986, Chapter 1.

25 As of 1 January 1988, see J.-B. Marie, 'International instruments relating to human rights', *Human Rights Law Journal*, IX, 1988, p. 113.

26 A system of periodic reports is also provided for in the 1973 Convention on the Suppression and Punishment of the Crime of Apartheid. Text in Brownlie, *Basic Documents*, p. 164. Under Article 9 these reports are considered by a group of three members of the Commission on Human Rights who are also 'representatives of the States Parties to the ... Convention'. On 1 January 1988 there were eighty-six parties to this Convention; see Marie, 'International instruments'.

27 Marie, *ibid.*

28 For the text of the Convention, see Brownlie, *Basic Documents*, p. 94.

29 See, for example, J. Loranger, 'Convention on the Elimination of All Forms of Discrimination against Women', *Canadian Yearbook of International Law*, XX, 1982, p. 349 and Meron, *Human Rights Law-Making*, Chapter 2 (with references to previous literature).

30 Meron, *ibid.*, p. 66. Article 5(b) is open to the same objection since it requires States: 'To ensure that family education includes a proper understanding of maternity as a social function and the recognition of the common responsibility of men and women in the upbringing and development of their children, it being understood that the interest of the children is the primordial consideration in all cases.'

31 As of 1 January 1988. See Marie, 'International instruments'.

32 Meron, *Human Rights Law-Making*, p. 53.

33 See *Report of the Committee on the Elimination of Discrimination against Women*, 42 UN GAOR Supp. (No. 38), paras 57–60, UN doc. A/42/38 (1987), noted in *American Journal of International Law*, LXXXII, 1988, p. 607, n. 13.

34 For the text of the Declaration, see Brownlie, *Basic Documents*, p. 35. For the text of the Convention, see *Human Rights Law Journal*, V. 1984, p. 349.

35 The scope of the Convention may usefully be compared with that of the Inter-American Convention to Prevent and Punish Torture, which covers similar ground but uses different language. For the text of the latter, see Council of Europe, *Human Rights Information Sheet*, No. 20, Strasbourg, 1987, p. 139. On 1 January 1988 four States were parties to the Inter-American Convention, which is in force. It should be noted, however, that apart from a general supervision to be exercised by the Inter-American Commission, there are no means of implementation in this Convention.

36 As of 1 January 1988. See Marie, 'International instruments'.
37 Argentina, Austria, Denmark, France, Luxembourg, Norway, Spain, Sweden, Switzerland, Togo; see Marie, *ibid.*
38 See Council of Europe *Human Rights Information Sheet*, No. 21, Strasbourg, 1988, p. 117.
39 See Resolution 32/130 of 16 December 1977.
40 See R. S. Clark, *A United Nations High Commissioner for Human Rights*, The Hague, 1972 and R. StJ. Macdonald, 'A United Nations High Commissioner for Human Rights: the decline and fall of an initiative', *Canadian Yearbook of International Law*, X, 1972, p. 40.
41 See Resolutions 32/130 and 33/105.

CHAPTER 4

The protection of human rights in Europe

I. The European Convention on Human Rights

1. The origin and history of the Convention

The factors which led the United Nations to concern itself with the protection of human rights had a similar effect in Europe.

One such factor was a natural reaction against the Nazi and Fascist systems which had provoked the Second World War and wrought such havoc on millions of lives during the course of that conflict. The denial of human rights was not merely an incidental result of these systems; it was a deliberate instrument of policy and even a precondition of their ascendancy. If the dictators had built their empires by suppressing individual freedoms, then an effective system for the protection of human rights would, it was thought, erect a bulwark against any recrudescence of dictatorship.

Another stimulus was that in the post-war years it soon became evident that the democratic systems of Western Europe needed protection, not only against a possible revival of the pre-war dictatorships, but also against another kind of regime which had captured control of half the continent. The principles championed by the French Revolution, some of which were enshrined in the Bill of Rights and earlier in Magna Carta, were menaced by a new political philosophy in which the so-called dictatorship of the proletariat gave all power to the State and reduced the individual to insignificance. The preservation of democracy and the maintenance of the rule of law required, as Robert Schuman put it, foundations 'on which to base the defence of human personality against all tyrannies and against all forms of totalitarianism'. Those foundations were the effective protection of the rights of man and fundamental freedoms.

As early as August 1941 the Atlantic Charter proclaimed the famous Four Freedoms and also (which is sometimes forgotten) the right of self-determination. These principles were reaffirmed in the Declaration of the twenty-six United Nations on 1 January 1942, and three years later came the well known provisions of the United Nations Charter. These texts, however, were proclamations of a very general nature. It was left to the Congress of Europe at The Hague in May 1948 to announce:

> We desire a united Europe, throughout whose area the free movement of persons, ideas and goods is restored;
>
> We desire a Charter of Human Rights guaranteeing liberty of thought, assembly and expression as well as the right to form a political opposition;
>
> We desire a Court of Justice with adequate sanctions for the implementation of this Charter;
>
> We desire a European Assembly where the live forces of all our nations shall be represented.

The essence of this message lay in the words 'guaranteeing' and 'sanctions'. Something more was required than declarations of intention. An organised system was needed to ensure the collective guarantee of human rights in the proposed European Union.

The task of designing such a system was taken up by the Consultative Assembly of the Council of Europe during its first session in August and September 1949. The Statute creating the Council of Europe had been signed earlier in the year. It laid down that the maintenance and further realisation of human rights and fundamental freedoms were one of the means for achieving the aim of the Council, which is a greater unity between its members, and Article 3 of the Statute reinforced this commitment by making respect for human rights a condition of membership. In August 1949 the Assembly's Committee on Legal and Administrative Questions met to study a proposal for the establishment of 'an organisation within the Council of Europe to ensure the collective guarantee of human rights' and before the end of the session presented its conclusions in the famous Teitgen Report of September 1949. The Committee proposed that a list of ten rights from the Universal Declaration should be the object of a collective guarantee; that the member States should bind themselves to respect the fundamental principles of democracy and to hold free elections; and that a European Commission for Human Rights and a European Court of Justice should be established, the former to hear complaints of alleged violations and attempt conciliation, the latter to take decisions as to whether a violation had occurred.

This is not the place to describe in detail the negotiation of the Convention on Human Rights.[1] It is enough to note that the Committee of Ministers of the Council of Europe appointed two separate governmental committees which met during the first half of 1950. After further consultation of the Assembly in the summer of that year, the Convention was signed in Rome by the Foreign Ministers in November.[2] The rights guaranteed are substantially the same as those proposed by the Assembly in the previous year and the organs of control are a Commission and a Court of Human Rights. However, the right of individuals to lodge complaints with the Commission was made conditional on the express acceptance of this procedure by the State concerned. Moreover, the possibility of bringing a case before the Court was made conditional on the State concerned agreeing to accept the Court's jurisdiction, and the Committee of Ministers of the Council of Europe was brought in as the final arbiter in cases which are not referred to the Court.

The Convention entered into force on 3 September 1953, when ten ratifications had been deposited. There are now twenty-one contracting parties: Austria, Belgium, Cyprus, Denmark, France, the Federal Republic of Germany, Greece, Iceland, Ireland, Italy, Liechtenstein, Luxembourg, Malta, the Netherlands, Norway, Portugal, Spain, Sweden, Switzerland, Turkey and the United Kingdom. In November 1988 San Marino became the twenty-second member of the Council of Europe and signed the Convention.

The Convention records in its Preamble that it was concluded in order 'to take the first steps for the collective enforcement of certain of the rights stated in the Universal Declaration'. Further steps were envisaged and were not long in coming. In the summer of 1950, even before the Convention was signed, the Assembly had proposed the inclusion of three additional rights which were subsequently included in the First Protocol, signed in March 1952, and which entered into force two years later.

Four further Protocols were concluded between the years 1963 and 1966. The Second Protocol, of May 1963, grants the Court a limited competence to give advisory opinions, while the Third

Protocol, of the same date, modifies the procedure of the Commission, by abolishing the system of sub-commissions. Since they affect the institutions of the Strasbourg system, these protocols required ratification by all parties to the Convention and came into force in 1970. The Fourth Protocol, securing four additional rights, required only five ratifications to enter into force, and this was achieved in May 1968. The Agreement relating to Persons participating in the Proceedings of the Commission and the Court came into force in 1971, and the Fifth Protocol, concerning the procedure for the election of members of the Commission and the Court, which required ratification by all contracting parties, entered into force in 1974.

In recent years three more Protocols have been added. The Sixth Protocol, which concerns the abolition of the death penalty, was concluded in April 1983 and entered into force on receiving its fifth ratification in March 1985. The Seventh Protocol was agreed in November 1984. It confers five additional rights and came into force in November 1988 when it had received seven ratifications. The Eighth Protocol deals with the procedure of the Commission and the Court. It was concluded in March 1985, but, like the earlier protocols of this type, requires ratification by all the parties to the Convention.

The States which drew up the Convention in 1950 initiated a legislative process which is clearly still continuing. With each year that passes the current Protocols obtain progressively wider adherence. In due course no doubt the latest Protocol will come into force and, of course, further rights may be added in the future. Against this general background the scope of the Convention as it stands today can now be considered in more detail.

2. *The rights guaranteed*

The first article of the Convention provides: 'The High Contracting Parties shall secure to everyone within their jurisdiction the rights and freedoms defined in Section I of this Convention.' The obligation assumed by each State is therefore not limited to protecting the rights of its own nationals, nor even to protecting those of the nationals of the other contracting parties. The obligation extends to all persons within the jurisdiction, whatever their nationality or legal status, and however short their length of stay.[3] It will be noted, however, that the obligation, though extensive as regards the category of the beneficiaries, is strictly limited to the rights and freedoms defined in the first part of the Convention.

The rights defined include, as we shall see shortly, the civil and political rights which are the hall-mark of a democratic society. Yet they do not include every right one might wish to see guaranteed in an ideal community. Should the list have been made more extensive when the Convention was drafted? This point was considered by M. Teitgen when he presented his proposals in September 1949. He said on that occasion:

> The Committee on Legal and Administrative Questions had first to draw up a list of freedoms which are to be guaranteed. It considered that, for the moment, it is preferable to limit the collective guarantee to those rights and essential freedoms which are practised, after long usage and experience, in all the democratic countries. While they are the first triumph of democratic regimes, they are also the necessary condition under which they operate.
>
> Certainly, professional freedoms and social rights, which have themselves an intrinsic value, must also in the future be defined and protected. Everyone will, however, understand that it is necessary to begin at the beginning and to guarantee political democracy in the European Union and then to co-ordinate our economies, before undertaking the generalisation of social democracy.[4]

The Convention thus set out only the basic civil and political rights, though others were to be added later. As a result, many individual applications to the Commission have to be rejected because the applicant alleges the violation of a right which, however necessary or desirable, is not covered by the Convention or its Protocols. This has happened with applications based on the denial of the right to a pension, the right to a nationality, the right to practise as a lawyer, the right to reside in one's own country, the right to a career in the public service, the right to political asylum, the right to be compensated for Nazi persecution, the right to a passport, the right to social security benefits, and many others.

Part I of the Convention sets out twelve rights and freedoms which are specifically guaranteed. These are:

1 The right to life (Article 2).
2 Freedom from torture and inhuman or degrading treatment or punishment (Article 3).

3 Freedom from slavery and servitude (Article 4).
4 The right to liberty and security of the person (Article 5).
5 The right to a fair trial (Article 6).
6 Protection against retroactivity of the criminal law (Article 7).
7 The right to respect for private and family life, the home and correspondence (Article 8).
8 Freedom of thought, conscience and religion (Article 9).
9 Freedom of expression (Article 10).
10 Freedom of assembly and association (Article 11).
11 The right to marry and found a family (Article 12).
12 The right to an effective remedy if one's rights are violated (Article 13).

The First Protocol adds three further rights:

13 The right to property (Article 1).
14 The right of parents to ensure the education of their children in conformity with their own religious and philosophical convictions (Article 2).
15 The right to free elections (Article 3).

The Fourth Protocol adds four more rights:

16 Freedom from imprisonment for debt (Article 1).
17 Liberty of movement and freedom to choose one's residence (Article 2).
18 Freedom from exile and the right to enter the country of which one is a national (Article 3).
19 Prohibition of the collective expulsion of aliens (Article 4).

The Sixth Protocol adds one further right:

20 Prohibition of the death penalty in time of peace (Articles 1 and 2).

The Seventh Protocol adds five further rights:

21 The right of an alien not to be expelled from a State without due process of law (Article 1).
22 The right to appeal in criminal cases (Article 2).
23 The right to compensation for a miscarriage of justice (Article 3).
24 Immunity from being prosecuted twice for the same offence (Article 4).
25 Equality of rights and responsibilities of spouses as regards matters of a private law character between them and in their relations with their children (Article 5).

The twenty-five rights and freedoms are, of course, defined, sometimes in considerable detail. In many articles the first sentence or paragraph contains a general affirmation of the right, often based on the text of the Universal Declaration, and the following paragraphs set out the limitations to which that right may be subjected. For example, the right to liberty can be restricted after conviction by a competent court, or in the event of lawful arrest or detention. Several other rights, such as freedom of expression, freedom of assembly and freedom of association, may be limited in the interests of national security, public safety, protection of the rights and freedoms of others, and so on. However, the limitations are carefully formulated and, in general, permitted only when they are prescribed by law and necessary in a democratic society to safeguard some aspect of the public interest.

Articles 14–18 of the Convention relate to the exercise of the rights guaranteed. Article 14 contains a widely drawn prohibition against discrimination. Article 15 permits the suspension of some, though not all, rights 'in time of war or other emergency threatening the life of the nation', but only 'to the extent strictly required by the exigencies of the situation' and after a notice of derogation has been filed with the Secretary-General of the Council of Europe. Article 17 provides that 'nothing in this Convention shall be interpreted as implying ... any right to engage in any activity or perform any act aimed at the destruction of any of the rights and freedoms set forth herein'. And Article 18 stipulates that the restrictions which are permitted under the Convention may not be applied for any purpose other than those for which they have been prescribed.

The rights and freedoms just described are all civil and political rights. As we saw in Chapter 1, however, there are other rights which the State should protect and which many regard as no less important, namely economic, social and cultural rights. The Council of Europe 'began at the beginning', as M. Teitgen proposed in 1949, but when the Convention and First Protocol had been concluded, turned its attention to what he had called 'the generalisation of social democracy'. The result was the European Social Charter of 1961, to which we will return in Chapter 7.

3. The system of international control

The rights discussed above are secured by the contracting parties' undertaking to ensure them to 'everyone within their jurisdiction'.

However, the authors of the Convention did not consider that by itself this obligation was sufficient. They therefore provided something more, an institutional guarantee. For this purpose they decided to create a Commission of Human Rights and a Court of Human Rights, and also to make use of the existing governmental organ of the Council of Europe, the Committee of Ministers.

(a) **The European Commission of Human Rights** The Commission consists of as many members as the High Contracting Parties. In fact there is normally one national of each State, although this is not mandatory. They act in an individual capacity and, in contrast with the members of the UN Commission on Human Rights, not as governmental delegates. The Commission elects its own President. Under Article 24 of the Convention any party may refer to the Commission an alleged breach of the Convention by any other party.

The system of international control established by Article 24 is valuable, but if it stood alone, would not be adequate. That is because the object of the Convention is not to protect States but individuals. As we pointed out when discussing the Optional Protocol to the UN Covenant on Civil and Political Rights, if a violation occurs the real party in interest is the individual whose rights have been denied, and in most cases this will be the result of acts by organs or agencies of his own government. Under traditional international law the individual has no *locus standi*, on the theory that his rights will be championed by his government. But how can his government be his champion when *ex hypothesi* it is the offender? What is necessary, therefore, is to give the individual access to an international organ which is competent to afford him a remedy even against the government of his national State.

The great merit of the European Convention on Human Rights is that it contains just such a procedure. This was a remarkable innovation in international law; so much so indeed, that some governments hesitated to accept it. The right of individual petition was therefore made optional, and so applies only in relation to States which have expressly declared that they accept it, in accordance with the provisions of Article 25 of the Convention. To their credit the twenty-one contracting parties have all agreed to this procedure with the result that the remedy is now available to over 300 million people.

Since its creation in 1954 the Commission has been competent to examine cases brought by one State against another. However, only eleven inter-State applications have been lodged so far. They fall into six groups: two cases brought by Greece against the United Kingdom in 1956 and 1957, relating to the situation in Cyprus at a time when the island was a British colony; a case brought by Austria against Italy in 1960, concerning the trial for murder of six young men who were members of the German-speaking minority in the South Tyrol; two cases brought by Denmark, Norway and Sweden against Greece in 1969 and 1970 (the Netherlands being a joint applicant in the first case), relating to the situation in Greece after the *coup d'état* of April 1967; two cases brought by Ireland against the United Kingdom in 1971 and 1972, relating to the situation in Northern Ireland; three cases brought by Cyprus against Turkey in 1974, 1975 and 1977, concerning the situation in Cyprus following the Turkish intervention in 1974; and finally a case brought by Denmark, France, the Netherlands, Norway and Sweden against Turkey in 1982, relating to the situation in that country under the military regime.

The Commission acquired its competence to consider individual applications in July 1955 when six States had recognised the right of individual petition, that is the right of redress given by Article 25 to 'any person, non-governmental organisation or group of individuals claiming to be the victim of a violation by one of the High Contracting Parties of the rights set forth in this Convention'. The overwhelming importance of this right, as compared with the inter-State procedure, may be seen from the fact that the Commission has now registered more than 12,000 individual applications.[5]

The first task of the Commission when it considers an application is to decide whether it is admissible. Here strict rules apply. Article 26 of the Convention lays down two conditions which apply both to inter-State cases and to individual applications. The Commission may deal with a case only after all domestic remedies have been exhausted, unless no such remedies are available or they are unreasonably delayed, and within a period of six months from the date of the final decision at the national level. Moreover, under Article 27, which applies only to individual cases, the Commission must reject as inadmissible any application which is anonymous, substantially the same as a matter already examined by the

Commission or through another international procedure, incompatible with the provisions of the Convention or manifestly ill-founded, or which constitutes an abuse of the right of petition. There are therefore seven separate grounds on which an application may be declared inadmissible, and bearing in mind that it is open to anyone to attempt to set the machinery of the Convention in motion by writing to Strasbourg, it is hardly surprising that the great majority of individual applications are rejected at this stage. Already, however, more than 500, or about four per cent, have been held to be admissible.

The ground of inadmissibility which is most difficult to apply is that of 'manifestly ill-founded'. The Commission is not competent to decide that an application is ill-founded on the merits because that is a decision for the Committee of Ministers or the Court. However, it must reject an application as inadmissible if the fact that it is ill-founded is 'manifest'. Where is the line to be drawn between these two concepts? This is clearly a matter of difficulty and of delicacy. An English lawyer would be tempted to say that a case is manifestly ill-founded if there is no *prima facie* appearance of a violation. The Commission itself has said:

> In a long series of previous decisions the Commission has consistently acted on the principle that an application should be declared inadmissible as being manifestly ill-founded only when a preliminary examination of the case does not disclose any appearance of a violation of the Convention.[6]

In its early days the Commission was very cautious and a high proportion of applications was rejected on this ground. Today it is less restrictive and so more survive this initial scrutiny and pass to the next stage.

If the Commission declares a case to be admissible, Article 28 of the Convention requires it to undertake an examination of the application 'with a view to ascertaining the facts'. This examination is carried out 'together with the representatives of the parties', which means in practice a hearing of a judicial nature with the individual applicant and the respondent government represented by counsel on a footing of complete equality. The difference between the procedure of the European Commission of Human Rights and that of the UN Human Rights Committee established by the Covenant on Civil and Political Rights described in Chapter 2, is thus strikingly apparent.[7]

Article 28 of the Convention also authorises the Commission where necessary to undertake an investigation, for which the State or States concerned are obliged to 'furnish all necessary facilities, after an exchange of views with the Commission'. It should be noted that the consultation concerns the modalities of the investigation, that is the date, the place, and the detailed arrangements, but not the major question of whether an investigation is necessary. On that point there is no discussion. By ratifying the Convention, the States concerned have accepted the obligation to agree to an investigation if the Commission so desires. Again, the difference between the European procedures and those of the United Nations is striking.

The most impressive example of an investigation carried out *in situ* was in the *Greek case* in 1969. A sub-commission met in Athens in March of that year and heard thirty-four witnesses to allegations of torture in Greece. It visited and photographed the premises of the Security Police and also heard twenty witnesses on the question of a state of emergency, including three former Prime Ministers, the chief of the armed forces, and the Director-General of Security.[8]

When the Commission has completed its investigation, Article 28(b) of the Convention requires it to try to secure a friendly settlement of the matter 'on the basis of respect for human rights as defined in this Convention'. About ten per cent of the individual applications found to be admissible are settled by this method,[9] which was also used in the inter-State case against Turkey in 1985. In the event of a friendly settlement the Commission draws up a report, which is published, containing a brief statement of the facts and of the solution reached (Article 30). If a friendly settlement is not achieved, the Commission draws up a detailed report, setting out the facts and stating its opinion as to whether the facts found disclose a violation of the Convention. Article 31 entitles the Commission to include whatever proposals it thinks fit and the report is then transmitted to the Committee of Ministers of the Council of Europe.[10]

(b) The Committee of Ministers The Committee of Ministers consists of the Ministers for Foreign Affairs or their deputies, of the member States of the Council of Europe.[11] It is essentially a political organ, yet judicial or quasi-judicial functions were conferred on it by the Convention. Article 32 provides that if a case is not referred to the Court of Human Rights, the Committee of Ministers shall decide whether or not a violation has occurred. It takes this decision by a two-thirds majority, although its important decisions in other spheres require unanimity.

The Committee does not have the power to order a government to take remedial measures. However, paragraph 2 of Article 32 requires it to prescribe a period of time during which the State concerned must take the measures required by the Committee's decision. In other words, if the Committee decides that a violation has occurred, it is for the respondent government to draw its own conclusions and take the necessary remedial action within the time fixed by the Committee. The contracting parties agree to be bound by the Committee's decision (Article 32, paragraph 4).

A sanction is provided in paragraph 3 of Article 32. If the government concerned has not taken satisfactory measures within the prescribed period, the Committee is required to decide what further action is necessary and to publish the report of the Commission. This sanction is more powerful than it may seem, because no government of a democratic State can be unconcerned at the publication of a report by a competent and impartial international organ announcing to the world that it is violating its human rights obligations. Moreover, in the last resort the Committee of Ministers has another more powerful sanction at its disposal. Article 8 of the Statute of the Council of Europe empowers the Committee to expel any member for violation of Article 3 of the Statute, which requires respect for the rule of law and the protection of human rights and fundamental freedoms. It is obvious, therefore, that the Committee of Ministers disposes of strong means of pressure, should this be necessary, to ensure compliance with its decisions.[12]

(c) The European Court of Human Rights The Court contains as many judges as the number of members of the Council of Europe (Article 38). Its current membership is therefore twenty-two. The judges act in complete independence, and must possess the same personal and legal qualifications as the members of the International Court of Justice at The Hague (Article 39(3)). The Court, like the Commission, elects its own President.[13]

The jurisdiction of the Court is contingent. A case may be

referred to it only by the Commission or a State and not by an individual applicant (Article 44), and then only if the defendant State has accepted the Court's jurisdiction. This may be done *ad hoc* for a particular case (Article 48), or by a general declaration accepting the jurisdiction of the Court in accordance with Article 46 of the Convention. Twenty States have made such declarations to date, that is to say all the contracting parties except Turkey.

Article 43 of the Convention provides that for each case brought before it the Court shall consist of a chamber of seven judges, which shall include as *ex officio* members the President or the Vice-President and the judge who is a national of any State party concerned, with the remaining judges chosen by lot. This is the normal procedure. However, under Rule 50 of the rules of procedure a chamber may relinquish jurisdiction in favour of the plenary Court if the case pending before it 'raises one or more serious questions affecting the interpretation of the Convention'. Moreover, such relinquishment is obligatory if there is a possibility of conflict with a previous judgement of a chamber or of the plenary Court. In practice this happens quite frequently, with the result that about one case in three is heard by the plenary Court.

The jurisdiction of the Court extends to all cases concerning the interpretation and application of the Convention submitted to it (Article 45), but the case must be submitted within a period of three months after the report of the Commission has been transmitted to the Committee of Ministers (Article 47). It is then for the Court to decide whether or not the facts found constitute a violation of the Convention.

If a violation has occurred, the Convention does not say whether the Court has the power to order remedial measures. This contrasts with the American Convention on Human Rights, which, as we shall see shortly, specifically confers such powers on the Inter-American Court. In the absence of an equivalent provision, the European Court has concluded that it lacks this power and in a number of cases has made the point that it is for the respondent State, not the Court, to decide upon the measures needed to implement its obligations. Article 50 of the Convention, on the other hand, specifically empowers the Court to give 'just satisfaction' or damages to an injured party if the internal law of the country concerned does not afford an adequate remedy. This has proved very important and, though a decision upholding a complaint does not invariably include an award of compensation, if loss can be proved the Court will generally award an applicant damages, as well as reimbursement of his costs and expenses.

The contracting parties undertake to abide by the decision of the Court in any case to which they are parties (Article 53). Moreover, the judgement of the Court is transmitted to the Committee of Ministers of the Council of Europe, which has the responsibility of supervising its execution (Article 54). This means in practice that the representative of the government concerned will explain to the Committee what action his government has taken in order to give effect to the judgement of the Court – for example, by amending its legislation or paying damages to an injured party – and the Committee will decide whether such action satisfies the requirements of the situation. In this respect the powers of the European Court of Human Rights are less extensive than those of the Inter-American Court or the Court of Justice of the European Communities, both of which can make an order for compensation which is directly enforceable in the country concerned. Nevertheless, the European system works reasonably well in practice and the requirement that a government should explain to the Committee of Ministers what action it has taken to comply with the Court's judgement is undoubtedly of value.

4. *The application of the Convention*

Many substantial volumes have been published reproducing decisions and reports of the European Commission of Human Rights, decisions of the Committee of Ministers and judgements of the Court. It is obviously impossible to summarise this voluminous case law in the present chapter. To indicate the kinds of cases which arise and convey the flavour of Strasbourg jurisprudence, we shall therefore summarise the two most important inter-State cases and review a number of typical individual applications. We shall then suggest some conclusions which can be drawn in the light of experience with the Convention to date.

(a) The Greek case In April 1967 there was a *coup d'état* in Greece. The following month the permanent representative of Greece addressed a letter to the Secretary-General of the Council of Europe in which he invoked Article 15 of the Convention and stated that the application of various articles of the Greek constitution had been suspended in view of internal dangers threatening public order and the security of the State. In subsequent letters in May and September the Greek government gave further information in regard to Article 15

In September 1967, in identical applications to the European Commission, the governments of Denmark, Norway and Sweden, after referring to the suspension of the provisions of the Greek constitution, submitted that by various legislative measures and administrative practices the Greek government had violated Articles 5, 6, 8, 9, 10, 11, 13 and 14 of the Convention. In relation to all these allegations they contended that the government had failed to show that the conditions of Article 15 of the Convention permitting measures of derogation were satisfied. In an application later in the same month the government of the Netherlands made submissions which corresponded in substance to those of the first three applicant governments. The four applications were therefore joined by the Commission in October.

In its written observations in reply in December, the respondent submitted that the Commission was not competent to examine the applications because they concerned the actions of a revolutionary government. It also stated with regard to Article 15 of the Convention that, in accordance with the Commission's jurisprudence, a government enjoyed a 'margin of appreciation' in deciding whether there existed a public emergency threatening the life of the nation and, if so, what exceptional measures were required. In January 1968 the Commission declared the four applications admissible.[14] In a further joint memorial in March 1968 the three Scandinavian governments extended their original allegations to Articles 3 and 7 of the Convention and Articles 1 and 3 of the First Protocol. In May 1968 these further allegations were also declared admissible.

The hearings which followed lasted some eighteen months and more than eighty witnesses were heard in Strasbourg and Athens. As already mentioned, an inspection was made and photographs were taken of the Security Police building in Athens. More than 300 pages of the Commission's report were devoted to the question of torture and many victims were heard as witnesses. Acting throughout with scrupulous objectivity, the Commission required corroboration of the allegations made, offered the government every opportunity to rebut the evidence, and even examined the possibility that many of the accounts of torture had been fabricated in an elaborate attempt to discredit it.

After carefully reviewing the evidence at its disposal, the Commission concluded that torture had been inflicted in eleven cases and that there were indications, *prima facie* cases, or strong indications, in seventeen other cases in which the sub-commission had been prevented from completing its investigation. It also found that there was a practice of torture and ill-treatment by the Athens Security Police of persons arrested for political reasons and that the Greek authorities, confronted with numerous and substantial complaints and allegations of torture and ill-treatment, had failed to take any effective steps to investigate them or remedy the situation.

The Commission, of course, also examined the other allegations made by the applicant governments. It concluded that in April 1967 there had not been a public emergency threatening the life of the nation; as a consequence the Greek derogations under Article 15 were invalid. The Commission also ruled that there were violations of nine other articles of the Convention and the First Protocol, including the right to liberty, the right to a fair trial, freedom of association, and the right to free elections. Its conclusions were contained in a report which was transmitted to the Committee of Ministers of the Council of Europe in November 1969.[15]

Consideration of the *Greek case* was complicated by the fact that two parallel procedures were being pursued in the Council of Europe at the same time. On the one hand, there was the case brought before the Commission under Article 24 of the Convention. On the other, the Consultative Assembly of the Council of Europe, on the basis of certain articles of the Statute, had recommended that the Committee of Ministers should expel the Greek government from the organisation. The relevant provisions were Article 3, which requires that every member must respect the rule of law and protect human rights, and Article 8, the effect of which is that a State which has seriously violated Article 3 may be suspended from membership. While the lengthy proceedings under Article 24 of the Convention were continuing before the Commission, the Assembly considered that there was already a strong case for holding that the Greek government had violated Article 3 of the Statute. It therefore concluded that the Committee of Ministers should act under

Article 8 without waiting for the result of the proceedings before the Commission and in January 1969 addressed a recommendation to this effect to the Committee.[16] When the Ministers met in London in May 1969 strong pressure was put upon them to implement this recommendation. Knowing that the report of the Commission was nearly ready, they promised a decision at their next session.

This was held in Paris in December 1969. The Commission's report had been sent to governments in November. Its contents were therefore known to the Ministers, even though it was not formally on the agenda of the meeting, because Article 32 of the Convention provides that a period of three months shall elapse, during which the case may be referred to the Court, before the Ministers can take a decision.

At their meeting in December the Ministers discussed both the situation in Greece and whether the country could remain a member of the organisation. At a dramatic meeting, during which a draft resolution for the suspension of Greece was circulated and received a wide measure of support, the Greek Foreign Minister announced that his government had decided to withdraw from the Council of Europe and denounce the Convention on Human Rights. However, the denunciation of the Convention could take effect only after the expiry of a period of six months and the denunciation of the Statute at the end of the following year. Moreover, as regards proceedings under the Convention, Article 65(2) makes it clear that denunciation has no effect on duties or obligations arising out of events occurring before the denunciation becomes effective. Consequently, the Committee of Ministers adopted a resolution in which they took note of the Greek declarations and drew the conclusion that Greece would cease to participate in the work of the Council of Europe immediately.

The Committee of Ministers was still required by Article 32 of the Convention to take a decision on the report of the Commission. This they did at their next session in April 1970. They endorsed the opinion of the Commission and decided that Greece had violated ten articles of the Convention on Human Rights and the First Protocol. At the same time they expressed the hope that democratic liberties would be restored in the near future and that Greece would then rejoin the Council of Europe. Happily the situation in Greece was restored with the return to democratic government in 1974, after which Greece resumed its membership of the Council of Europe and once more ratified the European Convention.

The *Greek case* is certainly the most serious situation the Convention institutions have had to deal with and demonstrates both the strengths and the limitations of the Strasbourg system. The fact that Greece was a party to the Convention did not prevent the *coup d'état*, or the large scale violations of human rights which were among its consequences. Human rights agreements can reinforce and consolidate democracy; what they cannot do is guarantee that liberty will always prevail when powerful forces are ranged against it. But if the Convention, like other human laws, is vulnerable to overwhelming social or political forces, its existence is far from meaningless. In the *Greek case* it supplied both a standard against which the conduct of the government could be measured and an objective procedure for assessment. Even more important, it made the conduct of affairs within Greece a legitimate subject for international concern. The withdrawal of Greece from the Council of Europe, which was the direct result of that organisation's commitment to human rights, had the effect of isolating the State and strengthening its democratic forces. Thus, following the coup, the inter-State procedure worked just as intended, to expose oppression in a way that left no room for doubt and to bring pressure to bear for a return to democratic values.

(b) The Northern Ireland case Physical maltreatment was also one of the issues raised in the case of *Ireland* v. *United Kingdom*. The Irish government lodged this application in December 1971 and filed two supplementary memorials in March 1972. The Commission decided to treat the first supplementary memorial as part of the original application, but to register the second as a new application.

The government referred to the Civil Authorities (Special Powers) Act, Northern Ireland, 1922, and the connected statutory rules, regulations and orders and submitted that this legislation was in itself a failure by the United Kingdom to comply with the obligation in Article 1 of the Convention to secure to everyone within its jurisdiction the rights and freedoms defined in Section 1.

The application further referred to the taking into custody of persons on or after 9 August 1971 under the Special Powers Act and alleged that they were subjected to treatment which constituted torture and inhuman and degrading treatment and punishment contrary to Article 3 of the Convention. The Irish government also claimed that internment without trial, as carried out in Northern Ireland subsequent to 9 August 1971, constituted a violation of Article 5 (the right to liberty and security of the person) and Article 6 (the right to a fair trial). In addition, the applicant government alleged that the powers of detention and internment were exercised in a discriminatory manner, contrary to Article 14 of the Convention.

On the question of torture or inhuman treatment the Irish government complained particularly about the methods of interrogation used by the British security forces in Northern Ireland, including hooding, noise, standing against a wall, deprivation of sleep and limited diet. In this respect the British government had already conceded a tactical advantage. In 1971 the Home Secretary had appointed a committee of enquiry to look into allegations of brutality in Northern Ireland arising out of procedures known as 'interrogation in depth'. In its report, known as the 'Compton Report', the committee described in detail the techniques used by the security forces. In March 1972, as a result of a further report by a group of Privy Counsellors, known as the 'Parker Report', the Prime Minister announced in the House of Commons that the government had decided that the use of the techniques in question would be discontinued. This action to stop the use of questionable methods of interrogation was certainly commendable. However, it put a powerful argument in the hands of the Irish government which could now quote official British sources describing the methods of interrogation employed, criticism by, among others, a former Lord Chancellor, the decision of the Prime Minister to stop their use, and the possibility, even if remote, of further recourse to them in future.

In October 1972 the Commission declared the first application admissible, but decided to strike the second application off the list. Examination of the merits then began. After an exchange of memorials, hearings on the merits took place in October 1973, and again in December of that year. Witnesses put forward by the Irish government were heard by three delegates of the Commission in December 1973 and February 1974, and those put forward by the British government on several occasions in 1974. For reasons of security some witnesses were heard at an air force base at Stavanger in Norway, and others in London in February 1975. In all 118 witnesses were heard by the delegates of the Commission in the course of this case.

The Commission sent its report to the Committee of Ministers in February 1976.[17] It expressed the opinion that the measures for detention without trial were not in violation of the Convention, because they were 'strictly required by the exigencies of the situation' and were therefore covered by the derogation made by the British government under Article 15. Moreover, the Commission found that the powers of detention and internment had not been applied in a discriminatory manner. On the other hand, it considered that the use of the five techniques for 'interrogation in depth' constituted a violation of Article 3 of the Convention prohibiting torture and inhuman treatment.

In March 1976 the Irish government referred the case to the European Court of Human Rights, the first, and so far the only, inter-State case to be so referred. Oral hearings took place in two stages in the following year and the Court's judgement was given in January 1978.[18] In its judgement the Court made a distinction between torture, on the one hand, and inhuman and degrading treatment, on the other. It held that the techniques of interrogation which had been used in Northern Ireland constituted inhuman and degrading treatment in violation of Article 3, but that they did not occasion suffering of the degree of intensity and cruelty implied by the word 'torture'. The Court agreed with the Commission that the measures of detention and internment without trial were covered by the derogation made under Article 15 of the Convention and that these measures had not been exercised in a discriminatory manner.

Despite certain similarities, the *Irish case* shows the inter-State procedure functioning in an altogether different situation from that which prompted the *Greek case*. In the latter, as we have seen, totalitarian forces had taken over and use of the Convention was a way of encouraging a return to democracy. In the *Irish case*, on the other hand, the question was how far a government may go when it is committed to democratic values, but confronted with the intractable problem of terrorism. By exonerating the respondent's actions under Article 15 the Court and the Commission recognised that an exceptional situation can justify measures which would not otherwise be permissible. However, by upholding the claim under

Article 3 the Strasbourg institutions again demonstrated the value of the inter-State procedure and underlined one of the Convention's basic principles, that in a democracy the end does not always justify the means.

(c) Some individual applications Since the European Commission of Human Rights began work in 1954 it has declared admissible more than 500 individual applications. About one-tenth formed the object of a friendly settlement within the meaning of Article 28 of the Convention, and as many more have been settled by some informal arrangement.[19]

The remainder, apart from some cases still under examination, have been the object of reports to the Committee of Ministers under Article 31 of the Convention. Many of these cases have been decided by the Committee of Ministers and more than 100 have been referred to the Court. As already explained, a case may be referred to the Court only if the respondent government has accepted its jurisdiction either in general terms or on an *ad hoc* basis. But nearly all the governments which have accepted the right of individual petition have also accepted the compulsory jurisdiction of the Court. Consequently, it is usually possible for a case which has its origin in an individual petition to be referred to the Court.

It is for the Commission or the government concerned to decide, within three months of the transmission of the Commission's report to the Committee of Ministers, whether or not a case should go to the Court. There are no rules setting out the criteria on which this decision should be based. Generally speaking, however, one may say that if the Commission is unanimous or nearly unanimous in expressing the opinion that no violation has occurred, the tendency is to leave the case with the Committee of Ministers. In such cases the Committee has always confirmed the Commission's opinion. On the other hand, the Commission or the government concerned, or both of them, will tend to refer a case to the Court in three circumstances: if the Commission is narrowly divided in its opinion, if the Commission considers that a violation has occurred, or if the case raises an important question of interpretation.

As a result, if we wish to obtain a general view of the application of the Convention but have to be selective in doing so, we can find the best examples in the case-law of the Court. And since space precludes an examination of that case-law in detail, we shall limit ourselves to outlining the issues in some of the more significant applications.[20]

The first case considered by the Court was the *Lawless case*, decided in 1961. It concerned the detention without trial in Ireland of a suspected member of the Irish Republican Army in the exercise of special powers conferred by the Offences against the State Act, 1940. The Irish government had made a derogation under Article 15 of the Convention, claiming the existence of a state of emergency. The Court held that the derogation was justified and there was no violation.[21] The issues in *Lawless* were very similar to those arising under Articles 5 and 6 in *Irish case*. There, as we have seen, the Court held that British measures against the IRA could be justified under Article 15. Cases like these, involving emergency situations, are fortunately rare, but when they occur present the Court with particularly delicate problems.

Most of the Court's early cases concerned the right to personal liberty in situations where there was no emergency. Here the Court had to decide the precise scope of the right and, in particular, whether conduct which would certainly be unacceptable in some States could nevertheless be regarded as within the Convention. Thus, five early cases arising out of individual applications brought against the Federal Republic of Germany (*Wemhoff*) and against Austria (*Neumeister, Stögmuller, Matznetter, Ringeisen*) all concerned prolonged periods of detention on remand awaiting trial – in several cases for two years, in one case for three years. The Court decided on the facts that there was no violation as regards *Wemhoff* and *Matznetter*[22] but there was violation in the cases of *Neumeister, Stögmuller* and *Ringeisen*.[23] Subsequently, on requests for 'just satisfaction' Neumeister was awarded his costs[24] and Ringeisen a substantial sum as compensation.[25] As a result of these cases both the Federal Republic of Germany and Austria amended their law on detention before trial.

The *Golder case* in 1975 concerned the right of access to a court of law. The applicant, who was serving a sentence of imprisonment in the United Kingdom, wished to see a lawyer with a view to bringing a civil action against one of the prison warders. Permission to do so was refused. The Court found a violation of the Convention, because the right to a fair trial was held to imply the right of access to a court.[26] Subsequently, the Home Secretary announced to Parliament a change in the prison rules in order to comply with the judgement.

Golder is one of the Court's most important cases because, apart from its immediate consequences, it demonstrated the possibility of extending the scope of the Convention by an imaginative interpretation of its provisions. Shortly afterwards, in the *Airey case*, the Court went even further and held that the Convention had been violated because the prohibitive costs of obtaining a judicial separation in Ireland meant that, although there was no formal barrier, the applicant had been deprived of an effective right of access to a court.[27] As bold pieces of judicial legislation, both decisions were controversial, and while the right of access to the courts is now firmly established in the Strasbourg jurisprudence, the proper approach to interpretation of the Convention can still give rise to controversy.[28]

In the year after *Golder* the Court had to decide a rather different question relating to the scope of the Convention's guarantees. In the *Engel case*, which concerned the Netherlands, one of the issues was whether the rules in the Convention about the right to a fair trial apply to disciplinary proceedings in the armed forces. On the question of principle the Court gave a positive answer, but nevertheless distinguished certain forms of disciplinary measures in the armed forces from deprivation of liberty as generally understood. Certain minor violations, however, were established.[29] One of the applicants received a token indemnity and certain amendments were introduced into the law and practice of military discipline in the Netherlands.

As might be expected, judicial proceedings and the scope of the right to a fair trial have provided the subject of many other cases. The *König case* concerned prolonged proceedings before administrative tribunals in the Federal Republic of Germany, which constituted a violation of the Convention.[30] The case of *Luedicke, Belkacem and Koç* involved the obligation to provide free interpretation for the defendant in a criminal case if he does not understand the language used in court. The requirement that the applicants should reimburse the cost of interpretation in the Federal Republic was here also held to constitute a violation.[31] In the *Winterwerp case* there was violation by the Netherlands because there was no possibility of recourse to a court for a person confined to a psychiatric hospital.[32] On the other hand, in the *Schiesser case* it was decided that the applicant's detention in Switzerland by order of the district attorney, on suspicion of having committed a series of aggravated thefts, was not a violation of the Convention.[33]

Another important group of cases has concerned the right to respect for private and family life, home and correspondence. The *Klass case* concerned the clandestine control of correspondence and telephone calls in the Federal Republic of Germany. While such action clearly interferes with the right to respect for correspondence and for private life, the Court held that in the circumstances it was justified in the interests of safeguarding national security and preventing disorder or crime.[34] On the other hand, in the *Marckx case* the Court held that certain provisions of Belgian law relating to children born out of wedlock, particularly as regards rights of inheritance, put them at a disadvantage as compared with legitimate children, and therefore violated the Convention.[35]

A notable feature of the *Marckx case* was the emphasis which the Court placed on its duty to interpret the Convention in the light of current attitudes towards illegitimacy rather than ideas which were prevalent when the Convention was drawn up. The Court also made the point that the Convention is not just concerned with restraining interference with rights, but in certain circumstances requires governments to take positive steps to promote them. Like the concept of implied rights which proved so significant in *Golder*, these principles reflect an approach to interpretation with enormous creative potential, and while the Court has recognised that it can only go so far, it has often used them to extend the scope of the Convention.[36]

Trade union freedoms were first considered by the Court in three cases decided in 1975 and 1976. In the *National Union of Belgian Police* and the *Swedish Engine Drivers' Union* cases the Court decided that the recognition of the right to form and join trade unions did not imply an obligation on the State to negotiate with those unions about matters of concern to their members.[37] In the *Schmidt and Dahlström case*, similarly, the Court held that the refusal to give retroactive effect to a wage settlement to members of a union which had taken strike action was not a violation of the Convention.[38]

The Court returned to the question of trade union law in 1981 when it decided the case of *Young, James and Webster*, which raised the difficult issue of the 'closed shop'. The applicants complained that they had been dismissed for refusing to join a union which was a condition of employment in the British railway industry. The Court held that they were entitled to compensation for violation of their rights under Article 11, despite the fact the Convention does not expressly provide for 'freedom of non-association'.[39] The Court was careful to state that its ruling did not relate to the institution of the closed shop in general, but rather to its legitimacy in the particular case. Like the *Golder case*, however, the judgement shows the Court's ability to develop the law in the individual's interests, as well as the impact of its decisions on the domestic plane.

Freedom of expression is one of the most basic rights in a democratic society, but obviously cannot be unlimited. In almost all the cases in which this freedom has been invoked the Court has had to decide whether the action complained of indicates that it has been infringed, or whether what is clearly a limitation of freedom of expression can be justified on one of the grounds set out in the Convention. In dealing with this issue, which is typical of the way adjudication in the field of human rights often requires individual rights to be assessed against the background of the general interest, the Court has made use of a concept which has been mentioned earlier, the margin of appreciation. In the *Handyside case*, for example, the applicant complained that his conviction in the United Kingdom for publishing an obscene book violated his right to freedom of expression. However, the Court decided that in the absence of a uniform approach to issues of sexual morality among the members of the Council of Europe, the question was not whether the Court agreed with the conviction, but whether the actions complained of had exceeded the bounds of reasonableness. Deciding that the authorities were entitled to regard the book as morally pernicious, the Court held that in view of their margin of appreciation no violation of the Convention had occurred.[40]

The margin of appreciation is a useful concept and has been applied in many other areas.[41] Its relevance and application, however, depend very much on the Court's view of the particular issue. An important case in which it did not help the government was the *Sunday Times case*, decided in 1979. The applicants claimed that a court order prohibiting the publication of an article concerning 'thalidomide children' (children who were born deformed by reason of their mothers having taken thalidomide as a tranquilliser during pregnancy) constituted a violation of the right of freedom of expression. The order had been made on the ground that the article in question might prejudice the court proceedings then pending against the manufacturers of the drug. The European Court held that where the authority of the judiciary is concerned the margin of appreciation is much narrower than in cases involving morality such as *Handyside*. It concluded that the United Kingdom had violated the Convention and subsequently ordered payment of a substantial sum to the applicants for their costs.[42] The United Kingdom then enacted legislation to bring English law into line with the judgement.

Some of the Court's most interesting cases have concerned another issue central to the work of a human rights tribunal, discrimination. Now the Convention's prohibition on discrimination is complementary to the other substantive provisions in the sense that it can be applied only where the facts fall within the ambit of one or more of the other articles. Moreover, even when this condition is fulfilled, a difference of treatment can be justified by showing that it has an 'objective and reasonable justification'. Here, not surprisingly, there is often scope for a margin of appreciation, although, as in the cases on freedom of expression, the scope for this will vary. In the *Rasmussen case*, for example, the Court held that although under Danish law a man's right to refer an issue of paternity to the courts was subject to time limits, whereas a woman's was not, there was no violation of the Convention because the difference could be justified by the interests of the child and came within the margin of appreciation.[43] In the case of *Abdulaziz, Cabales and Balkandali*, on the other hand, it reached the opposite conclusion. There the question was whether the United Kingdom was justified in having different admission requirements for the wives and husbands of immigrants, and the Court, emphasising that sex discrimination can be justified only in the most exceptional circumstances, decided that, despite the margin of appreciation, the Convention had been violated.[44]

The cases mentioned so far were mainly concerned with the rights and freedoms protected by the original Convention. However, there have also been numerous cases involving the provisions of the First Protocol. The right to property, for example, which is protected by Article 1, has been considered by the Court on several occasions.

This right is subject to important limitations and, as with the issue of freedom of expression, most of the cases have concerned the relation between the right and its qualifications. In *Sporrong and Lönnroth* (1982), for example, the Court decided that the applicants' rights had been violated by Swedish expropriation permits, which prevented them from selling or using their land, and held that this entitled them to compensation.[45] In 1986, however, the Court held in the *James case* that the compulsory transfer of property under the Leasehold Reform Act did not give rise to a violation[46] and shortly afterwards in the *Lithgow case* reached the same conclusion as regards the nationalisation of shipyards in the United Kingdom.[47] In both of the later cases the Court pointed out that the power of the State to take measures in the public interest, which is expressly preserved by Article 1, means that it is harder to establish a violation of this provision than of most articles of the Convention.

Another right guaranteed by the First Protocol is the right of parents to ensure education and teaching in conformity with their religious and philosophical convictions (Article 2). Like most of the Convention's provisions, this article requires a balance to be struck between the powers of the State and the rights of the individual and so can give rise to difficult questions of interpretation. In the *Danish Sex Education case* in 1976 the Court held that the Danish legislation on this subject, which provided for information to be given to school children in an objective manner, did not violate the Convention, even though some parents objected.[48] In *Campbell and Cosans* (1982), on the other hand, it held that in similar circumstances the use of corporal punishment in a Scottish school did violate Article 2.[49]

The *Campbell and Cosans case* also raised the question of whether the corporal punishment which was objected to could be regarded as 'inhuman or degrading treatment or punishment', thereby contravening Article 3. The Court held that in the circumstances it could not, although in its earlier decision in the *Tyrer case* (1978) it had decided that the birching of a juvenile which had been ordered by a court in the Isle of Man did constitute a violation of this provision.[50]

It is perhaps appropriate to conclude this overview of individual applications by mentioning a number of recent cases in which the Court has had to consider the scope of the right to marry in

Article 12. In the *Rees case* in 1986 it decided that this provision refers to traditional marriage between persons of the opposite biological sex. Thus, the United Kingdom had not violated the Convention by making it impossible for a person who had undergone a sex-change operation to marry a person of his former sex.[51] In the *Johnston case*, later in the same year, the Court decided that by guaranteeing the right to marry the Convention does not impliedly guarantee a right to divorce, with the result that Ireland, a country in which divorce was prohibited in the Constitution, was not in breach of its obligations.[52] Shortly afterwards, in the case of *F.* v. *Switzerland* (1987), the Court decided by a narrow majority that Switzerland had violated Article 12 when a man who had been married and divorced three times already, was prohibited from remarrying for a period of three years.[53]

Those who drafted the Convention would probably have been as surprised by the ruling in *F.* v. *Switzerland* as to see Article 12 being relied upon by the applicant in *Rees*. As with some of the other issues we have considered, however, the cases on the right to marry show that the Convention can sometimes be used in unexpected ways, and reinforce the point made earlier, that in interpreting its provisions the Court does not regard itself as circumscribed by the ideas of 1950, but is prepared to treat the Convention as a living and changing instrument.

(d) An appraisal A summary of leading cases cannot present a complete picture of the extraordinarily rich case-law of the Commission and Court, but can perhaps convey an impression of the European Convention in action. An assessment of the record must begin by recognising the crucial significance of co-operation by governments with both the Commission and the Court, without which the system could not function effectively. It is also interesting to note the great variety of problems which have arisen – and innumerable other questions have been raised in applications brought before the Commission which have not been mentioned – involving nearly all the rights and freedoms protected by the Convention and its Protocols. Moreover, experience with the Convention shows that no State should be immune from scrutiny to check that its judicial and other authorities are complying with the obligations it has accepted under treaties for the protection of human rights. All the States which have accepted the right of individual petition have seen cases against them brought before the Commission and the majority have also had cases referred to the Court. No administration is free from the possibility of error, even in countries which, when we look around the world, are unquestionably among those with the best record for the administration of justice and the protection of civil liberties.

These reflections would seem to justify two conclusions. First, that a system of international control like that of the European Convention is both necessary and desirable, even for States which respect the rule of law and possess constitutional guarantees of human rights and fundamental freedoms. Secondly, that, as has been often stated, the system established by the Convention is the most effective that has yet been introduced anywhere in the world.

When the European Convention had been in force for twenty-five years, the Committee of Ministers of the Council of Europe reaffirmed the importance it attaches to the Convention and its confidence in the Commission and the Court, and decided to give priority to exploring the possibility of extending the list of rights protected, notably by including rights in the social, economic and cultural fields.[54] This work is under way.

But if there are grounds for satisfaction, there is an important corollary which should not be forgotten. The European system has been able to function effectively because the governments concerned have been willing to co-operate with the Strasbourg organs, and the States to which the system applies genuinely wish to secure the effective exercise of human rights on their territories. The problems which come before the European Commission and Court, important as they may be for the individuals concerned, are with few exceptions of only marginal significance when compared with the massive and flagrant violations of human rights which occur in other parts of the world. The systematic torture of political prisoners, arrests of persons who then 'disappear', confinement of dissidents to psychiatric institutions, imprisonment of human right activists, these and other practices which are prevalent elsewhere pose problems which are immeasurably more serious than those which constitute the day-to-day business of the European organs.

It follows that a member of the Inter-American Commission on Human Rights would be impressed by the functioning of the European system, but might reflect that it has comparatively little relevance to the problems of massive violations in certain Latin American countries with which his Commission has to deal. What is true for Latin America applies with even greater force in certain other regions of the world. If an analogy may be drawn without trivialising the issue, it is fine to have a referee in a football match when all the players know what game is being played and intend to respect the rules. But if there is no agreement on these matters, what is needed is not a referee but a fundamental change in attitude. Thus, much work remains to be done before we can expect to see regional arrangements for the protection of human rights, comparable to the European system, in other parts of the world.

5. Comparison of the European Convention with the United Nations Covenant on Civil and Political Rights

The member States of the Council of Europe which are also members of the United Nations participated in the preparation of the UN Covenants and voted for their adoption in 1966. It was therefore only natural that the parties to the European Convention should compare the Covenant on Civil and Political Rights with the European instrument and examine the question of ratification in the light of their experience at Strasbourg. Such an examination was necessary not only to review the obligations which States assume by ratifying the United Nations Covenant, but also to decide such questions as the rules which would apply in the internal law of States that accept the direct applicability of treaties and which international forum is competent to adjudicate in cases involving rights which are protected by both the Covenant and the Convention.[55]

Settling the relationship between the two treaties is a problem which concerns all States which are parties to the European Convention. Since it is a common problem, it was natural that a joint study should be undertaken. For measures which can provide a solution to the problems raised for one State can probably also do so for another. Thus, it was desirable that if possible the parties to the Convention should adopt a common attitude towards ratification of the United Nations Covenant and any special arrangements which might be necessary to safeguard the European system. The Committee of Ministers of the Council of Europe therefore decided that a study of these matters should be undertaken. The work was entrusted to the body which was then known as the Committee of Experts on Human Rights, and largely made up of lawyers from government departments dealing with human rights matters.[56]

The problems which arise may be divided into two categories: those which concern the rights guaranteed and those relating to the machinery for their enforcement. In other words, questions of substance and questions of procedure. These require separate consideration.[57]

(a) The enumeration and definition of the rights guaranteed As we have seen, the European Convention and its Protocols protect twenty-five separate rights, while the United Nations Covenant on Civil and Political Rights protects twenty-three. As might be expected, many of the rights protected by the two instruments are the same and their definitions are substantially similar. This is all the more natural since work on the Covenant had already begun when the European Convention was prepared. Those who worked on the drafting of the latter in the spring of 1950 therefore had available – and made use of – the work already done at that stage by the United Nations Commission on Human Rights.

Although many of the definitions are substantially the same, in some instances the same rights are included but the definitions differ considerably. It is easy to appreciate that these differences may be very important for States which are, or have it in mind to become, parties to both instruments. They must consider whether obligations under the United Nations Covenant are more or less extensive than those under the European Convention and, if they are more extensive, whether the state of their national law is satisfactory.

A third category is constituted by those rights which are provided for in the United Nations Covenant but not in the European Convention, or vice versa. This might seem a simple situation where no particular problems should arise. But as we shall see, it is less simple than it would appear, because in some cases rights which are not expressly included in the Convention have been held to be implied, while in others they are covered by other conventions promoted by the Council of Europe to which many of the same States are parties.

(i) Rights included in both instruments in substantially similar terms Eleven rights are included in both instruments in substantially similar terms. They are the following, the reference in each case being to the article in the United Nations Covenant by which the right is protected:

Article 7 Freedom from torture and inhuman treatment.
8 Freedom from slavery, servitude and forced labour.
9 The right to liberty and security of the person.
11 Freedom from imprisonment for failure to fulfil a contractual obligation.
12 The right to freedom of movement.
15 Protection against retroactivity of the criminal law.
17 The right to privacy.
18 The right to freedom of thought, conscience and religion.
19 The right to freedom of expression.
21 The right of peaceful assembly.
22 The right to freedom of association.

Although these rights are defined in substantially similar terms, in some instances there are differences between the definitions which may be important. As regards the right to liberty and security of the person, for example, Article 9 of the United Nations Covenant prohibits simply 'arbitrary arrest or detention', while Article 5 of the European Convention prohibits arrest or detention except for six sets of circumstances which are specifically defined (after conviction by a competent court, for non-compliance with the lawful order of a court, etc.). The question therefore arises whether there is a correspondence between the prohibition of 'arbitrary arrest or detention' and the more elaborate European formula. It appears that 'arbitrary' is intended to mean 'unlawful and unjust'[58] and that it would therefore prohibit arrest or detention which might be permitted under some systems of law but which, by international standards, would not be considered 'just'. This could hardly apply, however, in the six cases permitted by Article 5 of the European Convention, and so even though the two definitions are not identical, no conflict should arise.

Similarly, Article 9, paragraph 2 of the United Nations text requires that when a person is arrested he shall be informed of the reasons 'at the time of his arrest', while the European requirement is that he should be informed 'promptly'. The requirement of the Covenant may be thought to impose the stricter obligation. It seems, however, that the underlying intention, and consequently the obligation, is much the same, so that here also, it is appropriate to think of these as rights which are defined in substantially similar terms.

(ii) Rights with regard to which there are important differences in the definitions Here we are dealing with four rights:

The right to life (Article 6).
The right to a fair trial (Article 14).
The right to marry (Article 23).
Political rights (Article 25).

The right to life. Article 6 of the Covenant protects the right to life. Its first paragraph reads: 'Every human being has the inherent right to life. This right shall be protected by law. No one shall be arbitrarily deprived of his life.' Again we find that the United Nations text uses the word 'arbitrarily', which was rejected during the drafting of the European Convention on the ground that it was too general or vague. The European text states explicitly that 'no one shall be deprived of his life intentionally save in the execution of a sentence of a court following his conviction of a crime for which this penalty is provided by law'. It continues by permitting restrictions on the right in the case of death resulting from the use of force which is no more than absolutely necessary in three cases: in defence against unlawful violence; in order to effect arrest or prevent escape; and for the purpose of quelling a riot or insurrection. As in the case of liberty and security, it would appear that the intention and the effect of the two texts are similar and that the restrictions permitted under the Convention would not be considered 'arbitrary' within the meaning of the Covenant.

The more important differences are found in the subsequent paragraphs of Article 6. They are plainly intended to ensure that the death penalty should be restricted as far as possible and eventually abolished. Paragraph 2 begins, 'In countries which have not abolished the death penalty, sentence of death may be imposed only for the most serious crimes ...', and paragraph 6 states that 'Nothing in this article shall be invoked to delay or to prevent the abolition of capital punishment by any State Party to the Covenant.' In this respect the Covenant is distinctly more progressive than Article 2 of the European Convention, and one may wonder whether the reintroduction of the death penalty, when it has once been abolished, would be consistent with the Covenant. A further difference is that the Covenant prohibits the death penalty for persons under eighteen years of age and for pregnant women; it also provides for the right to seek pardon or commutation of the sentence. There are no corresponding provisions in Article 2, even though the practice of the few European States which retain capital punishment is generally in conformity with these requirements.

The treatment of the right to life in Article 2 of the European Convention must now be read in the light of the prohibition of the death penalty in time of peace which is the subject of the Sixth Protocol. This, of course, goes much further than the Covenant, with the result that while the latter initially reflected a more liberal spirit, the position has now been reversed. However, not all the parties to the Convention have ratified the Protocol. For those which have not, the obligations of the Covenant are more extensive and the possibility of incompatibility remains.

The right to a fair trial The second article where there are differences between the two texts deals with what is perhaps the most important right of all: the right to a fair trial and due process of law. Article 14 of the Covenant opens with the general affirmation 'All persons shall be equal before the courts and tribunals'. This, though unexceptionable as a general principle, is not to be found in the European Convention.

The main statement of the right is rather similar in the two instruments. Article 14 of the Covenant provides: 'In the determination of any criminal charge against him, or of his rights and obligations in a suit at law, everyone shall be entitled to a fair and public hearing by a competent, independent and impartial tribunal established by law'. There are, however, three differences between this text and the corresponding sentence in Article 6 of the European Convention. First, the United Nations text uses the expression 'rights and obligations in a suit at law', whereas the Convention speaks of 'civil rights and obligations'. The French versions are identical in the two instruments (*droits et obligations de caractère civil*), which suggests that the English words are intended to have the same meaning. In the case-law of the Convention, however, the concept of 'civil rights and obligations' has generated a complex and controversial jurisprudence and as yet it is unclear whether the Covenant will (or ought) to be interpreted similarly.[59]

The second difference in the two definitions is that the European text includes, while the United Nations text omits, a requirement that the hearing must be 'within a reasonable time'. A later paragraph of the United Nations text provides that a trial on a criminal charge must take place 'without undue delay' (Article 14, paragraph 3). Thus, both instruments provide this guarantee in criminal matters, but only the European Convention covers civil proceedings.

The third difference is that while both texts provide for hearing by 'an independent and impartial tribunal established by law', the United Nations text adds the requirement that the tribunal shall be 'competent'. The intention was to make it clear that all persons should be tried by courts whose jurisdiction has been previously established by law and thus avoid arbitrary proceedings. However, this notion is already included or implied in 'independent ... tribunal established by law' and so the difference here seems of minor importance.

The second paragraph of Article 14 affirms the presumption of innocence in terms which are almost identical with those used in the European Convention.

The third paragraph sets out the rights of the defence in criminal proceedings. It is generally similar to Article 6(3) of the European Convention.

The United Nations Covenant then continues with four further paragraphs, setting out additional provisions regarding the right to a fair trial: paragraph 4, protecting the special position of juveniles; paragraph 5, on the right of a convicted person to appeal; paragraph 6, on the right to compensation for miscarriage of justice; and paragraph 7, laying down that no one may be tried twice for the same offence. None of these points is covered in the European Convention, except that Article 6 contains a provision which authorises an exception to the general stipulation of public trials 'where the interests of juveniles ... so require', while the other principles have recently been introduced in the Seventh Protocol.

The right to marry Article 23 of the Covenant proclaims the right to marry and found a family. In one respect it is less positive than the corresponding article in the European Convention because it states that the right 'shall be recognised', whereas Article 12 of the Convention provides that men and women of marriageable age 'have the right to marry and to found a family'. In other respects, however, the provisions of the United Nations Covenant are more far-reaching.

In the first place the Covenant starts with a general affirmation of principle, comparable to that of a number of national constitutions: 'The family is the natural and fundamental group unit of society and is entitled to protection by society and the State.' Secondly, the European text recognises the right 'according to the national laws governing the exercise of this right' and so incorporates by reference certain restrictions on the right permitted by national law, in case of insanity or hereditary disease, for example. There is no provision permitting restrictions in the Covenant, although the difference here may be more apparent than real. Convention case-law has made it clear that any restrictions in national law must not interfere with the 'substance' of the right.[60] Conversely, the kinds of restrictions permissible under Article 12 could easily be regarded as implied limitations in the Covenant. Thus, in practice the difference between the two texts is not likely to be significant. Thirdly, the United Nations text continues, 'no marriage shall be entered into without the free and full consent of the intending spouses'. This is an additional guarantee not found in the Convention, though it is no doubt partly compensated for by the reference to national law. Fourthly – and this is the most important point – Article 23, paragraph 4 of the Covenant provides for 'equality of rights and responsibilities of spouses as to marriage, during marriage and at its dissolution'. There is nothing comparable in the European Convention, and the absence of any reference to the dissolution of marriage has been given by the Court as a reason for refusing to read a right to divorce into the Convention.[61] It should be noted, however, that words similar to those of Article 23 are to be found in Article 5 of the Seventh Protocol. As with the principles of Article 14 then, now that this Protocol is in force a significant discrepancy between obligations under the two treaties has been removed, though only, of course, for States which have accepted both the Covenant and the Protocol.

Political rights Here again, Article 25 of the Covenant is considerably more extensive. Article 3 of the First Protocol to the European Convention provides: 'The High Contracting Parties undertake to hold free elections at reasonable intervals by secret ballot, under conditions which will ensure the free expression of the opinion of the people in the choice of the legislature.' The United

Nations text, on the other hand, provides that 'every citizen shall have the right and the opportunity without ... distinction ... and without unreasonable restrictions' to exercise the following activities:

(a) To take part in the conduct of public affairs, directly or through freely chosen representatives.
(b) To vote and to be elected at genuine periodic elections ...
(c) To have access, on general terms of equality, to public service in his country.

The Covenant thus contains several provisions not included in the Convention. As regards the right to vote, it is more positive in form and of wider application. It would seem not to be limited to the election of the legislature but also to cover, for example, local elections, a matter on which the scope of the European Convention is unclear.[62] The right 'to take part in the conduct of public affairs ... through freely chosen representatives' is harder to understand. If it means the right to vote, there is no problem; but this is covered by the following paragraph, so it presumably means something else. Does it then refer to the 'conduct of public affairs' by the executive branch of the government? In most countries the citizen does not directly elect the members of the executive and the same would apply *a fortiori* to the judiciary. Its content therefore remains somewhat obscure. The third paragraph, on access to the public service on general terms of equality, is also something new. It is not mentioned in the European Convention and on several occasions applications have been rejected for alleging violation of this right.[63] This is therefore a point on which the Covenant clearly affords wider protection than the Convention and which the parties to the latter, who left out this right quite deliberately, have had to bear in mind when deciding whether to ratify the Covenant.

(iii) Rights included in the Covenant but not in the Convention or vice versa Eight rights are included in the United Nations Covenant but not in the Convention, and three are found in the European instrument, but not in the United Nations text.

The first article of both Covenants proclaims that 'All peoples have the right of self-determination.' This involves the right to determine freely their political status, to pursue freely their economic, social and cultural development, and to dispose freely of their natural wealth and resources. States parties to the Covenant undertake to promote the realisation of this right.

The Third Committee of the General Assembly hesitated for a long time about the inclusion of this article, which had not been proposed by the Human Rights Commission and which, as we have pointed out, presents a thorny problem of interpretation. Its distinct character is evidenced by the fact that it is put at the beginning of each Covenant, as a single article constituting Part I, and not in sequence with the other rights protected.

A later article relates to 'ethnic, religious or linguistic minorities'. Persons belonging to such minorities 'shall not be denied the right, in community with the other members of their group, to enjoy their own culture, to profess and practise their own religion, or to use their own language' (Article 27). This raises some of the same problems as Article 1, though it will be observed that the rights are conferred on the 'persons belonging to such minorities' and not on the minority groups as such.

While there is no corresponding article in the European Convention, at one stage the Consultative Assembly of the Council of Europe proposed that a provision on the rights of minorities should be included in the Fourth Protocol, which was then being drafted.[64] The text proposed went further than Article 27 of the Covenant, because to the rights included there relating to culture, language and religion it added 'to establish their own schools and receive teaching in the language of their choice'. However, the governments did not feel able to accept this proposal[65] and the Fourth Protocol was completed without any reference to the rights of minorities. The Covenant text is therefore the most far-reaching to date on this subject and protection of minorities under the Convention still awaits specific provision.

Another provision of the Covenant which has no counterpart in the European Convention is Article 10, which provides that 'All persons deprived of their liberty shall be treated with humanity and with respect for the inherent dignity of the human person.' It continues by providing for the separation of accused persons from convicted persons and of juveniles from adults, and asserts that the essential aim of the penitentiary system shall be the reformation and social rehabilitation of prisoners. The principles to be observed in the treatment of prisoners generally correspond to those set out in the Standard Minimum Rules for Prisoners adopted by the

United Nations in 1955, many of which have been further developed in Council of Europe texts in more recent years.

Mention should also be made of the other articles of the Covenant protecting rights not included in the European Convention and its Protocols. These are:

Article 13, which contains certain procedural safeguards for an alien who is under threat of expulsion. There is no corresponding provision in the European Convention, and a proposal to include such a provision was rejected when the Fourth Protocol was being drafted. However, this matter is now covered in Article 1 of the Seventh Protocol and so, as with equality of spouses, this omission is now in the process of being remedied.

Article 16, on 'the right to recognition everywhere as a person before the law', and Article 26, on equality before the law and the right to the equal protection of the law. As with the right of self-determination, these are excellent statements of political principle, but as legal texts are conspicuously lacking in precision.

Article 20 of the Covenant provides categorically that 'any propaganda for war shall be prohibited by law', and continues by demanding a similar prohibition of 'any advocacy of national, racial or religious hatred that constitutes incitement to discrimination'. The Convention on the Elimination of All Forms of Racial Discrimination of 1965 covers some of the same ground, but the Covenant is wider in scope because of its reference to 'national ... or religious hatred'.

Article 24 deals with the rights of the child, which include the right to special measures of protection without discrimination, the requirement of registration immediately after birth, the right to a name, and the right to acquire a nationality.

Finally, we must note three rights which are protected in the European system but which are absent from the United Nations Covenant. The first is the right of property, which is protected by Article 1 of the First Protocol to the Convention. Even though this text was carefully drafted so as to make it acceptable to socialist governments engaged in nationalisation, and even though the right of property was included (as Article 17) in the Universal Declaration, no similar provision was found acceptable in the forum of the United Nations.[66] Secondly, the Fourth Protocol to the European Convention contains in its Article 3 a prohibition of exile in the terms: 'no one shall be expelled ... from the territory of the State of which he is a national.' Thirdly, the Fourth Protocol to the European Convention also prohibits in Article 4 the collective expulsion of aliens. Since collective expulsion is very unusual, the practical importance of this provision is limited. It would nevertheless be useful to have a practice which can cause enormous suffering and misery prohibited by the United Nations Covenant.

(b) The machinery of international control The major problem for States which are parties to the European Convention and have ratified or are thinking of ratifying the United Nations Covenant and its Optional Protocol relates to the measures of implementation, in other words, the system of international control.

The coexistence of the two sets of provisions in the two instruments raises the question whether a State which has ratified both instruments and made a declaration under Article 41 of the UN Covenant, and which wishes to bring a case against another State which is similarly bound, can choose between the two systems or use them both in turn. This problem was envisaged when the texts were drafted. Article 44 of the Covenant lays down that its provisions shall not prevent States from using other methods of settling disputes, which would clearly include those available under the European Convention. The corresponding provision in the European Convention (Article 62) does not permit, except by special agreement, the submission of a dispute arising out of the interpretation or application of the Convention to a means of settlement other than those provided for in the Convention.

It follows that States which are parties to the European Convention should utilise the European machinery for disputes relating to human rights and not refer them to the United Nations, and that this is fully consistent with Article 44 of the Covenant. It is also consistent with the principle set out in Article 33 of the United Nations Charter, which recognises the regional settlement of disputes as complementary to United Nations procedures. However, the proposition that European States should utilise the European machinery in preference to that of the Covenant needs qualification in two respects. First, it applies only to disputes about the alleged violation of a right which is included in substantially similar terms in both instruments. Secondly, it applies only to the disputes of the European States *inter se* and for obvious reasons does not prevent them from accepting the United Nations machinery in relation to disputes with other States. This conclusion as regards the procedure for dealing with inter-State disputes was proposed by the Committee of Experts on Human Rights to the Committee of Ministers of the Council of Europe and approved by the latter in a resolution adopted in 1970.[67]

Different problems arise when we come to consider applications or communications by individuals. The coexistence of the two sets of implementation measures clearly raises certain problems for those States which have accepted the procedure of Article 25 of the European Convention and also ratified the United Nations Optional Protocol, particularly the question of whether an individual can choose between the two systems or use both of them in turn. Article 5, paragraph 2, of the Optional Protocol provides that:

> The Committee shall not consider any communication from an individual unless it has ascertained that:
> (a) the same matter is not being examined under another procedure of international investigation or settlement;

Article 27, paragraph 1(b) of the European Convention states:

> The Commission shall not deal with any petition submitted under Article 25 which:
> . . .
> (b) is substantially the same as a matter which has already been examined by the Commission or has already been submitted to another procedure of international investigation or settlement and if it contains no relevant new information.

From these provisions it appears that the European Commission can never consider a complaint previously lodged with the United Nations Committee, unless new evidence is produced. The UN Committee, on the other hand, cannot consider an application already lodged with the European Commission while the European procedure continues, but would seem to be free to do so once that procedure has terminated.

Since the underlying object of both instruments is to secure the protection of the individual, it is reasonable that a person who believes that his rights have been violated should have a choice between the European procedure and the United Nations procedure and be allowed to use whichever he considers most favourable to his case. However, it is more difficult to accept that he should be able to use both procedures in turn. Of course, if he makes a mistake and addresses himself to the wrong forum – for example, by complaining to the European Commission of the violation of a right which is not protected by the European Convention but which is included in the United Nations Covenant – then he should be allowed to correct his mistake and make a new application to the proper body. But in the case of a right which is guaranteed by both instruments, reasons of public policy militate against a series of successive international remedies.

Our conclusion, then, is that an individual who wishes to bring a case against a State which has accepted the optional procedures under Article 25 of the European Convention and the Protocol to the Covenant should in principle have the right of choice between the two methods of bringing his case before an international organ. However, except in the case of an honest mistake as to the appropriate forum, he should accept the consequences of his decision and not have the possibility of going from one forum to the other. This would apply in both directions. The attempt to 'appeal' from the United Nations Committee to the European Commission already seems to be barred by Article 27(1)(b) of the European Convention. An attempt to 'appeal' from the European organs to the United Nations Committee is at present barred by Article 5(2) of the Optional Protocol for as long as the European proceedings continue, but not thereafter. What is required, therefore, is a device to extend the scope of Article 5(2) so as to give it the same effect as Article 27(1)(b). This can be done either by a reservation when ratifying the Optional Protocol or by a declaration of interpretation. Which method is preferable is a technical question it is unnecessary to examine here.

This solution was proposed to the Committee of Ministers by the Committee of Experts on Human Rights, which drew up a text that could be used either as a reservation or as a declaration of interpretation. The Ministers agreed with the conclusions of the Committee of Experts and transmitted their text to the member governments of the Council of Europe so that they could use it, if they wished, when ratifying the Optional Protocol to the UN Covenant.[68] Several of them have in fact done so.

The effect of the reservation suggested by the Committee of Experts was considered by the Human Rights Committee in the case of *A. M.* v. *Denmark* (1982).[69] The author of a communication to the Committee had already applied to the European Commission which had ruled his application inadmissible on the ground that it was manifestly ill-founded. The Committee decided that although it would have been competent to consider the case under Article 5(2) alone, it was prevented from doing so by a reservation under which Denmark excluded from its jurisdiction matters which had already been considered by the Commission. In drawing this conclusion the Committee took a broad view of the reservation and rejected the argument that a case which the Commission holds to be inadmissible cannot be said to have been considered.

The Committee adopted a rather similar approach in *V. O.* v. *Norway* (1984). There the question was whether the matter which was before the Committee was the same matter that had earlier been considered by the Commission. The Committee decided that it was, despite the fact that the relevant provisions of the European Convention differed in some respects from the corresponding articles of the Covenant, and, even more important, that in his communication to the Committee, the claimant invoked certain rights in the Covenant which have no counterpart in the Convention. Again, therefore, the Committee seemed more concerned to give the reservation its maximum effect than to allow the individual the possibility of a second hearing. While this approach is no doubt satisfactory from the point of view of States which are parties to the Convention and the Covenant, it is open to objection on wider grounds. One member of the Committee dissented in the earlier case and further controversy on this issue can be anticipated.

Before leaving this topic, it should perhaps be pointed out that the question of harmonising obligations in the field of human rights and reconciling the various systems of control is in no way confined to the relation between the Covenant on Civil and Political Rights and the European Convention. As we shall see in later chapters, exactly the same problems arise when one compares obligations under the American Convention with the Covenant, and where arrangements exist for measures of implementation, similar questions of fairness and *locus standi* arise. Moreover, it is not only in relation to the Covenant that the issue of compatibility is presented. We have seen in Chapter 3 that the Convention on the Elimination of All Forms of Discrimination and other United

Nations instruments create obligations and offer procedural possibilities and these, like the provisions of the Covenant, may not always be easy to reconcile with regional arrangements, or for that matter with each other.

Difficulties of this kind are inevitable when the law relating to human rights has developed in an unco-ordinated manner and over a relatively short period of time. In a sense, then, these are the problems of success which is not to say that the present situation is satisfactory. Like other complex problems, however, the solution to the problem of co-ordinating the various human rights instruments depends not on a dramatic break-through of some kind, but on a patient analysis of specific difficulties. As far as the European Convention is concerned, the solution proposed by the Committee of Experts and now implemented is a constructive first step. Further measures would be useful, especially in relation to substantive obligations. It should not be beyond the wit of man – and, more particularly, of lawyers – to work out adequate measures of harmonisation of the two systems, the European and the universal, the more so as the fundamental objective of both of them is the same: the protection of freedom, rights and the rule of law throughout the world.[70]

II. The European Convention for the Prevention of Torture

In January 1981 the Consultative Assembly of the Council of Europe recommended that the Committee of Ministers should invite member States to hasten the adoption and implementation of the draft Convention against Torture which was being prepared by the United Nations Commission on Human Rights. As we saw in the previous chapter, the Convention was adopted by the General Assembly in December 1984 and subsequently opened for signature. In the meantime, however, the Legal Affairs Committee of the Council of Europe had approved a draft European Convention on Torture and passed it on to the Committee of Experts for the extension of the rights embodied in the European Convention. On the instructions of the Committee of Ministers, the Committee of Experts reviewed the draft and after extensive consultations adopted a final text. After consulting the Assembly, the Committee of Ministers adopted this text and the result, the European Convention for the Prevention of Torture and Inhuman or

Degrading Treatment or Punishment, was opened for signature on 27 November 1987 and came into force on 1 February 1989.[71]

The purpose of the Convention is to create a procedure for supervising the treatment of persons deprived of their liberty with a view to strengthening, where necessary, the protection of such persons from torture and from inhuman or degrading treatment or punishment. To this end the Convention creates a Committee which may visit any place within the jurisdiction of the parties where persons are deprived of their liberty by a public authority.

The first part of the Convention, which consists of Articles 1 to 3, defines the function of the Committee and lays down the parties' obligation to co-operate with it.

The second part, Articles 4 to 6, deals with the membership and procedure of the Committee. The European Committee for the Prevention of Torture and Inhuman or Degrading Treatment, as the new body is known, has as many members as there are parties to the treaty. They must be suitably qualified and serve in their individual capacity. They are elected by the Committee of Ministers for a period of four years and may be re-elected. The Committee meets in camera and draws up its own rules of procedure.

The heart of the Convention is the third section, which consists of Articles 7 to 14 and which deals with the organisation of visits and the specific responsibilities of the Committee. It is important to appreciate that although the Committee is given wide powers to visit prisons and other places of detention, it is not the intention that it should perform any judicial functions. It is therefore not its task to judge whether violations of treaty obligations have occurred, but rather to study the situation in the place visited, draw up a report on the facts found, and make appropriate recommendations. As the explanatory report to the Convention puts it, 'The purpose of the Committee is not to condemn States, but, in a spirit of co-operation and through advice, to seek improvements, if necessary, in the protection of persons deprived of their liberty.'[72]

In accordance with the above aim, the information gathered by the Committee in relation to a visit, its reports and its consultations with the State concerned are confidential. However, a report can be published at the request of a party and, more important, if a State fails to co-operate or refuses to improve the situation in the light of the Committee's recommendations, 'the Committee may decide by a majority of two-thirds of its members to make a public statement on the matter' (Article 10(2)). In addition, and as a way of ensuring that the Committee's work becomes known, notwithstanding its confidential nature, the Committee must annually submit 'a general report on its activities' to the Committee of Ministers for publication.

The remaining provisions deal with the privileges and immunities of members of the Committee and various technical matters. Article 17 contains a saving clause in the usual form, providing that the Convention cannot be invoked as a justification for restricting the protection granted under other international instruments, or at the domestic level. Article 17(3), however, lays down that: 'The Committee shall not visit places which representatives or delegates of Protecting Powers or the International Committee of the Red Cross effectively visit on a regular basis by virtue of the Geneva Conventions of 12 August 1949 and the Additional Protocols of 8 June 1977 thereto.' This therefore recognises that although the new Convention is not limited to time of peace, in cases of armed conflict the Geneva Conventions have priority of application.[73] The Convention required seven ratifications to bring it into force (Article 19) and is not subject to reservations (Article 21).

The usefulness of the Convention will naturally become fully apparent only when the new committee begins its work. In general terms, however, the value of an instrument of this kind is already clear. As we have seen, the supervisory system established by the European Convention on Human Rights operates on the basis of inter-State complaints under Article 24 and individual complaints under Article 25. Important as these are for ensuring that States respect their obligations under Article 3, they require an alleged violation to have occurred and so operate after the event. There is therefore value in non-judicial machinery of an essentially preventive character, which is what the new Convention aims to provide.[74] When the United Nations Convention was being drawn up a preventive mechanism of this kind was proposed,[75] but, as noted earlier, the text which was adopted creates a Committee against Torture with other functions. It is thus not surprising that the members of the Council of Europe, several of whom are parties to the United Nations Convention, considered it appropriate to produce a regional Convention.

III. The Helsinki Agreement and human rights

The Conference on Security and Co-operation in Europe was formally opened at Helsinki on 3 July 1973 and continued at Geneva from September 1973 to July 1975.[76] It was concluded at Helsinki on 1 August 1975. The thirty-five participants included all the European States from East and West, irrespective of their size, except Albania, and also the United States and Canada. The Holy See and the three 'mini-States' of Liechtenstein, Monaco and San Marino participated on a basis of equality with the USA and the USSR.[77]

The final session in Helsinki from 30 July to 1 August 1975 was attended by the heads of State or government of nearly all the participating States. The Final Act was signed on 1 August 1975. It comprised four sections concerning respectively: (1) Questions relating to Security in Europe; (2) Co-operation in the fields of Economics, of Science and Technology and of the Environment; (3) Co-operation in Humanitarian and other fields; (4) the 'Follow-up' to the Conference.[78]

1. The Final Act

The first thing to be noted about the Final Act of the conference is that it is not a treaty but a declaration of intentions. It does not use the standard formulation of a treaty and set out undertakings of States. Instead it says, 'The High Representatives of the participating States have solemnly adopted the following,' and continues, 'The participating States will respect each other's sovereign equality . . .'; 'The participating States regard as inviolable all one another's frontiers . . .'; 'The participating States will respect the territorial integrity of each of the participating States' and so on.

At first sight it may seem that there is little difference between States' acceptance of an obligation to do certain things and a statement that they will do certain things. But the difference is more than a lawyer's quibble and there are key differences between a legal undertaking and a declaration of intention. On the domestic constitutional plane, in most countries a treaty is not binding unless it is ratified by the legislature. However, the Helsinki Final Act did not require ratification and so was not submitted to the various national parliaments. On the international plane, non-observance of a treaty constitutes a breach of international law, incurs State responsibility, and can, in theory, form the object of proceedings before the International Court of Justice. No such consequences result from the non-observance of a declaration of intention.

This does not mean that the Helsinki Final Act is unimportant or can be violated with impunity. It sets out moral and political obligations of States, but these are something distinct from obligations binding in international law. As a result, it is inaccurate, from a legal point of view, to speak of the 'Helsinki Agreement'. However, since the expression has come into current use, and is more convenient than the full title 'Final Act of the Conference on Security and Co-operation in Europe', it will be used here on the understanding that the word 'agreement' is used in its popular, but not in its legal, sense.

The second thing to be noted about the Final Act is that it is mainly concerned with international security and relations between States. For reasons which are generally known it was not possible to conclude a peace treaty at the end of the Second World War, and during the period of the 'Cold War' it was evident that no mutually satisfactory definition of relations between East and West was possible. However, after some years of 'détente', the new 'Ostpolitik' of Chancellor Willy Brandt, the agreement between the two Germanies and the admission of both of them to the United Nations, some new arrangements for coexistence between East and West seemed feasible. For years the Soviet Union had been seeking recognition of its Western frontiers as established after the end of the war, and Mr Brezhnev had made this a central issue of his foreign policy. The difficulty was that there was little that the Western powers were likely to receive in return. They had no territorial claims to make – apart from the Germans, who knew in advance that the reunification of Germany was not to be expected – and they recognised that fundamental political changes in the direction of liberalisation were excluded. What they tried to obtain, therefore, were certain modest concessions as regards respect for human rights, freedom of movement and freedom of information between East and West, in the hope that these could be the beginning of a gradual liberalisation of authoritarian regimes.

This leads us to a third preliminary point, which concerns the human rights provisions of the Final Act. Since the Act is concerned with relations between States and the interests of States, the provisions concerning human rights do not seek to protect the individual as such. Thus, the Final Act does not follow the method of the Universal Declaration or of the UN Covenants in providing that 'Everyone has the right to ...' a certain number of fundamental rights and freedoms. Instead, it provides that 'The participating States will respect human rights and fundamental freedoms ...'. In accordance with the whole philosophy of the Final Act, it is the action of States which is the objective and not the situation or behaviour of individuals.

The first three sections of the Final Act are commonly known as three 'baskets'. The most important for our purpose is 'Basket I', which starts off with a *Declaration on Principles guiding Relations between Participating States*. This sets out ten fundamental principles which it is relevant to list. They are:

1 Sovereign equality and respect for the rights inherent in sovereignty.
2 Avoidance of the threat or use of force.
3 Inviolability of frontiers.
4 Territorial integrity of States.
5 Peaceful settlement of disputes.
6 Non-intervention in internal affairs.
7 Respect for human rights and fundamental freedoms, including freedom of thought, conscience, religion and belief.
8 Equal rights and self-determination of peoples.
9 Co-operation among States.
10 Fulfilment in good faith of obligations under international law.

Each of these principles is explained in some detail in the Final Act. It is perhaps significant that Principle No. 7 concerning human rights and fundamental freedoms has the longest explanatory text, running to eight paragraphs in all. It makes four main points. First, 'The participating States will respect human rights and fundamental freedoms'. Here, particular mention is made of freedom of thought, conscience, religion and belief. Secondly, the participating States say that they will 'promote and encourage the effective exercise of civil, political, economic, social, cultural and other rights and freedoms'. It should be noted that this very widely drawn reference to civil rights and other freedoms is preceded by the words 'promote and encourage'. It thus falls well short of an affirmative statement that the participating States will 'respect' these rights and freedoms. It brings to mind Article 1(3) and Article 55 of the Charter of the United Nations, which speak of 'promoting and encouraging respect' for human rights and fundamental freedoms, thereby emphasising intentions for the future rather than immediate implementation.

The third main point in the text is its statement that the participating States will respect the rights of national minorities, which recalls Article 27 of the Covenant on Civil and Political Rights. The fourth and final point is that there are two references to the human rights work of the United Nations. Paragraph six provides that the participating States will endeavour 'jointly and separately, including in co-operation with the United Nations, to promote universal and effective respect' for these rights and freedoms. This recalls (and substantially repeats) Article 56 of the Charter. Finally, in paragraph eight, the participating States declare that they 'will act in accordance with the purposes and principles of the Charter of the United Nations and with the Universal Declaration of Human Rights'. This paragraph continues by referring specifically to their 'obligations as set forth in the international declarations and agreements in this field, including *inter alia* the International Covenants on Human Rights, by which they may be bound'.

To summarise, then, the *Declaration on Principles guiding Relations between Participating States* includes respect for human rights, alongside other principles such as the inviolability of frontiers, the peaceful settlement of disputes and avoidance of the use of threat of force. Principle No. 7 is wide in its scope, because the second paragraph refers to the effective exercise of all categories of rights and freedoms, but limited in its effect, because, like the Charter, it contains expressions of intention to 'promote and encourage' instead of affirmative statements of a determination to 'respect' human rights. Some of its provisions would appear to be tautologous in the sense that they reaffirm existing obligations. However, this is not a criticism, because the constant reaffirmation of the obligation to respect human rights, always provided it is taken seriously, may help to impress that obligation more securely in the consciousness of governments and of the general public.

'Basket III' is also relevant to our purpose, but may be summarised more briefly. It is entitled *Co-operation in Humanitarian and other Fields* and contains four sections. The first relates to 'human contacts' and, among other matters, deals with reunification of families, marriages between citizens of different States, travel, tourism, meetings of young people, and sport. The second section, which if implemented could be of great importance, concerns the free flow of information. The participating States 'make it their aim to facilitate the freer and wider dissemination of information of all kinds' and set out a number of steps to be taken, relating to oral, printed, filmed, and broadcast information. These include measures 'to facilitate the improvement of the dissemination on their territory of newspapers and printed publications ... from the other participating States', and measures 'to improve the conditions under which journalists from one ... State exercise their profession in another ... State'. Basket III concludes with two short sections about co-operation and exchanges in the fields of culture and education.

2. *Post-Helsinki developments*

The signature of the Final Act of the conference was much more widely acclaimed, and its contents more widely publicised, in the East than in the West. This was no doubt for the reason already mentioned, that the Soviet Union had a greater interest in the successful conclusion of the conference, because it represented an official acceptance by the West of her territorial acquisitions during the Second World War. What had been agreed by three powers at Yalta – and a good deal more than that – had now been accepted as permanent, thirty years later, by the whole of Europe, plus the United States and Canada. This was a real achievement for Soviet diplomacy.

One might have thought that it would mark the beginning of a new era of détente and co-operation in Europe. However, this was not to be.

The publicity given to the Final Act led many there to believe that its provisions on human rights would be implemented and that an era of liberalisation was about to begin. The well-informed knew that all the East European States had already ratified the United Nations Covenants (except Poland, which did so subsequently) and thus accepted obligations in international law to respect human rights. With these two significant developments, it was hardly surprising that politically conscious individuals looked to their governments to allow a freer flow of information and greater liberty of expression, even if they were not so optimistic as to expect the right to form a political opposition.

The most striking example of this sentiment was in Czechoslovakia, where nearly 500 intellectuals and others subscribed to a human rights manifesto which they called 'Charter 77'. It took as its point of departure Czechoslovakia's ratification of the two United Nations Covenants on Human Rights and the reaffirmation of the Covenants in the Final Act of the Helsinki conference. The Charter welcomed accession to those agreements, but continued, 'Their publication, however, serves as a powerful reminder of the extent to which basic human rights in our country exist, regrettably, on paper alone.' A series of examples was then given of various rights which are proclaimed and supposed to be protected by the Covenants but are in fact systematically violated in Czechoslovakia. They include freedom of expression, freedom of information, freedom of religion, freedom of association, the right to form trade unions, the right to privacy, and the right to leave any country including one's own.

'Charter 77' struck a responsive chord in other Eastern European countries. In Yugoslavia Milovan Djilas, a former leader of the Communist party, appealed to West European Communist parties to support the Charter and the movement for human rights not only in Czechoslovakia but also in his own country, where he said that proportionally there were as many political prisoners as in the Soviet Union. Similar repercussions were observed in East Germany, in Poland, and in Romania.

But the most important reaction was in the Soviet Union itself. A committee was established to supervise the application of the Helsinki Agreement, under the chairmanship of Youri Orlov. The detention of Alexander Guinzbourg led to the signing of a manifesto by 248 supporters. Andrei Sakharov, who had formed the Soviet Committee on Human Rights nearly ten years earlier, continued his struggle in unprecedented ways, including an American television interview, a personal letter to President Carter and a letter to all the heads of State or government who had signed the Helsinki Agreement. President Carter replied, 'You may be assured that the American people and our government will maintain their firm engagement to promote respect for human rights not only in our country but also abroad.'

Sakharov was constantly harassed and in 1980 exiled to Gorkhi. Vladimir Boukovski, having been liberated and exiled in December 1976 after twelve years in prison, in exchange for the Chilean Communist leader Luis Corvalan, was received by President Carter in February and testified to a Congressional committee that none of the human rights provisions of the Helsinki Agreement was respected in the USSR. Andrei Amalrik, a dissident historian exiled in 1976, spoke to the press in Paris as a representative of the committee on the application of the Helsinki Agreement in the same sense as Boukovski in Washington. In 1980 he was killed in a car accident on his way to attend the second 'follow-up' conference in Madrid.

Following the Soviet invasion of Afghanistan in December 1979, repression was intensified.[79] The number of emigrants allowed to leave the Soviet Union fell sharply, groups which had been set up to monitor implementation of the Helsinki Agreement were extinguished, while religious and minority groups were harassed. Similar action was taken by governments in Eastern Europe. In Poland the attempt to assert the right to freedom of association through the Solidarity movement was suppressed. In Czechoslovakia the Charter 77 movement was attacked and in Romania the persecution of dissidents was accompanied by a particularly vicious campaign directed at the country's many national minorities.

In accordance with the provisions of the 'Fourth Basket' of the Helsinki Final Act a follow-up meeting to the 1975 Conference was held in Belgrade between October 1977 and March 1978. However, little was achieved in the field of human rights.[80] A further conference was held in Madrid in 1980. When that year opened, the international atmosphere was sombre. Détente had been thwarted by the Soviet invasion of Afghanistan in December 1979, which was promptly condemned, not only by the Western powers but also by the non-aligned countries. In the spring of 1980 serious doubts were felt in many quarters as to whether it was possible or desirable to hold the Madrid conference at all. (The partial boycott of the Olympic Games in Moscow was another symptom of the same reaction.) Yet preparations for the conference continued, since none of the intended participants wished to assume the responsibility for a break in relations.

After a great deal of argument over the agenda, the conference began in 1980 and was scheduled to finish in March 1981. By that date, however, no agreement was in sight either on matters of substance or a final communiqué. The proceedings dragged on into the summer months, but still with no significant progress in securing the more effective observance of the human rights provisions of the Final Act. The proceedings were then adjourned for a time, after which the meeting was reconvened and a concluding document was eventually agreed.[81]

A further follow-up conference began in Vienna in November 1986. Although East–West relations were now much improved, the proceedings, like those of the Madrid conference, were held up by disagreements in which the issue of human rights was once more prominent. The conference therefore again overran and instead of finishing, as planned, in the middle of 1987 was not concluded until January 1989. The final document, however, marked a considerable advance because in addition to provisions on security, trade, culture, education and the environment, it included a more elaborate commitment to human rights than any of its predecessors[82] and, for the first time in a CSCE text, a human rights monitoring procedure.[83]

The Vienna conference was followed by meetings on human rights in Paris and Copenhagen. By the time of the Copenhagen meeting in June 1990 a political revolution had taken place in the East, with liberalisation in the Soviet Union and the overthrow of communism in Eastern Europe clearing the way for the emergence of popular governments and the reunification of Germany. In this dramatically changed situation the Copenhagen meeting was able to adopt a wide ranging Concluding Document as a further step in the CSCE process.[84]

Another meeting in Paris in November 1990 resulted in the Paris Charter for a New Europe.[85] This creates a comprehensive institutional framework for the CSCE and, among other innovations, establishes a regular schedule of meetings. In accordance with the schedule various meetings have been held subsequently in which issues of human rights have been addressed. These include meetings in Moscow in September 1991 and in Oslo in November. In addition, the fourth follow-up meeting has been scheduled for Helsinki, where the CSCE process began, in 1992.

In terms of follow-up arrangements, then, those who saw the Helsinki Agreement as the first step in a progressive elaboration of agreed objectives in the field of human rights had to wait longer than they might have anticipated. But though the process begun at Helsinki was slow to achieve formal consolidation, the effect of the Final Act on the political and intellectual climate of Eastern Europe has turned out to be profound.

Speaking on the tenth anniversary of the signing of the Helsinki

Final Act, the British Foreign Secretary, Sir Geoffrey Howe, posed the question 'whether far-reaching and ambitious documents of this kind, agreed between countries ideologically opposed and having very different systems of government, can advance in a practical way the cause of understanding and peace between nations ... (and) the prospects of human liberty'.[86] Experience to date in relation to the Helsinki Agreement suggests that they can, so long as it is recognised that what is ultimately important is not the document but the attitude of governments towards it. While the Final Act and the follow-up conferences certainly raised expectations in Eastern Europe, no improvement with respect to human rights was possible as long as the communist regimes there refused to treat their undertakings seriously. The Gorbachev era brought first the withdrawal of Soviet power from the region, then at the end of 1991 the break-up of the Soviet Union itself. Although enormous problems remain to be solved, in the light of these developments there is now a real opportunity to implement the principles of the Helsinki Agreement and consolidate human rights across the whole of Europe.

Notes

1 The negotiations are described more fully in A. H. Robertson, 'The European Convention for the Protection of Human Rights', *British Year Book of International Law*, XXVII, 1950, p. 145 and in *Human Rights in Europe*, second edition, Manchester University Press, 1977, pp. 1–21.

2 Among the many books which have been published on the Convention are: F. G. Jacobs, *The European Convention on Human Rights*, Oxford, 1975; A. H. Robertson, *Human Rights in Europe* (cited *supra*, n. 1); P. Van Dijk and G. J. H. Van Hoof, *Theory and Practice of the European Convention on Human Rights*, Deventer, 1984; J. E. S. Fawcett, *The Application of the European Convention on Human Rights*, second edition, Oxford, 1987; and J. G. Merrills, *The Development of International Law by the European Court of Human Rights*, Melland Schill Monographs in International Law, Manchester University Press, 1988. For other books and articles about the Convention, see the bibliography published annually in the *Yearbook of the Convention on Human Rights*; a separate bibliography with annual supplements is published by the Directorate of Human Rights of the Council of Europe. The text of the Conventions and Protocols may be found in many books and collections, including *Yearbook of the European Convention on Human Rights*, I, 1955–57, p. 4 and I. Brownlie, *Basic Documents on Human Rights*, second edition, Oxford University Press, 1981, p. 242.

3 In a number of member States the normative provisions of the Convention are directly applicable and can be applied by natural courts, see H. Golsong, 'The

European Convention on Human Rights before domestic courts', *British Year Book of International Law*, XXXVIII, 1962, p. 445 and A. Z. Drzemczewski, *European Human Rights Convention in Domestic Law*, Oxford University Press, 1982.

4 Consultative Assembly, *Official Reports*, 7 September 1949, p. 217.

5 On 1 January 1987 the number of individual applications registered was 12,327.

6 See *Yearbook of the European Convention on Human Rights* IV, 1961, p. 196 and Fawcett, *Application*, pp. 371–3.

7 For a comparison of the two bodies by T. Opsahl, who was a member of both the European Commission and the Human Rights Committee, see 'The protection of human rights in the Council of Europe and in the United Nations', *European Yearbook*, XXIV, 1978, pp. 92–118.

8 Robertson, *Human Rights in Europe*, pp. 177–8.

9 See Van Dijk and Van Hoof, *Theory and Practice*, pp. 101–10.

10 The functions and procedure of the Commission are described in more detail *ibid.*, pp. 53–110. See also Robertson, *Human Rights in Europe*, pp. 139–92.

11 Austria, Belgium, Cyprus, Denmark, France, Germany (Fed. Rep.), Greece, Iceland, Ireland, Italy, Liechtenstein, Luxembourg, Malta, Netherlands, Norway, Portugal, San Marino, Spain, Sweden, Switzerland, Turkey, United Kingdom.

12 The functions and procedure of the Committee of Ministers under the Convention on Human Rights are described more fully in Robertson, *Human Rights in Europe*, pp. 237–67 and Van Dijk and Van Hoof, *Theory and Practice*, pp. 161–74.

13 The functions and procedure of the European Court of Human Rights are described in greater detail in Robertson, *ibid.*, pp. 193–236 and Van Dijk and Van Hoof, *ibid.*, pp. 111–60.

14 *Yearbook*, XI, 1968, pp. 690–728.

15 *Yearbook*, XII *bis*: the *Greek case.*

16 Recommendation 547, *Texts adopted by the Assembly*, January 1969; *Yearbook of the Convention*, XII, 1969, p. 126.

17 *Yearbook*, XIX, 1976, p. 512.

18 *Publications of the Court*, Series A, No. 25, 1978.

19 A convenient, though unofficial, source of information on the case-law of the Commission is *Stock-taking on the European Convention on Human Rights*, published periodically by the Commission's Secretary.

20 A survey of the latest decisions of the European Court is published each year in the *British Year Book of International Law.*

21 Series A, Nos. 1, 2 and 3 (1960–61).

22 Series A, Nos. 7 (1968) and 10 (1969).

23 Series A, Nos. 8 (1968), 9 (1969) and 13 (1971).

24 Series A, No. 17 (1974).

25 Series A, Nos. 15 (1972) and 16 (1973).

26 Series A, No. 18 (1975).

27 Series A, No. 32 (1979).

28 See Merrills, *Development of International Law*, pp. 63–88.

29 Series A, No. 22 (1976).

30 Series A, No. 27 (1978).

31 Series A, No. 29 (1978).

32 Series A, No. 33 (1979).
33 Series A, No. 34 (1979).
34 Series A, No. 28 (1978).
35 Series A, No. 31 (1979).
36 See Merrills, *Development of International Law*, pp. 89–112.
37 Series A, Nos. 19 (1975) and 20 (1976).
38 Series A, No. 21 (1976).
39 Series A, No. 44 (1981).
40 Series A, No. 24 (1976).
41 See Merrills, *Development of International Law*, pp. 136–59 and T. A. O'Donnell, 'The margin of appreciation doctrine', *Human Rights Quarterly*, IV, 1987, p. 474.
42 Series A, No. 30 (1979). For the legislative response, see S. H Bailey, 'The Contempt of Court Act 1981', *Modern Law Review*, XXXXV, 1982, p. 301.
43 Series A, No. 87 (1984).
44 Series A, No. 94 (1985). It should be noted, however, that the response of the British Government to this decision was to remove the element of discrimination by removing the preferential treatment of wives and placing them on the same footing as husbands. See J. G. Merrills, 'Decisions on the European Convention on Human Rights during 1985', *British Year Book of International Law*, LVI, 1985, pp. 335, 352.
45 Series A, No. 52 (1982).
46 Series A, No. 98 (1986).
47 Series A, No. 102 (1986).
48 Series A, No. 23 (1976).
49 Series A, No. 48 (1982).
50 Series A, No. 26 (1978).
51 Series A, No. 106 (1986).
52 Series A, No. 112 (1986).
53 Series A, No. 128 (1987).
54 *Declaration on Human Rights* of 27 April 1978, *Yearbook*, XXI, 1968, p. 82; see also A. Berenstein, 'Economic and social rights: their inclusion in the European Convention on Human Rights – problems of formulation and interpretation', *Human Rights Law Journal*, II, 1981, p. 257.
55 By 1 January 1988 only five States parties to the European Convention had not also ratified the UN Covenant on Civil and Political Rights: Ireland, Liechtenstein, Malta, Switzerland and Turkey.
56 It is now called the Steering Committee on Human Rights.
57 Some of the matters examined in this section were discussed in greater detail in the first edition of this book at pp. 80–110. See also A. H. Robertson, 'The United Nations Covenant on Civil and Political Rights and the European Convention on Human Rights', *British Year Book of International Law*, XXXXV, 1968–69, p. 21. The report of the Committee of Experts comparing the rights protected in the two treaties was published by the Council of Europe as doc. H(70)7, September 1970. The relevant decisions of the Committee of Ministers are published in *Yearbook*, XIII, 1970, pp. 70–6.
58 Report of the Secretary General of the United Nations on the draft Covenants, doc. A/2929 of 1 July 1955, Chapter VI, para. 3.

59 For the legislative history of this provision, see Robertson, *Human Rights in Europe*, pp. 68–72. For its interpretation in the case-law of the Commission and Court, see Fawcett, *Application*, pp. 133–45 and Van Dijk and Van Hoof, *Theory and Practice*, pp. 238–43.
60 See the *Rees case*, Series A, No. 106, para. 50.
61 See the *Johnston case*, Series A, No. 112, para. 52.
62 For consideration of the scope of Article 3 of the First Protocol, see the *Mathieu-Mohin and Clerfayt case*, Series A, No. 113 (1987), discussed in Merrills, *Development of International Law*, pp. 113–16.
63 See, for example, the *Glasenapp case*, Series A, No. 104 and the *Kosiek case*, Series A, No. 105 (1986).
64 Recommendation 285 of 28 April 1961.
65 *Sixteenth Report of the Committee of Ministers* (1965), paras 301–2. The *Belgian Linguistics case*, (Series A, No. 6), was then under consideration by the European Commission of Human Rights.
66 The Commission on Human Rights found it impossible to agree on a text, and at its tenth session in 1954 adjourned consideration of the question *sine die*, see doc. A/2929, 1955, Chapter VI, para. 195.
67 *Yearbook* XIII, 1970, pp. 70–6. By 1 January 1988 the following parties to the European Convention had accepted the optional procedure for inter-State cases under Article 41 of the UN Covenant: Austria, Belgium, Denmark, Germany (Fed. Rep.), Iceland, Italy, Luxembourg, Netherlands, Norway, Spain, Sweden, United Kingdom.
68 By 1 January 1988 the following parties to the European Convention had ratified the Optional Protocol: Denmark, France, Iceland, Italy, Luxembourg, Netherlands, Norway, Portugal, Spain, Sweden.
69 For discussion of this and subsequent cases, see P. R. Ghandi, 'The Human Rights Committee and the right of individual communication', *British Year Book of International Law*, LVII, 1986, pp. 201, 229–32.
70 For further discussion of these issues see T. Meron, *Human Rights Law-Making in the United Nations*, Oxford, 1986. A quite distinct problem of co-existence concerns the relationship between the system established by the European Convention on Human Rights and the provisions affecting human rights of Community law, i.e. the legal system set up by the Treaty of Rome, 1957, establishing the European Economic Community. For discussion of this problem see Robertson, *Human Rights in Europe*, pp. 286–291.
71 For the text of the Convention, see Council of Europe, *Human Rights Information Sheet* No. 21, Strasbourg, 1988, p. 50. The Convention obtained the seven ratifications needed to bring it into force in 1988 and on 10 November of that year had been ratified by the following States: Ireland, Luxembourg, Malta, Netherlands, Sweden, Switzerland, Turkey, and the United Kingdom.
72 *Explanatory Report*, para. 20.
73 It should be noted, however, that the new Committee will be able to visit places of detention if the ICRC does not visit them 'effectively' or 'on a regular basis', see *Explanatory Report*, para. 93.
74 It is only necessary to recall the situations which prompted the *Greek case* and the *Irish case*, discussed earlier, to appreciate the value of a system of preventive investigation.

75 Costa Rica submitted a draft optional protocol to this effect which was not adopted. See *Explanatory Report*, para. 2.

76 For a contemporary view of the Conference, see D. G. Scrivner, 'The Conference on Security and Cooperation in Europe: implications for Soviet-American détente', *Denver Journal of International Law and Policy*, VI, 1976, p. 122. For discussion of the Final Act of the Conference, with particular reference to its treatment of human rights, see H. S. Russell, 'The Helsinki Declaration: Brobdingnag or Lilliput?', *American Journal of International Law*, LXX, 1976, p. 242.

77 In addition, statements were made to the conference by representatives of Algerial, Egypt, Israel, Morocco, Syria, and Tunisia. One section of the Final Act relates to 'Security and Cooperation in the Mediterranean'.

78 The full text of the Final act, which is very long (about 80,000 words), may be found in various official publications. Extensive extracts are given in *Keesing's Contemporary Archives*, 1–7 September 1975, pp. 27 and 301–8, in *European Yearbook*, XXXIII, 1977, p. 211; and in Brownlie, *Basic Documents*, pp. 320–77.

79 See G. Edwards, 'The Conference on Security and Cooperation in Europe after ten years', *International Relations*, VIII, 1984, pp. 397, 403–4.

80 The proceedings of the Belgrade Conference were more fully described in the second edition of this book at pp. 125–6. See also W. W. Bishop and others, 'Human rights and the Helsinki Accord – a five year road to Madrid,' *Vanderbilt Journal of Transnational Law*, XIII, 1980, p. 249.

81 See G. Edwards, 'The Madrid Follow-Up Meeting to the CSCE', *International Relationas*, VIII, 1984, p. 49.

82 For the text of the Concluding Document see *Human Rights Law Journal*, X, 1989, p. 283. The Concluding Document was also published in the United Kingdom as Cm 649 in March 1989. For discussion of the treatment of human rights in the Document see A. Bloed and P. van Dyke, *The Human Dimension of the Helsinki Process*, Dordrecht, 1991 and D. McGoldrick, 'Human rights developments in the Helsinki process', *International and Comparative Law Quarterly*, XXXIX, 1990, p. 923.

83 See the editors' essay, 'Supervisory mechanism for the Human Dimension of the CSCE', in Bloed and van Dyke, *Human Dimension*, p. 74 and F. Coomans and L. Lijnaad, 'Initiating the CSCE supervisory procedure', *ibid.*, p. 109.

84 See McGoldrick, 'Human rights developments', pp. 935–9 and A. Bloed, 'A new human rights catalogue: the Copenhagen Meeting of the Conference on the Human Dimension of the CSCE', in Bloed and van Dyke, *Human Dimension*, p. 54.

85 The text of the Paris Charter is in *Human Rights Law Journal*, XI, 1990, p. 379. For an analysis of the Charter see E. Schlager, 'The procedural framework of the CSCE: from the Helsinki consultations to the Paris Charter, 1972–1990', *Human Rights Law Journal*, XII, 1991, p. 221.

86 Quoted in Edwards, 'The Conference on Security and Cooperation', p. 401.

CHAPTER 5

The American Convention on Human Rights

1. The origin and history of the Convention

The origins of the movement for Latin American unity can be traced back to the early years of the nineteenth century, when the Latin American republics achieved their independence. By 1825 this had been recognised by the United States and then by Britain, while the proclamation of the Monroe doctrine prevented European intervention in American affairs.

As early as 1822 Simon Bolivar proposed a 'meeting of plenipotentiaries of the Americas' with a view to establishing a confederation of the newly independent republics. As a result of further proposals which he made in December 1824, the 'First Congress of American States' was held in Panama in June and July 1826. It produced a 'Treaty of Perpetual Union, League and Confederation' between the participating States, but this ambitious project was stillborn, because it was ratified by only one State. Subsequently, the 'First International American Conference', held at the invitation of the United States and attended by seventeen American republics, was held in Washington from October 1889 to April 1890. It was here that the International Union of American Republics was founded, commonly known as the Pan American Union. Its principal functions were to promote economic co-operation and the peaceful settlement of disputes and so arrangements were made for the collection and publication of information on production, trade and customs regulations.

Between the beginning of the twentieth century and the outbreak of the Second World War eight conferences of American States were held at irregular intervals, but with increasing frequency, in various Latin American capitals. This period also saw the opening in 1910 of the 'House of the Americas' in Washington, as the headquarters of the Pan American Union. During the Second World War three meetings of consultation of the Foreign Ministers took place, in 1939, 1940 and 1942, to discuss the problems confronting the American republics as a result of the war, in an attempt to protect them from subversion in what came to be known as 'the political defence of the hemisphere'. The third of these meetings recommended that the American republics should sever diplomatic relations with the Axis powers.

The Inter-American Conference on Problems of War and Peace was held in Mexico in February and March 1945 to consider, among other matters, the organisation of the Inter-American system in the post-war world. Its conclusions were instrumental in the adoption at the San Francisco conference a few months later of Chapter VIII of the UN Charter on 'Regional arrangements'. The Inter-American Conference in Rio de Janeiro in 1947 was principally devoted to the question of the maintenance of continental peace and security, and its outcome, the Inter-American Treaty of Reciprocal Assistance, signed in Rio on 2 September 1947, is still the basic instrument of collective security of the Inter-American system.

At the ninth Inter-American Conference at Bogotá in 1948, the American States undertook a review of their methods of co-operation and reorganised the whole system. The 'Charter of Bogotá' adopted on this occasion furnished the new constitutional instrument that was needed and thereby established the Organisation of American States (OAS).

The Charter announces in its first article that the OAS is a regional agency within the United Nations. It continues by laying down the essential purposes of the Organisation, which include: to strengthen peace and security, to ensure the peaceful settlement of disputes, to provide for common action in the event of aggression, and to promote economic, social and cultural development.

There follow two important chapters on 'Principles' and 'Fundamental Rights and Duties of States'. These reaffirm the significance of international law and fundamental human rights, declare that an act of aggression against one constitutes aggression against all American States, and emphasise the principle of non-intervention to which the American republics have traditionally attached great importance. The Charter then provides separate chapters on the pacific settlement of disputes, on collective security, and on economic, social and cultural standards.[1]

Another basic text adopted at Bogotá was the American Declaration on the Rights and Duties of Man. While it is, for the most part, on rather similar lines to the Universal Declaration of the United Nations, it is worth noting that it was adopted in May 1948, that is to say, seven months before the Universal Declaration, and that it contains no less than ten articles setting out the duties of the individual citizen in addition to twenty-eight articles proclaiming his rights.

The Bogotá Conference gave new life, as well as new institutions, to the OAS. The Inter-American Conference was established as the supreme policy-making organ. New councils (Economic and Social, Cultural, Juridical) were organised and started their work; whilst the existing Council of Permanent Representatives in Washington continued as the organ of direction for current business.

A meeting of consultation of the Ministers for Foreign Affairs, held at Santiago in 1959, resulted in further initiatives in the field of human rights. The Ministers adopted a 'Conclusion' containing the following statement:

> ... eleven years after the American Declaration of the Rights and Duties of Man was proclaimed, the climate in the hemisphere is ready for the conclusion of a Convention – there having been similar progress in the United Nations Organisation and in the union known as the Council of Europe in the setting of standards and in the orderly study of this field, until today a satisfactory and promising level has been reached.

The document instructed the Inter-American Council of Jurists to prepare a draft Convention on Human Rights and a draft Convention for the creation of an Inter-American Court for the Protection of Human Rights, along with other appropriate organs. It also resolved to create an Inter-American Commission on Human Rights of seven members elected as individuals by the Council of the OAS from panels of three candidates presented by the governments. Accordingly, the Inter-American Council of Jurists met in Santiago later in the year and prepared a draft Convention, which was largely based on the European model.

This draft Convention was considered at the Second Special Inter-American Conference held in Rio de Janeiro in 1965. In fact the conference considered three drafts; one prepared by the

Inter-American Council of Jurists in 1959, and two revised drafts presented by Chile and by Uruguay which took account of developments since 1959, particularly the European Social Charter of 1961 and the three Protocols to the European Convention of 1963. The Chilean text added a striking innovation in its Article 19, designed to prevent military *coups d'état*; the right of the electorate to be represented and governed by their legally elected representatives. The Uruguayan draft, on the other hand, gave particular attention to economic and social rights. It was soon evident, however, that the competent committee of the Rio conference could not produce a new draft Convention in the short time at its disposal. It was therefore agreed that the three drafts should be referred to the Council of the Organisation and that the latter, after hearing the views of the Inter-American Commission on Human Rights, should produce a new draft Convention. This would then be sent to the governments for their comments, after which the Council would call a special conference to produce a final text and open it for signature.

The Rio conference resolved that, pending the conclusion of the new Convention on Human Rights, the existing Commission on Human Rights should be authorised to consider complaints from individuals alleging violation of certain basic rights, viz. the right to life and liberty, freedom of opinion and expression, the right to a fair trial, protection from arbitrary arrest, due process of law, equality before the law without discrimination, and freedom of religion. The Commission would have the right, when considering such complaints, to request information from and make recommendations to governments and, in certain cases, to publish reports on the action taken.

A Third Special Inter-American Conference was held in Buenos Aires in February 1967, with the object of revising the Charter of the OAS. Most of its decisions do not concern the subject matter of this book[2] but one which does related to the Inter-American Commission on Human Rights.

The Inter-American Commission, which, as we have seen, was originally created by a resolution of the Foreign Ministers at Santiago in 1959, becomes in the amended Charter a statutory organ of the OAS 'whose principal function shall be to promote the observance and protection of human rights and to serve as a consultative organ of the Organisation in these matters'. The revised Charter goes on to say that the structure, competence and procedure of the Commission will be determined in an Inter-American Convention on Human Rights. Pending the conclusion of the new Convention, the existing Commission on Human Rights would discharge the functions set out in the Charter (Article 150).

In accordance with the decisions taken at Rio de Janeiro in 1965, the Council of the OAS requested the Inter-American Commission on Human Rights to examine the various drafts for the proposed Convention and submit its own proposals on the matter. This was duly done. In the meantime the General Assembly of the United Nations, in December 1966, approved the text of the UN Covenants. The Council of the OAS then asked its member governments whether they still wished to go ahead with the preparation of a separate Inter-American Convention now that the UN Covenants had been completed. The majority of member governments said that they did. Accordingly, at the beginning of October 1968 the Council of the OAS submitted to member governments the revised draft Convention prepared by the Inter-American Commission on Human Rights, inviting their comments. When these had been received a Specialised Conference on Human Rights was held in San José, Costa Rica, in November 1969 to produce a final text.

Nineteen of the twenty-four member States of the OAS were represented at the conference, the absentees being Bolivia, Barbados, Haiti, Jamaica and Cuba. There were observers from various non-member States and from certain international organisations, including the United Nations, UNESCO, the ILO and ODECA. The members of the Inter-American Commission on Human Rights also attended, together with three 'special advisers' who were invited as expert consultants on account of their knowledge of the European Convention and its system.[3]

The American Convention on Human Rights otherwise known as the 'Pact of San José', was drafted at this conference and signed on 22 November 1969.[4] It entered into force on 18 July 1978, on the deposit of the eleventh instrument of ratification. At the time of writing it has been ratified by Argentina, Barbados, Bolivia, Colombia, Costa Rica, Dominican Republic, Ecuador, El Salvador, Grenada, Guatemala, Haiti, Honduras, Jamaica, Mexico, Nicaragua, Panama, Peru, Surinam, Uruguay, and Venezuela.

2. *The rights protected*

The undertaking of the States in Article 1 of the American Convention is to 'ensure to all persons subject to their jurisdiction the free and full exercise' of the rights and freedoms recognised therein. The limitation 'within their territory', which is found in the UN text, is thus not included in the American Convention. The obligation is otherwise very similar to that contained in the UN Covenant, that is to say it is intended, in principle, to be of immediate application; and Article 2 provides that contracting parties will adopt such legislative or other measures as may be necessary in cases where the rights and freedoms are not already ensured in their domestic law.

Twenty-six rights and freedoms are protected by the American Convention. Twenty-one of these are included in the UN Covenant on Civil and Political Rights. They are:

The right to life.
Freedom from torture and inhuman treatment.
Freedom from slavery and servitude.
The right to liberty and security.
The right to a fair trial.
Freedom from retroactivity of the criminal law.
The right to respect for private and family life.
Freedom of conscience and religion.
Freedom of thought and expression.
Freedom of assembly.
Freedom of association.
Freedom to marry and found a family.
Freedom of movement.
The right to free elections.
The right to an effective remedy if one's rights are violated.
The right to recognition as a person before the law.
The right to compensation for miscarriage of justice.
The right to a name.
The rights of the child.
The right to a nationality.
The right to equality before the law.

The five rights and freedoms included in the American Convention but not in the United Nations Covenant are:

The right of property.
Freedom from exile (though the Covenant provides in Article 12 that

'No one shall be arbitrarily deprived of the right to enter his own country').
Prohibition of the collective expulsion of aliens.
The right of reply.
The right of asylum.

On the other hand, the provision in the UN Covenant on the rights of minorities (Article 27) has no counterpart in the American Convention.

A comparison of the provisions of the American Convention with those of the European Convention and its Protocols, reveals that the principal rights included in the American but not in the European text are: the right of reply, the rights of the child, the right to a name and to a nationality, and the right of asylum. On the other hand, the right to education, contained in the First Protocol to the European Convention is not specifically protected by the American text.

The definitions of the American Convention are generally closer to those of the United Nations Covenant on Civil and Political Rights than to the European Convention, though there are several differences which are sometimes due to following the European model. As one would expect, many articles provoked long and lively discussion at the San José conference, for example those on the right of property, the right of asylum, the rights of illegitimate children, and on the prohibition of propaganda for war, which is included, as an exception, in the article on freedom of expression. A departure from the earlier texts is to be found in Article 4 on the right to life, which states: 'This right shall be protected by law, and, in general, from the moment of conception.' Whether this means that, as a general rule, abortion is a violation of fundamental rights has proved controversial.[5] On a number of occasions delegates maintained that it would be better to follow the United Nations texts and so avoid conflicting definitions at the regional and universal levels. Generally, however, this argument was rejected, on the ground that since the American States had decided to go ahead with the conclusion of their own Convention after the UN Covenants had been completed, it was appropriate to introduce modifications in the light of circumstances in the American republics.

Two of the most important rights guaranteed in the UN

Covenant and in the two regional Conventions are the right to liberty and security, including freedom from arbitrary arrest, and the right to a fair trial. The draft submitted to the San José conference contained provisions defining these rights which gave less protection than Articles 9 and 14 of the UN Covenant and Articles 5 and 6 of the European Convention. The special advisers drew attention to these differences, and the conference agreed to change the provisions concerned. As a result, Article 7(5) now provides that 'any detained person shall be brought promptly before a judge ... and shall be entitled to trial within a reasonable time,' etc. In Article 8, on the right to a fair trial, the text submitted to the conference provided for 'a fair hearing' without further definition. The conference agreed to a proposal to strengthen this very important provision by adding the words 'by a competent, independent and impartial tribunal established by law' from the UN Covenant, together with the words 'within a reasonable time' from the European Convention.[6]

Another question which was discussed was whether the American Convention should also include economic, social and cultural rights. Now the Charter of the OAS, as amended by the Protocol of Buenos Aires, contains separate chapters on economic standards, on social standards and on educational, scientific and cultural standards. It also set up an Inter-American Council for Education Science and Culture and an Economic and Social Council. These councils have the task of promoting the standards set out in the Charter and may make recommendations. Moreover, the governments are required to send in annual reports. It was therefore decided not to list economic, social and cultural rights, as in the first UN Covenant and the European Social Charter, but to include a general undertaking by States to take appropriate measures to secure the rights generated by the standards set out in the OAS Charter. This undertaking is now contained in Article 26 of the Convention and, as a corollary, Article 42 requires governments to send the Inter-American Commission on Human Rights copies of their annual reports, so that it can monitor their performance.

3. *The system of international control*

The American Convention on Human Rights, like the European Convention, provides for two organs of control: a Commission and a Court. But there are important differences in the composition, functions and powers of the organs established under the two regional systems, as we shall see.

A problem which faced those who drafted the American Convention was that when they came to define the composition, functions and powers of the Inter-American Commission on Human Rights, they were not creating a new organ but conferring new functions and powers on an existing body. As already noted, the Inter-American Commission was created in 1959 by Resolution VIII of the meeting of consultation of the Ministers for Foreign Affairs at Santiago. Originally a promotional organ, it was granted limited powers to consider individual complaints at the Rio conference in 1965. Then, in 1967 the conference on the revision of the Charter transformed it into one of the statutory organs of the OAS, and decided that its structure and competence would be determined by the new Convention, which was being prepared.

As a result of this evolution the 1969 Convention was able to confer new functions and powers on the existing Inter-American Commission, but, of course, the new provisions would only apply in relation to States which ratified the new Convention. It was therefore also necessary to provide that the existing functions and powers of the Commission would remain and continue to be exercised in relation to States which did not ratify the new Convention. In other words, the Inter-American Commission would have a double mandate: that resulting from the Convention in relation to States parties to the Convention; and that resulting from the earlier decisions of 1959, 1965 and 1967 in relation to all members of the OAS, whether or not they ratified the Convention.

This was in fact what happened. And since the American Convention on Human Rights entered into force only on 18 July 1978, and some time had to elapse before its new functions could be effectively exercised, almost all the work of the Commission during the first twenty years of its existence was taken up with its 'old functions'. It is therefore useful to begin by considering the activities of the Commission outside the Convention.[7]

(a) The 'old functions' of the Inter-American Commission Following its creation in 1959, the Inter-American Commission drew up a Statute which was approved by the OAS Council in 1960. The Statute gave the Commission power to examine the human rights situation in OAS member States where flagrant and repeated violations were occurring; to request pertinent information of the governments concerned and, if necessary, to request their consent to visit their territory; to make such visits if the necessary consent was obtained; to put forward any recommendations it thought advisable and to prepare reports. It was not competent to take decisions on individual complaints of violation of human rights, but it could take account of such complaints as sources of information on the state of human rights in the countries concerned.

The competence to consider individual complaints of violation of a limited number of specific rights was conferred on the Commission, as already mentioned, by the Rio conference in 1965, and the Statute was amended accordingly. The new text empowered the Commission to examine communications submitted to it and any other available information, to request pertinent information from governments, to make appropriate recommendations, and to report on these activities to the Inter-American Conference. It will be noted that when the Commission utilises these procedures it can make recommendations and reports, but is still not authorised to take decisions.

In application of these provisions the Inter-American Commission has examined the situation of human rights in a considerable number of the Latin American republics. Sometimes this has been on the basis of complaints received and evidence obtained outside the country concerned, but sometimes its examination has also included on the spot visits and hearing of witnesses, including both governmental representatives and individual complaints. The results of these investigations have been incorporated in a series of 'country reports'.

Examples of the first category are a series of reports on the situation of human rights in Cuba which began in 1962. Regrettably, the Cuban government did not co-operate with the Commission when it was preparing these studies. A particularly striking case of visits on the spot, on the other hand, concerned the Dominican Republic when civil war was raging in 1965. Members of the Commission spent several months there and were able to intervene on behalf of detained persons and secure the release of prisoners on both sides as well as observance of other humanitarian measures. Another sort of humanitarian mission was undertaken by the Commission in 1980, when about twenty diplomats attending a reception at the Dominican embassy in Bogotá were held as hostages by a group of terrorists. As the result of an agreement negotiated with the government of Colombia, the Inter-American Commission supervised the release of the hostages and the evacuation of the terrorists and also undertook to monitor the trials of certain political prisoners.

Other 'country reports' produced by the Inter-American Commission in recent years concern the human rights situation in Haiti (1980, after a visit in 1978); Uruguay (1977); Chile (annual reviews from 1974 to 1980, one resulting from a visit in 1974); Panama (1978, after a visit during the previous year); Nicaragua (visit and report in 1978); El Salvador (visit in 1978, report in 1979); and Argentina (visit in 1979 followed by a report in 1980). In all these countries serious violations of human rights were found.[8]

The Commission's report on Argentina precipitated a major crisis in the OAS. It was considered by the General Assembly of the OAS, meeting in Washington in November 1980. The report was highly critical of the Argentine government and the United States proposed a resolution condemning the violations of human rights in that country. Argentina threatened to leave the Organisation if this was adopted, and was supported by Bolivia, Chile, Paraguay and Uruguay. The agenda of the conference included not only the special report on Argentina, but also the annual report of the Commission, which recounted serious violations of human rights in Chile, El Salvador, Paraguay and Uruguay. In the end the conference adopted a resolution in which it took note of the reports and made a general condemnation of countries which violate human rights but without naming any of them specifically.[9] At the same time, several countries, including Mexico, Venezuela, Colombia, Ecuador, and Peru, expressed their support for the Inter-American Commission and the conference requested it to undertake an investigation on the human rights situation in Bolivia.

As regards the complaints which it receives from individuals and groups, the Commission seems to be struggling with an uphill – some would say an impossible – task. This is partly due to the number of complaints received; for example, it opened more than 1,000 case files in one recent year.[10] To deal with this mass of applications the Commission holds only two regular sessions a year, totalling not more than eight weeks, though there is usually one additional or extraordinary session. Moreover, it has only seven members, all with other professional occupations, to cope with the volume of work. An even greater obstacle is the lack of effective co-operation from the governments concerned. For in the great majority of cases they reply to the Commission's enquiries with a minimum of information and are evidently seeking to cover up, rather than investigate, the violations brought to their attention.

In this difficult situation the Commission has adopted a rule to the effect that once a communication has been declared admissible, the facts alleged will be presumed to be confirmed if the government concerned fails to bring forward convincing evidence in rebuttal.[11] It is on the basis of this presumption, which is entirely reasonable in the circumstances, that the majority of the decisions of the Commission are reached on individual complaints.

The results of the Commission's work can be seen in its annual reports to the General Assembly of the OAS. As one example, about half the annual report for 1978 was devoted to the consideration of individual complaints. Out of more than 1,000 complaints received the Commission reported in detail on thirty-seven cases: five concerning Argentina, ten concerning Bolivia, twenty concerning Chile, and one each concerning Panama and Uruguay. They present a depressing picture of arbitrary arrest, detention without trial, interrogation accompanied by torture, exile without judicial process and a variety of similar violations. Co-operation of governments in investigating the complaints was minimal. In all cases except one, serious violations were established.[12]

From this brief summary two conclusions may be drawn. First, a great deal of the work of the Commission to date – and, no doubt, a considerable part of its work in the future – results from its 'old functions' which antedate the entry into force of the American Convention on Human Rights in 1978. Indeed, the Permanent Council of the Organisation recognised this in 1978 when it decided that the Commission should continue to apply its existing Statute and Regulations without change to those member States which are not parties to the Convention, and should apply any new Statute and Regulations that might be approved only to States that have ratified the Convention. Matters were taken a stage further at the ninth regular session of the General Assembly of the OAS in

October 1979, when a new Statute of the Commission was approved. This contained three separate articles on the functions and powers of the Commission. Article 18 deals with its powers with respect to all members of the OAS, which are mainly promotional, while Article 19 deals with its powers in relation to States which have ratified the Convention. The latter, as we shall see shortly, are principally concerned with its action on petitions and communications under the terms of the Convention and its relations with the Inter-American Court of Human Rights. Article 20 then sets out its powers in relation to States which have not yet ratified the Convention and authorises the Commission to continue to act in accordance with the old procedures.[13]

Our second conclusion is prompted by a comparison of the work of the Inter-American Commission on Human Rights with that of the European Commission of Human Rights described in the previous chapter. It is plain that they are immeasurably different. The two Commissions operate in quite different circumstances, one might almost say at quite different levels. The European Commission has, with very rare exceptions, been concerned with what might be called the finer points of human rights law. Questions, for example, such as what is a reasonable time in detention pending trial, what is the precise content of the right to a fair trial, what limitations may be placed on freedom of expression, what exactly are the implications of the right of freedom of association, and so on. Furthermore, when dealing with such problems the European Commission has almost always had the full co-operation of the governments concerned and the full support of its parent organisation, the Council of Europe. The Inter-American Commission, on the other hand, has had to deal with problems of a quite different order: arbitrary arrests on a massive scale, systematic use of torture, scores or hundreds of 'disappeared persons', total absence of judicial remedies, and other flagrant violations of civilised standards. In dealing with such cases it has found the governments concerned more like antagonists than willing partners, while at the General Assembly of the OAS the lip service paid to its work, and the genuine support of some governments, have not prevented others from expressing violent and destructive criticism.

When studying the development of international techniques for the protection of human rights, we must therefore remember that the problems confronting the Inter-American Commission are far graver than those in Western Europe, and give due recognition to the efforts of the Commission to expose the serious violations which occur and seek justice for the victims.

(b) The 'new functions' of the Inter-American Commission First, a few words about the organisation of the Commission, which is covered in Articles 34 to 40 of the Convention.

When the Convention was drawn up in 1969, it was decided to keep the number of members at seven, as in the original decision of 1959. They must be persons of high moral character and recognised competence in the field of human rights (Article 34). A proposal was made at the San José conference that the General Assembly of the OAS should have the power to enlarge the membership of the Commission when this was considered to be necessary. The proposal was rejected, however, apparently because it was feared that the possibility of such action by a political body might affect the independence of the Commission. While this is a real enough point, the fact remains that the burden of work falling on the seven members of the Commission under the present arrangements is excessive.

The Commission represents all the member countries of the OAS (Article 35). However, the members of the Commission sit in a personal capacity (Article 36) and this is, of course, essential to guarantee their independence.

There was a long discussion during the drafting of the Convention as to whether all member States of the Organisation or only contracting parties should have the right (a) to propose candidates, (b) to elect members, and (c) to have their nationals sit as members of the Commission. On the one hand, it was argued that if only a limited number of member States ratified the Convention, it was they who should decide on the membership of the organ whose full jurisdiction only they accept. On the other hand, it was pointed out that the Commission is an organ of the OAS as a whole (as a result of the Protocol of Buenos Aires) and that, consequently, all member States ought to participate in the election and be able to have their nationals sit as members. It was the second argument which prevailed. As a result, all member States may propose candidates and vote in the election by the General Assembly of the OAS. They may propose up to three candidates, with the unusual proviso that if they do, at least one must be of another nationality.

The term of office of members of the Commission is four years. However, they may be re-elected, but only once (Article 37). The necessary services are furnished by a specialised unit in the General Secretariat of the OAS (Article 40). The first election under the terms of the Convention took place at the ninth regular session of the General Assembly of the OAS in October 1979.

The next three articles of the Convention relate to the functions of the Commission. They repeat the 'old functions' of a promotional character conferred on the original Commission in 1959, which include the making of recommendations to member governments and requesting information from member governments on human rights matters, and the submission of an annual report to the General Assembly (Article 41). There is a provision which we noticed earlier for the examination by the Commission of governments' reports on compliance with the economic, social and cultural standards established by the OAS Charter (Article 42) and an undertaking by States parties to provide the Commission with information which it may request as to the manner in which their domestic law complies with the Convention (Article 43).

The new functions of the Commission are set out in Articles 44 to 47. It is competent to consider petitions from individuals, groups of individuals or non-governmental organisations alleging violation of the Convention by States parties (Article 44). But in contrast with Article 25 of the European Convention, acceptance of this competence is not optional but obligatory. In terms of the provision of effective international procedures for protecting human rights, the compulsory jurisdiction of the Commission under Article 44 is the outstanding feature of the American Convention.

Needless to say, the Commission's competence to receive individual petitions was not achieved without much discussion. When Article 44 was being examined in Commission II of the San José conference, Argentina proposed that the right of individual petition should be made optional and was supported by the delegate from Panama (who quoted the European Convention) and those from Nicaragua and the Dominican Republic. However, Chile, supported by Uruguay, the United States and others, and followed by Mexico, argued in favour of an obligatory provision. This view was accepted in the Commission by ten votes to none, with five abstentions, and subsequently in the plenary meeting.

Article 45 then deals with inter-State complaints. The working party of Commission II recommended by a majority that this should also be made an obligatory procedure. But in the plenary Commission Argentina and Mexico opposed it, supported by Nicaragua, while Brazil, Panama, Paraguay and the Dominican Republic abstained, with the result that the proposal was not carried. As a consequence, the procedure for inter-State complaints is optional. A declaration accepting the competence of the Commission may be made at any time and may be for a limited or unlimited period of time. A suggestion was made that it should also be possible for a State to make such a declaration accepting the competence of the Commission *ad hoc* for a particular case, and this also was accepted.

It is therefore evident that, as regards the competence of the Commission, the American Convention is the exact opposite of the European Convention. Acceptance of the right of individual petition follows automatically from ratification, whereas the procedure for inter-State complaints is optional. This is undoubtedly a major advance in establishing an effective system of international control, bearing in mind that a compulsory system of inter-State complaints could be politically explosive in the Latin American context.

The rules on admissibility (Articles 46 and 47) are generally similar to those contained in the European Convention. They include the requirement of exhaustion of domestic remedies and require that the petition should be filed within six months of the notification of the final domestic decision. In order to resolve the question of whether an applicant may bring his case successively before the UN Committee and the regional commission, the suggestion was made that a petition should be declared inadmissible if at an earlier stage it had been submitted to another procedure of international settlement. This was accepted and incorporated as Article 47(d).

Once the Commission has decided that a case is admissible, its first task is to establish the facts. It may undertake an investigation, for which the States concerned will furnish all necessary facilities (Article 48(1)(d)). An urgent procedure for emergency cases is set out in Article 48(2). The Commission then has the task of trying to bring about a friendly settlement. The procedure (Articles 48(1)(f) and 49) is broadly similar to that of the European Convention. If no friendly settlement is achieved, the Commission is required to draw up a report setting out the facts and stating its conclusions and may make such proposals and recommendations as it thinks fit (Article 50).

There was much discussion as to what should happen at the next stage. The draft submitted to the conference proposed that, if the case was not submitted to the Court within a period of three months, the Commission should take a final decision on the question of violation. However, this did not meet with general agreement, because many States were not willing to grant the Commission such extensive powers. Consequently the article was redrafted so as to provide that if, within a period of three months, the matter is not settled or submitted to the Court, the Commission may, by an absolute majority of its members, 'set forth its opinion and conclusions concerning the question submitted for its consideration'. It may also 'make pertinent recommendations' and fix a period of time within which the State concerned is to take the measures needed to remedy the situation. At the end of that period the Commission decides whether the State has taken adequate measures, and whether to publish its report (Article 51).

From the political point of view this was no doubt a wise compromise. From a lawyer's perspective, however, it must be noted that the American Convention still does not provide for a definite decision on the question of violation if a case does not go to the Court. Nevertheless, it does go a good deal further than the UN Covenant in this respect. Indeed, if the Commission expresses the opinion that a State has violated the Convention and sets a period of time within which remedial measures should be taken, then decides that adequate measures have not been taken and publishes its report with the reasons for its action, to all intents and purposes there is a decision on violation.

(c) **The Inter-American Court of Human Rights** The draft Convention submitted to the San José conference provided for the creation of an Inter-American Court of Human Rights, with the power to give a decision if a contracting party referred a case to it after the Commission had examined the matter and expressed its opinion. The jurisdiction of the Court, however, would be optional.

The first question the conference had to decide was whether a Court of Human Rights was desirable in the American context. The Mexican representative suggested that it would be premature, and stated that his government could not agree that such a body should be in a position to pass judgement on the legality of the acts of a State. He therefore urged that the Court should be omitted from the Convention altogether. However, many delegations took the opposite view and considered that a judicial organ was indispensable. The representative of Chile, for example, maintained that this would be the logical culmination of the process which had begun in 1948 with the proclamation of the American Declaration of the Rights and Duties of Man, and continued with the establishment of the Inter-American Commission on Human Rights in 1959. The United States also favoured the creation of the Court and pointed out that if its jurisdiction was optional, there would be no difficulty in accommodating States which were unwilling to accept it. At the end of the general discussion, it was agreed to establish an Inter-American Court of Human Rights with optional jurisdiction.[14]

The Court consists of seven judges, elected in an individual capacity from among jurists of the highest moral authority and recognised competence, and who possess the qualifications required for the highest judicial office (Article 52). In contrast with the procedure for the election of the members of the Commission, only the parties to the Convention may propose candidates and take part in the election. However, candidates may be of the nationality of any member State of the OAS, and, as with the Commission, the lists of three candidates put forward by the parties must include at least one who is not a national of the proposing State (Article 53).

The right to participate in the election of the judges is not limited to the States which have accepted the compulsory jurisdiction of the Court. Moreover, unlike the European Convention, there is no provision requiring a stated number of acceptances of the jurisdiction of the Court before the first election. As a result, it was possible to begin the procedure for setting up the Court shortly after the entry into force of the Convention in 1978. In fact the election took place in the course of the meeting of the General Assembly of the OAS in May 1979.

The judges are elected for a term of six years, and may be re-elected, but only once (Article 54). Article 58 left the choice of the seat of the Court to be determined by the General Assembly of the OAS. In July 1978, when it was known that the entry into force of the Convention was imminent, the General Assembly recommended that the Court should be based in Costa Rica.[15] This was subsequently confirmed by the States parties and was appropriate recognition of the fact that that country had acted as host to the conference which had drafted the Convention in 1969, was the first State to ratify the Convention in April 1970, and the first to accept the compulsory jurisdiction of the Court. It also called to mind that Costa Rica was the seat of the Central American Court of Justice when it was set up in 1907.

Article 55 deals with the question of the 'national judge', that is whether a judge who is a national of a party to a case should have the right to sit in a case in which his own country is involved. This involves as a corollary the question whether, if there is no 'national judge', the State concerned may appoint an *ad hoc* judge. This is, of course, the arrangement in both the International Court of Justice and the European Court of Human Rights. The Inter-American Commission on Human Rights had proposed that a judge who is a national of a party to a dispute should stand down and not participate in the proceedings. The Brazilian representative argued that this would be a more progressive arrangement and more likely to secure impartiality in the composition of the Court. This view, however, did not prevail. The final text therefore follows the traditional system of national and *ad hoc* judges (Article 55).

When the special advisers had explained the role of the European Commission in the proceedings of the European Court of Human Rights, it was decided to include an article in the American Convention providing that 'the Commission shall appear in all cases before the Court' (Article 57).

The Court appoints its own secretary (Article 58). Article 59 provides that the Court shall establish its own secretariat, which functions under the direction of the Secretary of the Court, but in accordance with the administrative regulations of the General Secretariat of the OAS to the extent that they are not incompatible with the Court's independence. The importance attached to such independence, a vital element in any system of judicial supervision, is therefore clear.

(d) The competence of the Court Only States parties and the Commission may submit cases to the Court (Article 61). Consideration was given to the idea of allowing an individual applicant to refer a case to the Court if he was dissatisfied with the opinion of the Commission, and the example of the Central American Court was mentioned as a precedent. Predictably, however, the system established by the European Convention was quoted on the other side, and several delegates stated that their governments would be unwilling to accept the right of individuals to activate the Court. A proposal to confer such a right was therefore rejected by a majority vote.

Under Article 62 of the Convention contracting parties may declare that they accept the jurisdiction of the Court unconditionally or on condition of reciprocity, and for an indefinite or for a limited period of time.[16] The suggestion was made, and accepted, that this should also be possible *ad hoc* and so the words 'or for specific cases' were added.

The delegate of Costa Rica proposed the insertion of an article authorising the Court to order interim measures 'in cases of extreme seriousness and urgency, and when it is necessary to avoid irreparable damage ...'. This was accepted and incorporated as paragraph 1 of Article 63.

The powers of the Inter-American Court are very wide and, as we shall see, significantly more extensive than those of the European Court. If it finds that there has been a violation, it may order that the injured party be reinstated in his rights and, where appropriate, can also order that the consequences of a violation should be remedied and damages paid (Article 63). Moreover, the contracting parties undertake to abide by the judgement of the Court, and an order for damages will be directly enforceable in the State concerned (Article 68). This last provision has no counterpart in the European Convention, but is comparable to the effect of judgements of the European Court of Justice under Articles 187 and 192 of the Treaty of Rome.

What is the ultimate sanction if a State refuses to comply with a judgement of the Court? Although there is not, and perhaps cannot be, any indefeasible sanction, the Inter-American Court is required to submit an annual report to the General Assembly of the OAS, indicating, in particular, cases in which a State has not complied with its judgements and making 'the pertinent recommendations' (Article 65). The making of an annual report is an unusual procedure for a judicial body, and it may not always be easy for the Court to know whether a State has fully complied with a judgement. However, Article 65 was introduced to provide at least some form of sanction. The reporting of a State for non-compliance to the General Assembly, which will be attended by several hundred delegates and receive wide publicity, is no doubt a procedure which most governments would prefer to avoid.

Article 64 of the Convention invests the Inter-American Court with wide powers to give advisory opinions.[17] Requests for advisory opinions may relate not only to the American Convention on Human Rights, but also to other treaties concerning the protection of human rights in the American States. All the organs of the OAS listed in Chapter X of the Charter (as amended by the Protocol of Buenos Aires) may consult the Court on matters within their competence.[18] In addition, any member State of the OAS may request and receive an opinion on the compatibility of any of its domestic laws with the American Convention on Human Rights or any other treaty relating to human rights in the American States. It is significant, moreover, that the right to request advisory opinions is not limited to contracting parties to the American Convention. The suggestion was made and accepted that this right should be given to all member States of the Organisation. The thinking here was that this procedure would be useful in permitting a State which is considering ratification to obtain an authoritative opinion on whether a particular domestic law might be incompatible with the Convention.

(e) **The work of the Court** When the Inter-American Court was given the authority to issue advisory opinions, it was hoped that this would enable it to play an active part in the Convention system, whether or not a substantial number of States accepted its jurisdiction and regardless of the Commission's readiness to refer cases to it. The wisdom of providing the Court with wide powers under Article 64 is now apparent, for not only has the Court handed down a number of important advisory opinions, but this aspect of its activity has so far proved much more significant than its contentious jurisdiction.

The Court's first advisory opinion was given in 1982 and others have followed at an average of just over one per year. The Court, it must be remembered, has no control over the volume of business, which depends entirely on the readiness of the States and the relevant organs of the OAS to refer cases to it. It is therefore interesting to note that of its first eight advisory opinions, five were given in response to requests by States (three by Costa Rica and one each by Peru and Uruguay), while three were in response to requests from the Inter-American Commission.

The cases to date, though relatively few in number, have already taken the Court into several quite different areas of the Convention. In its first case, which we shall call the *Other Treaties case*,[19] the question was the actual scope of the advisory jurisdiction and, in particular, the meaning of the reference in Article 64(1) to 'other treaties concerning the protection of human rights in the American States'. The request was made by the Government of Peru, which asked specifically whether 'other treaties' meant treaties adopted within the framework of the Inter-American system, or was more general and included, for example, the United Nations Covenants, or other human rights treaties to which American and non-American States may be parties.

The Court held that the broader view was correct, so that in principle any human rights treaty to which American States are parties can be the subject of an advisory opinion. The Court qualified this a little by pointing out that its advisory jurisdiction is permissive, and that there might be circumstances in which it would be proper to deny a request, for example if the issue in the case involved an obligation assumed by a non-American State.

The qualification is significant, but no less important are the reasons given by the Court for its main conclusion. For these include the assertion that the purpose of the Court's advisory role is 'to assist the American States in fulfilling their international human rights obligations'[20] and that the object of the American Convention is to integrate the regional and the universal systems of human rights protection. In the light of this reasoning and the Court's conclusion, it is possible that the advisory opinions of the American Court may one day provide a most valuable guide to the interpretation of a wide range of human rights treaties.

The Court's second case, also in 1982, again concerned the scope of its advisory jurisdiction, although not as the main issue. In the *Effect of Reservations case*[21] the Commission asked the Court to say when a State becomes a party to the American Convention if it ratifies or adheres to the Convention with one or more reservations. Before answering this question, however, the Court made the important jurisdictional ruling that the Commission was competent not only to request the present opinion but generally, since by virtue of its functions it enjoys 'an absolute right to request advisory opinions within the framework of Article 64(1) of the Convention'.[22]

The main issue, which raised a technical but very practical issue in the law of treaties, turned on whether reservations to the Convention are subject to acceptance by the other parties. The crucial article of the American Convention (Article 75) is unclear on the point, but the Court interpreted it as meaning that reservations are not subject to the acceptance of the other parties. It supported this conclusion by explaining that human rights treaties are not in the nature of bargains between States, involving a reciprocal exchange of rights and obligations, but have as their object and purpose:

> the protection of the basic rights of individual human beings, irrespective of their nationality, both against the State of their nationality and all other contracting States ... [T]he States [Parties] can be deemed to submit themselves to a legal order within which they, for the common good, assume various obligations, not in relation to other States, but towards all individuals within their jurisdiction.[23]

It is interesting to note that the character of the American Convention was an essential element in the Court's reasoning, and that in emphasising the special character of human rights treaties, the Court drew heavily on the earlier reasoning of both the International Court and the European Commission.[24]

The *Restrictions to the Death Penalty case*[25] in 1983 was another case with a double aspect. The case arose because the Commission had a disagreement with Guatemala over the scope of a reservation which the latter had made to Article 4(4) of the Convention, which concerns the imposition of the death penalty for political crimes. When the Commission asked the Court for an advisory opinion on the point, Guatemala argued that because the request related to a dispute involving Guatemala, and Guatemala had not accepted the jurisdiction of the Court in contentious cases, the question could not be answered by means of an advisory opinion.

This is a type of argument which the International Court of Justice has considered on several occasions[26] and which its predecessor, the Permanent Court, discussed as long ago as 1923.[27] The American Court referred to several of these cases in its opinion and held that since the request clearly fell within the sphere of competence of the Commission, the Court had jurisdiction to give the opinion requested.

Having established that it was competent, the Court had to consider the main issue in the case, which was the effect of Guatemala's obligations under Article 4(2). In dealing with these questions the Court emphasised the primacy of the text in interpreting both Article 4 of the Convention and the reservation, but also held that 'in interpreting reservations, account must be taken of the object and purpose of the relevant treaty'.[28] Bearing in mind that the Convention is a human rights treaty, the Court concluded that Guatemala's reservation should be construed in a way that was compatible with the object and purpose of the Convention, and (and this was the whole point of the case) which also left Guatemala's obligations under Article 4(2) intact.

The first case in which the Court was requested to determine the compatibility of a particular law with the Convention was the *Proposed Amendments case*[29] in 1984. Here Costa Rica asked the Court if certain amendments which were proposed to the naturalisation provisions of the Constitution would be compatible with Articles 17, 20, and 24, dealing with, respectively, the rights of the family, the right to a nationality, and the right to equal protection. Sensibly deciding that the case fell under Article 64(2) even though the proposed amendments were not yet 'laws', the Court found that in most respects the new arrangements would be compatible with the Convention, but ruled that one provision, which concerned naturalisation and discriminated between spouses, would contravene Articles 17(4) and 24.

The *Licensing of Journalism case*[30] in 1985 raised both a general question under Article 64(1) and a specific issue under Article 64(2). The general question was how far the compulsory licensing of journalists, a common practice in Latin America, is compatible with Article 13 of the Convention, which protects freedom of expression. The specific issue was whether the law regulating this matter in Costa Rica could be approved. In a long opinion reviewing the scope of freedom of expression, and making extensive use of case-law from the European Convention, the Court concluded that the compulsory licensing of journalists is incompatible with Article 13 if it denies any person access to the full use of the news media as a means of expressing opinions or imparting information. In the light of this principle it then ruled that the particular law was not compatible with the Convention.

The next three cases were all referred under Article 64(1) and raised general issues of varying importance. In the *Interpretation of 'Laws' case*[31] in 1986, Uruguay asked for an interpretation of Article 30 of the Convention which provides that restrictions on the enjoyment or exercise of its rights and freedoms may only be applied 'in accordance with laws enacted for reasons of general interest . . .'. The point on which the Court was asked to rule was whether the word 'laws' in this provision refers to laws in the formal sense, that is to legal norms passed by the legislature and promulgated in the way prescribed by the Constitution, or to laws in the material sense, that is as a synonym for the entire body of law, without reference to the procedure followed in the creation of the norm, or to the rank assigned to it in the particular system.

The Court held that the first view was correct and took the opportunity to explain both the link between human rights and democracy and the special significance of these concepts in the Americas. Explaining that the Convention 'has its own philosophy under which the American States "require the political organisation of these States on the basis of the effective exercise of democracy"',[32] the Court concluded that the word 'laws' in Article 30 'means a general legal norm, tied to the general welfare, passed by democratically elected legislative bodies established by the Constitution and formulated according to the procedures set forth by the constitutions of the States parties for that purpose.'[33]

The *Right of Reply case*[34] in the same year raised a narrower point. Here Costa Rica asked about the scope of Article 14, which guarantees the right of reply, and the Court gave a short opinion in which it explained the relation between this part of the Convention and the domestic law of the parties.

Finally, in the *Habeas Corpus case*[35] in 1987 the Commission asked the Court for an opinion on a point which, like the question in the *Interpretation of 'Laws' case*, concerned the scope of permissible limitations to the rights protected by the Convention. Article 27(1) of the American Convention authorises suspension of its guarantees in emergency situations and thus corresponds to Article 15 of the European Convention. However, Article 27(2) provides that the articles guaranteeing certain rights may not be suspended, and goes on to prohibit suspension 'of the judicial guarantees essential for the protection of such rights'. The Commission's question was whether, in view of its importance, the writ of habeas corpus is one such non-suspendable guarantee. The Court concluded that it is and supported this with reference to both the 'inseparable bond between the principle of legality, democratic institutions and the rule of law',[36] which it had identified in the *Interpretation of 'Laws' case*, and to the special position of emergency powers.

The Court also referred to 'the realities that have been the experience of some of the peoples of this hemisphere in recent decades, particularly disappearances, torture, and murder committed or tolerated by some governments'.[37] As the Court recognised, political conditions in many of the States which are parties to the American Convention make the scope of emergency powers an especially vital issue. Here, therefore, as in the *Licensing of Journalism* and *Interpretation of 'Laws'* cases, the Court's advisory opinion was able to develop and clarify the law on a matter of particular regional interest.

The Court's developing advisory jurisprudence stands in sharp contrast to the virtual neglect of its contentious jurisdiction. In 1981 the government of Costa Rica referred the *Gallardo case*[38] to the Court in circumstances which were unusual because the case had not been considered by the Commission. The government argued that it was entitled to waive this first stage of the proceedings, but the Court disagreed. In an important review of the role of the Convention organs the Court emphasised that the processing of a case by the Commission is more than a matter of convenience for the respondent, and constitutes an integral part of the Convention system. Since the Commission fulfils a vital and independent function, it was not open to a State to dispense with the first stage of the proceedings and refer a matter directly to the Court. The decision was undoubtedly correct, but the effect, of course, was to render the case inadmissible, with the result that the substantive point, which involved the murder of a person while in prison, was never examined.

Following the unsuccessful attempt to refer the *Gallardo case*, several years elapsed before the contentious procedure was used again. In its opinion in the *Licensing of Journalism case* in 1985 the Court indicated that the Commission could have raised the relevant point in contentious proceedings and stated that it should have done so, instead of leaving Costa Rica to seek an advisory opinion. Stung by the criticism that its neglect of the Court had damaged the delicate balance of the Convention, in April 1986 the Commission referred three cases to the Court.[39]

The cases, *Velásquez Rodríguez, Garbi and Corrales*, and *Cruz*, are all very similar and concern people who have disappeared in Honduras. Early in 1988 the Court was informed that one person who had given evidence and another who was due to do so had been murdered, and that the lives of other witnesses were in danger. It therefore issued two orders under Article 63(2) of the Convention requiring the Government of Honduras to adopt measures to protect the rights of witnesses and investigate the killings.[40] The problem of 'disappeared persons' is one with which the Inter-American Commission is all too familiar and the events just described are a reminder, if one is needed, of the problems confronting the Convention institutions. In its decision on the merits in the *Velásquez Rodríguez* case[41] in July 1988 the Court found that Honduras had violated its obligations to respect and ensure the right to personal liberty set forth in Article 7 of the Convention, the right to humane treatment in Article 5 and the right to life in Article 4. It also decided that Honduras was required to pay compensation to the next-of-kin of the victim. On all these points the Court was unanimous. In this case, unlike the Court's advisory opinions, factual as well as legal issues were significant and the judgement contains important material on the international rules of evidence. Now that the Commission has at last begun to refer contentious cases to the Court, further developments in this aspect of its jurisprudence can be expected.

4. *Other provisions of the Convention*

Article 70 provides for the privileges and immunities of members of the Commission and the Court. Throughout their term of office they enjoy the immunities extended to diplomatic agents. In the first draft their immunities were limited to the period during which they hold office; however, it was pointed out that the immunity accorded to judges and members of the Commission as regards the contents of their judgements and opinions should be absolute, so that they can act with the necessary independence. This view was generally accepted, and a second sentence was added to Article 70 to this effect.

Article 72 of the Convention deals with the budget of the Commission and the Court. It provides that the conditions under which the emoluments and expenses of the members are to be paid are to be set out in the respective Statutes of the two organs. The Statute of the Commission (Article 13) provides for expenses and fees; that of the Court (Article 17) for salaries and expenses. The actual amounts, as well as the general expenses of the Court and of the Commission, are fixed each year in the budget of the Organisation. The draft budget of the Court is drawn up by the Court itself and submitted to the General Assembly of the OAS by the Secretary-General, who has no power to amend it. This is to protect the independence of the Court *vis-à-vis* the Secretariat of the OAS, a concern that was also evident as we have seen, when the provisions relating to the Secretary of the Court (Article 58) and its Secretariat (Article 59) were drafted.

Article 73 of the Convention is very unusual. It relates to 'sanctions to be applied to the members of the Commission and the Court'. A provision was suggested by the representative of Argentina which would have allowed the General Assembly of the OAS to impose sanctions on members of those bodies for reasons which would be set out in their respective Statutes. This proposal caused some concern because it could obviously prejudice the independence of the judiciary. A revised version was subsequently adopted which admits the possibility of sanctions, but only on the proposal of the Commission or the Court themselves. While this is less objectionable, punitive provisions directed at individuals really have no place in a human rights convention.

Article 74 relates to ratification. The draft submitted to the conference provided that the Convention would enter into force when ratified by seven States. There was a general feeling that this number was too low, and finally the number was fixed at eleven. As mentioned earlier, this number was achieved in July 1978.

The question of reservations is dealt with by Article 75. During the negotiations some delegations argued that reservations should be permitted only in respect of constitutional provisions which are in conflict with the provisions of the Convention, because if a State were permitted to make a reservation whenever a provision of its domestic law was inconsistent with the Convention, the number of reservations would be excessive. In their view it was preferable that a State should amend its law before ratifying. On the other hand, it was argued that too rigid an attitude in this respect would make ratification more difficult, and probably slower, and might even prevent the entry into force of the Convention. The first point of view gained majority support in Commission II, but was not accepted by the plenary conference. Agreement was finally reached on a proposal of Uruguay which permits reservations 'in conformity with the provisions of the Vienna Convention on the Law of Treaties signed on 23 May 1969'. In fact it seems that the fears of some delegations were rather exaggerated. Although the Court has already had occasion to consider Article 75 in two of its advisory opinions,[42] of the States which have ratified the Convention, only an insignificant minority have made reservations.

5. Comparison with the UN Covenant and the European Convention

In Section 2 of this chapter we noted the similarities and differences in the rights protected in the American Convention, the UN Covenant on Civil and Political Rights, and the European Convention. We may therefore conclude with a brief comparison of the different systems of international control.

It is best to begin by considering the UN Human Rights Committee and the two regional Commissions. Attention has already been drawn to some of the differences between them. The position may be summarised as follows.

(a) Membership and election; sessions The Inter-American Commission has only seven members (Article 34). It is an organ of, and represents all the member countries of, the OAS (Article 35). It is elected by the General Assembly of the OAS (Article 36).

The UN Committee consists of eighteen members (Article 28 of the Covenant). It is elected by the States parties (Article 30) and has competence only in relation to the States parties. It is not an organ of the United Nations.

The European Commission has a number of members equal to the number of the High Contracting Parties (Article 20 of the European Convention). This means that at present there are twenty-one members. They are elected by the Committee of Ministers of the Council of Europe (Article 21). The functions of the Commission extend only to the contracting parties.

In all three cases the members serve in a personal capacity (Articles 36, 28, and 23 respectively).

The growth of the Strasbourg system has created a situation in which the European Commission is seriously overburdened,[43] and so it must be questionable whether the Inter-American Commission with only seven members is big enough to fulfil the functions imposed on it by the Convention, particularly as the number of individual applications increases.

All three bodies meet intermittently. The UN Committee usually holds three sessions a year, the Inter-American Commission two regular and often one additional session, the European Commission usually five plenary sessions a year. In all three cases there is a clear need for more frequent sessions in order to cope with the volume of work.

But then another problem arises. The great majority of the members of these bodies have other professional occupations and may not be able to devote more time to serve on the international organs. Is there a case for full-time membership on a salaried basis? Are the organisations concerned prepared to accept the consequential financial implications? These questions pose real problems, but are increasingly pressing.

(b) Competence of the three organs

(i) Reporting procedures This is the principal function of the UN Committee (Article 40). States parties to the American Convention report to the Inter-American Commission only in reply to a specific request for information (Article 41(d) and Article 43), except as regards economic, social and cultural rights, where there is an obligation to send the Commission copies of the annual reports prepared for the Inter-American Economic and Social Council and the Inter-American Council for Education, Science and Culture (Article 42).

Under the European Convention there is no automatic requirement of submitting reports to the Commission, but only, on request, to the Secretary-General of the Council of Europe (Article 57).

(ii) Inter-State communications This is an optional procedure in both the Inter-American and the UN systems (Article 45 of the American Convention; Article 41 of the UN Covenant). It contrasts sharply with the procedure under the European Convention,

according to which all contracting parties accept the jurisdiction of the European Commission to consider any breach of the Convention alleged by another contracting party (Article 24 of the European Convention).

The Inter-American Commission (Article 48), the UN Committee (Article 41) and the European Commission (Article 28) all have the task of trying to achieve a friendly settlement. If this fails, the Inter-American Commission draws up a report stating the facts and its conclusions, proposals and recommendations (Article 50). The European procedure is broadly similar (Article 31). The UN Committee must confine itself to a brief statement of the facts (Article 41, paragraph h).

The European procedure alone leads to a binding decision by the Committee of Ministers or the European Court of Human Rights, on the basis of the report of the Commission.

Also worth noting is the procedure under the UN Covenant (Article 42) for the appointment of an *ad hoc* Conciliation Commission for inter-State disputes, if both parties agree. This has no counterpart in the two regional Conventions.

(iii) Individual communications The biggest advance made by the American Convention on Human Rights is that acceptance of the procedure for individual petitions to the Inter-American Commission follows automatically from ratification of the Convention (Article 44). In other words, acceptance of this procedure is not optional but obligatory.

This contrasts with the procedure under the European Convention, whereby acceptance of the right of individual petition is optional (Article 25). However, all the contracting parties have now accepted this optional provision.

The UN Covenant on Civil and Political Rights contains no provision authorising the UN Committee to consider individual communications. Instead, this procedure is contained in an Optional Protocol. Currently thirty-nine States have ratified the Optional Protocol, out of eighty-seven which have ratified the Covenant.

All three instruments contain detailed rules about exhaustion of domestic remedies and other conditions of admissibility (American Convention, Articles 46 and 47; UN Optional Protocol, Articles 3 and 5; European Convention, Articles 26 and 27).

The Inter-American Commission has power to carry out an investigation on the spot, for the purpose of which 'it shall request, and the States concerned shall furnish to it, all necessary facilities' (Article 48, paragraph 2(d)). The UN Committee has no such power. The European Commission can carry out, if necessary, an investigation 'for the effective conduct of which the States concerned shall furnish all necessary facilities, after an exchange of views with the Commission' (Article 28(a)).

The conclusions of the three bodies after they have examined individual communications or petitions take the same form as when they have dealt with inter-State communications, as explained earlier.

As regards the judicial organs invested with responsibility in human rights matters, the possibility of comparison is limited to the two regional Courts, because the UN Covenant on Civil and Political Rights has no arrangements for judicial supervision.

We may summarise the points which arise in the comparison of the two Courts in the following way:

1. As regards the size of the Courts, there is a big difference: seven judges on the Inter-American Court (Article 52) and twenty-two on the European Court (Article 38), though the European Court often hears cases in a chamber of seven judges.

2. The European Court was established six years after the entry into force of the European Convention, that is after eight States had accepted its jurisdiction as compulsory (Article 56). Since there is no comparable provision in the American Convention, the Inter-American Court was set up in 1979 shortly after the Convention entered into force.

3. The jurisdiction of both courts is optional and extends only to States which have expressly declared that they accept it (Articles 62 and 46). They may do so for a limited or unlimited period of time, on condition of reciprocity, or on an *ad hoc* basis.

4. In both cases, only States and the Commission may refer a case to the court – not individual applicants (Articles 61 and 48).

5. As regards the effect of judgements, the Inter-American Court (Article 63) has considerably wider powers than the European Court (Article 50), but the procedure for supervision of the judgements of the European Court by the Committee of Ministers (Article 54) is important and likely to be more effective than that of annual reports by the Inter-American Court to the OAS General Assembly (Article 65).

6. The power of the Inter-American Court to order 'provisional measures' (Article 63, paragraph 2) is valuable, as its recent practice demonstrates, and has no counterpart in the European Convention.

7. The powers of the Inter-American Court to give advisory opinions (Article 64) are much wider than those conferred on the European Court by the Second Protocol to the European Convention. The Court's powers under Article 64 have already been used to good effect and to date constitute its main contribution to a developing human rights jurisprudence in the Americas.

Notes

1 The development of the Organisation of American States is more fully described in the first edition of this book at pp. 111–21.

2 The decisions of the Third Special Inter-American Conference are summarised in A. H. Robertson, 'Revision of the Charter of the O.A.S.', *International and Comparative Law Quarterly*, XVII, 1968, p. 346.

3 The three special advisers were M. Rene Cassin, President of the European Court of Human Rights, Professor Balladore-Pallieri, judge of the European Court and subsequently its President, and Professor A. H. Robertson, the original author of this book.

4 The text of the American Convention on Human Rights may be found in I. Brownlie, *Basic Documents on Human Rights*, second edition, Oxford, 1981, p. 391.

5 In its decision in the *Baby Boy case* in 1981 the Inter-American Commission on Human Rights was divided on this point. For the text of the Commission's decision, see *Human Rights Law Journal*, II, 1981, p. 110. For discussion of this case, see D. Shelton, 'Abortion and the right to life in the inter-American system: the case of "baby boy"', *ibid.*, p. 309.

6 An unfortunate change was made in Article 8(2) on the suggestion of the United States. This was to limit the presumption of innocence in criminal proceedings so that it applies only to persons 'accused of a serious crime'. This is, however, less damaging than it may appear because the Spanish text, which will be used by the majority of the contracting parties, uses the same words as Article 14(2) of the UN Covenant 'toda persona inculpada de delito …'. For a comparison of the rights protected by the two regional instruments, see J. Frowein, 'The European and American Conventions – a comparison', *Human Rights Law Journal*, I, 1980, p. 44.

7 In addition to the functions outlined in the text, the Commission now also performs a general supervisory role under Article 17 of the 1985 Inter-American Convention to Prevent and Punish Torture (see Chapter 3, n. 35). For discussion of the Commission's other work, see D. V. Sandifer, 'Human rights in the inter-American system', *Howard Law Journal*, XI, 1965, p. 508; L. R. Scheman, 'The Inter-American Commission on Human Rights', *American Journal of International Law*, LIX, 1965, p. 335; J. A. Cabranes, 'Human rights and non-intervention in the American system', *Michigan Law Review*, LXV, 1966–67,

p. 1147. On the American Convention in general, see P. P. Camargo, 'The American Convention on Human Rights', *Human Rights Journal*, III, 1970, p. 333.

8 The conclusions of the Inter-American Commission were also communicated to the Commission on Human Rights of the United Nations under the procedure established by ECOSOC Resolution 1159 (XLI) of 1967 – see, for example, doc. E/CN.4/1333/Add. 1 of 15 February 1979. On the practice of the Inter-American Commission, see Robert E. Norris 'Observations in loco; practice and procedure of the Inter-American Commission of Human Rights', *Texas International Law Journal*, XV, 1980, p. 46.

9 General Assembly of the OAS, Tenth Regular Session, AG/doc. 1348/80 of 27 November 1980.

10 At its forty-sixth session (March 1979) the Commission was seized of 425 new cases, involving 643 victims from sixteen countries. At its forty-eighth session (December 1979), 171 new cases, in addition to 4,153 new complaints which it had received during its 'on-site observation' in Argentina in September that year.

11 See H. Hannum (ed.), *Guide to International Human Rights Practice*, London, 1984, p. 118.

12 *Annual Report of the Inter-American Commission of Human Rights for 1978*, Washington, DC 1979, pp. 28–109. The one exception concerned Panama. The report of the Commission for 1979–80 recounts the proceedings in eleven cases in which the Commission found violations, nine concerning Argentina and two concerning Panama.

13 As the United States has yet to ratify the Convention, the old procedures were the basis of the Commission's jurisdiction in the *Baby Boy case* (see n. 5) and more recently in the *Application of death penalty on juveniles case* which contains an interesting treatment of customary international law and *ius cogens* in relation to human rights; see *Human Rights Law Journal*, VIII, 1987, p. 345.

14 See T. Buergenthal, 'The Inter-American Court of Human Rights', *American Journal of International Law*, LXXVI, 1982, p. 231.

15 Resolution AG/Res. 372 (VIII – 0/78) of 1 July 1978.

16 By 1 January 1988 the jurisdiction of the Court had been accepted by nine States: Argentina, Colombia, Costa Rica, Ecuador, Guatemala, Honduras, Peru, Uruguay and Venezuela.

17 See T. Buergenthal, 'The advisory practice of the Inter-American Human Rights Court', *American Journal of International Law*, LXXIX, 1985, p. 1.

18 The organs concerned are the General Assembly, the meeting of consultation of the Ministers of Foreign Affairs, the Councils, the Juridical Committee, the Commission on Human Rights, the General Secretariat, the specialised conferences, and the specialised organisations.

19 *'Other treaties' subject to the advisory jurisdiction of the Court*, Advisory Opinion No. OC-1/82 of 24 September 1982, Series A, No. 1. Text in *Human Rights Law Journal*, III, 1982, p. 140.

20 *Ibid*., para. 25.

21 *The effect of reservations on the entry into force of the American Convention*, Advisory Opinion No. OC-2/82 of 24 September 1982, Series A, No. 2. Text in *Human Rights Law Journal*, III, 1982, p. 153.

22 *Ibid*., para. 16.

23 *Ibid.*, para. 29.

24 See the *Reservations to the Convention on the Prevention and Punishment of the Crime of Genocide*, Advisory Opinion, 1951 I.C.J. Rep. 15 and *Austria* v. *Italy*, *European Yearbook of Human Rights*, IV, 1960, p. 116 at p. 140.

25 *Restrictions to the death penalty*, Advisory Opinion No. OC-3/83 of 8 September 1983, Series A, No. 3. Text in *Human Rights Law Journal*, IV, 1983, p. 339.

26 See, for example, the *Western Sahara*, Advisory Opinion, 1975 I.C.J. Rep. 12.

27 See the *Status of Eastern Carelia*, Advisory Opinion, 1923, P.C.I.J., Series B, No. 5.

28 *Restrictions to the death penalty case*, para. 65.

29 *Proposed amendments to the naturalization provisions of the Constitution of Costa Rica*, Advisory Opinion, No. OC-4/84 of 19 January 1984, Series A, No. 4. Text in *Human Rights Law Journal*, V, 1984, p. 161.

30 *Compulsory membership in an association prescribed by law for the practice of journalism*, Advisory Opinion, No. OC-5/85 of 13 November 1985, Series A, No. 5. Text in *Human Rights Law Journal*, VII, 1986, p. 74.

31 *The word 'laws' in Article 30 of the American Convention on Human Rights*, Advisory Opinion No. OC-6/86 of 9 May 1986, Series A, No. 6. Text in *Human Rights Law Journal*, VII, 1986, p. 231.

32 *Ibid.*, para. 30.

33 *Ibid.*, para. 38.

34 *Character and scope of the right of reply or correction recognised in the American Convention*, Advisory Opinion No. OC-7/85 of 29 August 1986, Series A, No. 7. Text in *Human Rights Law Journal*, VII, 1986, p. 238.

35 *Habeas corpus in emergency situations*, Advisory Opinion No. OC-8/87 of 30 January 1987, Series A, No. 8. Text in *Human Rights Law Journal*, IX, 1988, p. 94. Since this case the Court has delivered another advisory opinion concerned with the scope of Article 27 at the request of Uruguay. See *Judicial guarantees in states of emergency*, Advisory Opinion No. OC-9/87 of 6 October 1987, Series A, No. 9. Text in *Human Rights Law Journal*, *ibid.*, p. 204.

36 *Ibid.*, para. 24.

37 *Ibid.*, para. 36.

38 *Decision on the application of the Government of Costa Rica with regard to Viviana Gallardo et al.*, Decision of 13 November 1981, No. G 101/81. Text in *Human Rights Law Journal*, II, 1981, p. 328. For the Court's preliminary decision and for its decision closing the case, see *ibid.*, II, p. 108 and V, p. 77, respectively.

39 See Resolutions 22/86, 23/86 and 24/86, all of 18 April 1986. Texts in *Human Rights Law Journal*, VII, 1986, pp. 424, 427 and 428.

40 Orders of 15 January and 19 January 1988. Texts in *Human Rights Law Journal*, IX, 1988, pp. 104 and 105.

41 *Velásquez Rodríguez case*, Judgement of 29 July 1988. Text in *Human Rights Law Journal*, IX, 1988, p. 212.

42 The *Effect of reservations case* and the *Restrictions to the death penalty case*, see ns. 21 and 25 above.

43 See H. G. Schermers, 'Has the European Commission of Human Rights got bogged down?', *Human Rights Law Journal*, IX, 1988, p. 175.

CHAPTER 6

Regional co-operation on human rights elsewhere

I. The Permanent Arab Commission on Human Rights

The League of Arab States was founded in March 1945, shortly before the end of the Second World War, when seven countries, Egypt, Iraq, Jordan, Lebanon, Saudi Arabia, Syria, and Yemen, signed the Pact of the League of Arab States. The Pact described the purpose of the League as: 'the strengthening of the relations between the Member States; the co-ordination of their policies in order to achieve their independence and sovereignty; and a general concern with the affairs and interests of the Arab countries.' Article 2 of the Pact continued by providing for co-operation in economic and financial affairs, including commerce, agriculture and industry; communications of all sorts; cultural affairs; legal matters; social affairs; and health issues. The treaty deliberately established only loose ties between the members because they believed that this would facilitate the accession of other Arab States. However, Article 9 of the Pact authorised 'Member States which desire to establish closer co-operation and stronger bonds than are provided for by this Pact ... to conclude agreements for that purpose'.

The next significant step was the conclusion of a Treaty for Joint Defence and Economic Co-operation, which was signed by Egypt, Lebanon, Syria, Saudi Arabia and Yemen in 1950, by Iraq in 1951, by Jordan a year later, and by the remaining Arab countries at a summit conference in Alexandria in 1964. Thus were laid the foundations for a new international regional organisation, whose membership was soon to extend from the Atlantic Ocean to the Arabian Gulf.[1] The Joint Defence Treaty describes the Arab League as a regional organisation for the purposes of the United Nations Charter, and this has been recognised by the General Assembly which has granted the League observer status at UN meetings.[2] In addition, the Arab League has concluded agreements for co-operation with UNESCO, the ILO, FAO, and WHO.

Three quite separate developments led the Arab League to interest itself in human rights matters. The first arose out of its practice of co-operation with the United Nations. In August 1966 the Economic and Social Council invited four regional organisations, the Council of Europe, the Organisation of American States, the Organisation of African Unity, and the League of Arab States, to attend sessions of the UN Commission on Human Rights and to exchange information with it on their respective human rights activities.[3] At about the same time, the four regional organisations were urged to support the initiative of the United Nations in celebrating 1968 as International Human Rights Year and, as a corollary, were invited to attend the International Conference on Human Rights in Tehran, the Year's main event.[4] While the Council of Europe and the Organisation of American States already had their own human rights programmes, the Arab League had not, but now had an incentive to consider establishing one. In September 1966 the Council of the League decided to accept the invitation to participate in International Human Rights Year and soon appointed a committee of governmental representatives to consider how it should implement the decision.[5]

The second development was that early in 1967 the UN Commission on Human Rights decided to study the possibility of setting up regional Commissions in areas where they did not already exist.[6] Later that year the Arab League, like other regional organisations, was asked for its views on this proposal. Its reply made the following points:

1. The field of human rights is a vital one for strengthening links among countries which belong to a regional area.
2. As for the procedure of establishing regional commissions on human rights and specifying their functions, the League of Arab States believes that the proper foundations for setting up such regional commissions are the foundations on which a regional inter-governmental organisation is based. Thus the regional commissions should be established within the framework of international or regional inter-governmental organisations.

Having expressed these views to the United Nations, it was no surprise when the League subsequently gave further attention to the idea of establishing its own regional Commission on Human Rights.

The third development occurred at the International Conference on Human Rights at Tehran in 1968. A number of Arab countries sought to include on the conference agenda the question of 'respect and implementation of human rights in occupied territories', meaning the territories occupied by Israel during the war of June 1967. Now, whatever view may be taken about that war, there is no doubt that one result was that many thousands of people found themselves living under foreign occupation with some of their basic rights severely restricted. Consideration of this problem was included on the agenda of the Tehran conference, with the support of the majority of delegations. The concerted action of the Arab States at the conference, assisted by the Secretariat of the Arab League, thus demonstrated that it was possible to use human rights as a means of censuring Israel over its treatment of the inhabitants of the occupied territories.

The above developments led the Arab League to the conclusion that the time was ripe to set up its own Commission on Human Rights. The Council of the League decided to organise an Arab regional Conference on Human Rights in Beirut in December 1968, as part of its contribution to International Human Rights Year and used it to announce that it had decided to set up a Permanent Arab Commission on Human Rights.[7]

The rules of procedure which the League established for the Commission cover both procedural matters and its composition and functions. Each member State of the League is represented on the Commission, which means that its members are government officials, as in the UN Commission, and not independent persons serving in a personal capacity, as in the European and Inter-American Commissions. Other Arab States may be invited to attend, and representatives of the Gulf Emirates are invited as observers. The Council of the League appoints the Chairman of the Commission for a term of office of two years, which is renewable, and the Secretary-General of the League appoints the Commission's Secretary.

The functions of the Commission, like those of other Commissions of the League, are essentially to prepare draft agreements or other proposals for the Council. However, it has a power of initiative and may submit its own recommendations and suggestions to the Council. In accordance with this power, the Commission prepared a plan of action which was approved by the Council of the League at its session in September 1969. This programme is based on the principle that all matters relating to human rights in the Arab world fall within the competence of the Commission, particularly the co-ordination of joint action, the protection of the rights of the individual, and promoting respect for human rights in Arab countries in general. As one would expect, the Commission has given priority to the question of the rights of Arabs living in the occupied territories.

The programme is in two parts, relating respectively to action at the national level and action at the international level. As regards national action it includes the creation of national commissions on human rights, which would be linked to the Permanent Commission of the League; receiving reports from member States on their activities in the field of human rights and making recommendations; and, perhaps most important of all, undertaking preparatory work for a proposed Arab Charter of Human Rights. At the international level the Commission has concentrated on assisting the League and the delegations of member States at various conferences, including sessions of the UN Commission on Human Rights and the Working Group set up to investigate Israel's conduct in the occupied territories. The Commission also sends an annual report on its activities to the United Nations Commission, and its representatives played an active part in the UN seminar on the establishment of regional commissions on human rights with special reference to Africa, which was held in Cairo in 1969.

Information about the results achieved by the Commission is rather sparse. Its activities to date seem to have been mainly concerned with the situation in the occupied territories and this preoccupation is likely to continue. The Commission's terms of reference, like those of the UN Commission, are essentially to promote human rights, rather than to protect them, in contrast with the European Commission. Some work has been done on the proposed Arab Charter of Human Rights, but this has yet to produce action at the inter-governmental level. At a conference in Baghdad in 1979 the Union of Arab Lawyers proposed the conclusion of an Arab Convention on Human Rights which would guarantee fundamental rights as they are understood in an Islamic context. More recently, Arab jurists meeting at Syracuse approved the text of a Draft Charter of Human and Peoples' Rights in the Arab World.[8] This document, which was also envisaged as the basis for an Arab treaty, sets out civil and political rights, economic and social rights and a list of 'Collective Rights of the Arab People'. It also contains comprehensive arrangements for supervision and implementation, including both a new Commission on Human Rights and a Court. Like the earlier proposal for an Arab Convention, this latest document has no official status. While its appearance is therefore certainly of interest, no purpose would be served by describing its contents in detail. It should be noted, however, that though the Syracuse draft has no binding force, its basis was a draft prepared by the General Administration for Legal Affairs of the Secretariat General of the League of Arab States.

It is clear, then, that much remains to be done before the Arab world has a system comparable to the schemes of regional protection to be found elsewhere, but some evidence of progress is discernible.

II. The African Charter on Human and Peoples' Rights

1. The origin and history of the Charter

The advances which led to the establishment of regional organisations in Europe and America have also produced results in Africa. Between 1958 and 1962 the independent African States held a series of conferences. The conference in Lagos in 1962 approved a proposal for permanent machinery for economic and technical co-operation and Liberia suggested additional arrangements of a political character, including annual meetings of the Foreign Ministers and the appointment of a permanent secretariat. The following year a summit conference of heads of State and government held in Addis Ababa adopted the Charter of the Organisation of African Unity. Article II of the Charter includes among the aims of the OAU 'to promote the unity and solidarity of the African States', 'to eradicate all forms of colonialism from Africa' and 'to promote international co-operation, having due regard to the Charter of the United Nations and the Universal Declaration of Human Rights'. Although many national constitutions refer to, and sometimes incorporate, the provisions of the Universal Declaration, this was the first time that the constituent instrument of a new international organisation had done so. Article III of the Charter then proclaims a number of principles which all member States accept. These include the sovereign equality of all member States and non-interference in their internal affairs, and also 'absolute dedication to the total emancipation of the African territories which are still dependent' and 'a policy of non-alignment with regard to all blocs'.

Membership of the OAU is open to 'each independent, sovereign African State' (Article IV), although South Africa, which has never applied for membership, would presumably not be regarded as eligible.

The organs of the OAU are the Assembly of Heads of State and Government, which is the supreme organ and meets at least once a year; the Council of Foreign Ministers, which meets at least twice a year and whose principal function is to prepare or execute decisions of the Assembly; the General Secretariat; and a body called the Commission of Mediation, Conciliation and Arbitration. Article XIX of the Charter contains a specific undertaking about peaceful settlement of disputes and provided for the creation of the Commission by a separate Protocol. This instrument was concluded in 1964 and is considered an integral part of the Charter. The creation of this specifically African machinery represents an attempt to settle disputes on a regional basis without referring them to the Security Council, which is, of course, consistent with Articles 52 and 53 of the UN Charter.[9]

The headquarters of the OAU are at Addis Ababa, and this is also the seat of the Economic Commission for Africa of the United Nations which naturally encourages contacts between them.

The formation of an African Commission on Human Rights was first proposed at the African Conference on the Rule of Law, organised by the International Commission of Jurists in Lagos in 1961. The conference adopted the 'Law of Lagos', in which it declared that: 'in order to give full effect to the Universal Declaration of Human Rights, this Conference invites the African Governments to study the possibility of adopting an African Convention on Human Rights ...'. This was the first step in a process which extended over the next twenty years, and culminated in the adoption of an African Charter on Human and Peoples' Rights in 1981. To see the delicate issues inseparable from human rights law-making, it is interesting to trace the way in which this was achieved.

At the twenty-third session of the United Nations Commission on Human Rights in 1967 a proposal was tabled with the aim of encouraging the establishment of regional Commissions on Human Rights in those parts of the world where they did not already exist.[10] The most significant aspect of this proposal was that it was signed by the representatives of five African States[11] and clearly envisaged the creation of a Human Rights Commission in Africa.

The United Nations Commission decided to set up an *ad hoc* study group to consider the proposal and the group met in New York early in 1968. Its members were sharply divided on the question whether it was desirable to create regional commissions, with the East European members expressing their traditional view that such bodies were likely to interfere with matters which fall within the domestic jurisdiction of States, contrary to the principle of national sovereignty and in violation of Article 2(7) of the Charter. The contrary view, of course, was that once States have assumed international obligations to promote and respect human rights, as they had done in the Charter and were soon to do much more explicitly in the Covenants, these matters can no longer be regarded as exclusively within their domestic jurisdiction.

The report of the study group was largely a record of dissenting views, but there was agreement on one point. This was that if further regional Commissions were to be created, it should be on the initiative of the States in the region and not imposed by the United Nations.[12] In March 1968 the report was considered by the UN Commission which referred it for comment to the member governments and the regional organisations. In the reply which he sent to this request, the Secretary-General of the Council of Europe stated that, while it was not for him to say what advantages would be gained from the establishment of regional Commissions in other parts of the world, the European experience had shown that it was possible for a group of States in one region 'which have a common heritage of political traditions, ideals, freedom and the rule of law' to set up a more effective system for the protection of human rights than appeared to be possible on a world-wide basis.

By the time that the UN Commission came back to the matter at its twenty-fifth session in March 1969, two things had happened to change the situation and create a more favourable climate. The League of Arab States had set up the Permanent Arab Commission on Human Rights, which showed that the idea of regional

Commissions was gaining ground and had met with the support of a number of governments in Asia and North Africa. Furthermore, the government of the United Arab Republic had invited the United Nations to hold a seminar in Cairo as part of its programme of advisory services, to discuss the question of regional Commissions, with special reference to Africa.

This seminar took place in September 1969.[13] It was attended by participants from twenty African countries, as well as representatives of the Council of Europe and the Arab League.

There was a surprising amount of agreement on the desirability of establishing a regional Commission on Human Rights for Africa. The lead was taken by the delegation of the United Arab Republic whose positive stance was generally supported. If this was due in part to the desire to achieve a greater respect for human rights throughout the African continent, it was probably also significant that human rights had now become an accepted basis in the UN for attacking political opponents, whether over the Israeli-occupied territories, the practice of apartheid, the situation in Namibia, or other international controversies. Whatever the reasons, there was soon general agreement that an African Commission should be created.

The type of Commission which most of the participants had in mind was not one in the same mould as the European Commission, with its quasi-judicial functions, but rather a Commission for the promotion of human rights, more on the lines of the UN Commission, or the Inter-American Commission in its original form. The agenda drawn up by the UN Secretariat listed the following possible functions for the new Commission:

(a) Education and information activities.
(b) Undertaking research and studies.
(c) Performance of advisory services.
(d) Holding seminars and awarding fellowships.
(e) Fact-finding and conciliation.
(f) Consideration of communications from States, individuals and groups of individuals and the kind of action to be taken in response.

By the end of the discussion on the competence of the African Commission, it had been agreed to include the functions set out under points (a) to (d) above without reservation, and points (e) and (f) as optional provisions.

The other item for consideration was the means of establishing a regional Commission for Africa, and its geographical extent. On the second point, it was agreed that the Commission should include all African countries sharing the same political ideas, that is to say that it should cover the whole of Africa except those countries tainted with apartheid and colonialism. It was also agreed that the African Commission should be created by resolution of the Organisation of African Unity, rather than by the conclusion of a Convention. To this end it was decided to invite the Secretary-General of the UN to send the report of the seminar to the Secretary-General of the OAU with a request that he should communicate it to his member governments and place the question on the agenda of a forthcoming meeting of the OAU. At the same time the hope was expressed that the UN, interested Specialised Agencies and regional organisations would all lend their advice and assistance to the OAU if it decided to proceed with the project.

The report on the Cairo seminar was duly communicated to the UN Commission on Human Rights at its twenty-sixth session in 1970 and, as the participants had requested, to the Secretary-General of the Organisation of African Unity. The OAU, however, took no action at this stage.

The next step was a conference held in Addis Ababa in 1971 under the auspices of the United Nations Economic Commission for Africa and with the participation of the OAU. The matters discussed, which were the African legal process and the individual, related more to substantive issues of human rights than to the issue of new institutions, but the conference had been planned as a follow-up to the Cairo seminar, and repeated the recommendation for the establishment of a regional Commission on Human Rights for Africa.

Though this conference also was not followed by any practical action, the idea was kept alive at various subsequent meetings. One of these was the UN Seminar on the Study of New Ways and Means for Promoting Human Rights with Special Attention to the Problems and Needs of Africa, held in Dar-es-Salaam in 1973.[14] Two unofficial meetings which also discussed the question were the Third Biennial Conference of the African Bar Association in Freetown (Sierra Leone) in 1978, and a Seminar on Development and Human Rights organised by the International Commission of Jurists in Dakar in the same year.

An important step forward was taken by the Organisation of African Unity when the Assembly of Heads of State and Government adopted a 'Decision on Human Rights and Peoples' Rights in Africa', at the Assembly's sixteenth Ordinary Session, held in Monrovia in July 1979. In that decision the Assembly called on the Secretary-General of the OAU to 'organise as soon as possible in an African capital a restricted meeting of highly qualified experts to prepare a preliminary draft of an African Charter on Human Rights providing, *inter alia*, for the establishment of bodies to promote and protect human rights'.[15]

The decision stated that human rights 'are not confined to civil and political rights but cover economic, social and cultural problems', that special attention must be given to the latter, and that 'economic and social development is a human right'. The decision also called on the OAU Secretary-General to draw the attention of member States to 'certain international conventions whose ratification would help to strengthen Africa's struggle against certain scourges, especially against apartheid and racial discrimination, trade imbalance and mercenarism'.

Two months later the United Nations organised a further seminar on the establishment of regional Commissions on Human Rights, with particular reference to Africa, which was held in Monrovia in September 1979. This was attended by participants from thirty African countries, as well as observers from Specialised Agencies, regional organisations and non-governmental organisations.[16] It was naturally encouraged by the OAU decision taken the previous July about the preparation of an African Charter on Human Rights.

Widespread support was expressed for the idea of establishing an African Commission on Human Rights, but it was also suggested that the member States of the OAU did not show the political homogeneity which characterised the members of certain other regional organisations. The point was also made that they were primarily concerned with improving the living conditions and basic education of their peoples and that recommendations would only be made within the framework of the OAU decision adopted earlier by the heads of State.

It was accepted that the principle of non-interference in the internal affairs of a sovereign State should not exclude international action when human rights were violated in a particular State, but it was also considered that the functions of an African Commission on Human Rights should, in the beginning, be primarily promotional. As regards functions of protection, some participants stated that the Commission could be authorised to investigate alleged gross violations of human rights and to act as a mediator, but the majority maintained that it would be premature to admit individual petitions. At this first stage the priority was seen as to inform people and make them aware of their individual human rights, and the suggestion was made that here a useful role could be played by national and local institutions, as well as non-governmental organisations. Emphasis was also placed on the need to take account of the size of the African continent, the great number of African States, their cultural diversity, and the poor state of communications in many parts of Africa.

The seminar worked out a 'Monrovia proposal' for establishing an African Commission on Human Rights of sixteen members, elected by the Assembly of Heads of State and Government of the OAU to serve in their personal capacity. Its functions would be 'to promote and protect human rights in Africa'. It would apply 'the international law of human rights', including any specific African instruments on human rights and the relevant international texts. While the functions of the Commission would be mainly promotional, it could also study alleged violations, propose its good offices and make reports and recommendations to the OAU.

The seminar requested its chairman, the Minister of Justice of Liberia, to submit the Monrovia proposal to the Chairman of the OAU, President Tolbert of Liberia. The intention was obviously that the proposal should be considered by the meeting of experts which the OAU had already decided to convene with the task of preparing an African Charter on Human Rights.

Matters were not helped by the fact that President Tolbert and his government were overthrown a few months later by a military *coup d'état*. Nevertheless, the OAU meeting took place in the form of a Ministerial conference held in Bangui (Gambia) in June 1980. It was presented with a draft African Charter of Human and Peoples' Rights which had been prepared by a meeting of experts held in Dakar in 1979. This was a draft for an international Convention of sixty articles, containing both substantive and procedural provisions. However, the Ministerial conference in 1980 was able to examine only the first seven articles, with the result that a further meeting was held in January 1981. This completed work on the draft Charter, which was then submitted to the eighteenth summit meeting of the Organisation of African Unity, held in Nairobi in June 1981.

The summit meeting approved the Charter and opened it for signature on 26 June 1981. The Charter, which required ratification by a simple majority of the member States of the OAU, came into force in October 1986 and has now been ratified by thirty-five States.[17]

2. *The rights protected*

In Article 1 of the African Charter the parties agree to recognise the rights, duties and freedoms which it contains and 'to adopt legislative or other measures to give effect to them'. This is followed by a non-discrimination provision (Article 2) and a list of substantive articles with several unusual features. The first is that the Charter covers economic, social and cultural rights, as well as civil and political rights. This clearly distinguishes it from the European and American Conventions with their more traditional approach and reflects the importance which the African States attach to these issues. Secondly, as the title of the Charter indicates, its provisions are not limited to human rights in the sense of individual rights of both categories, but extend also to 'peoples' rights', that is to collective or 'third generation' human rights, as they are sometimes called. Here too the desire to move beyond the conceptual framework of the other regional conventions is apparent. Thirdly, the African Charter, again in contrast to the earlier instruments, includes provisions which express the idea that human beings can only realise their potential fully as a member of a group. While this is plainly linked to the idea of collective rights, its consequence is held to be that a person has duties, as well as rights in the community, so provisions to this effect are also included in the Charter.

(a) Civil and political rights The provisions relating to these rights are to be found in Articles 3 to 16 of the Charter, which guarantee the following rights and freedoms:

1. The right to equality before the law.
2. The right to respect for life and the integrity of the person.

3. Freedom from exploitation and degradation including slavery, torture and cruel, inhuman or degrading punishment.
4. The right to liberty and security of the person.
5. The right to a fair trial.
6. Freedom from retrospective punishment.
7. Freedom of conscience, including religious freedom.
8. The right to receive information and to express opinions.
9. Freedom of association.
10. Freedom of assembly.
11. Freedom of movement, including the right to asylum.
12. Prohibition of mass expulsion.
13. The right to participate in government.
14. The right of equal access to the public service.
15. The right of equal access to public property and to public services.
16. The right to property.

The list bears an obvious resemblance to the corresponding parts of the other regional conventions, as well as to the Covenant on Civil and Political Rights, and, of course, this is not accidental. It would be wrong to suppose, however, that the treatment of civil and political rights in the African Charter is identical to the earlier instruments. While a detailed comparison must be sought elsewhere,[18] two general observations, one commending the Charter's approach, the other critical, may be made.

In support of the Charter it can be seen that its list of civil and political rights includes all the rights covered by the original European Convention, except, rather curiously, the right to marry, some rights which were added by subsequent protocols, for example the right to participate in government and the right to property, and others such as the right of equal access to the public service, which have still to be recognised. Although the omitted rights are sometimes found in other conventions, there is no doubt that as regards the ground covered, the treatment of civil and political rights in the African Convention is quite extensive.

The criticism is that a comparison between the definition of certain rights in the African Charter and the equivalent provisions of other instruments, reveals the Charter to be drafted in a way that seems bound to produce difficulties. One problem is that in several cases the right concerned is defined inadequately. Article 4, for example, guarantees respect for life and the integrity of the person, then states vaguely 'No one may be arbitrarily deprived of this right'. Similarly, Article 6, potentially one of the most important provisions of the Charter, guarantees the right to liberty and security of the person, and concludes 'no one may be arbitrarily arrested or detained'. The question which springs to mind, but which is not answered in the Charter, is what does the word 'arbitrarily' mean in these provisions?

A related difficulty is that the Charter, like other human rights instruments, permits limitation of the rights guaranteed, but does so in terms which are again terse and often appear to emasculate the main provision. Thus, Article 9(2) provides that 'Every individual shall have the right to express and disseminate his opinions *within the law*', whilst Article 10(1) lays down that 'Every individual shall have the right to free association *provided he abides by the law*'. If the qualifying words are compared with the corresponding provisions of the other regional conventions the contrast is striking. Whereas they permit the limitation of rights only in carefully defined circumstances, the African Charter appears to define the right by reference to national law. Since the main purpose of human rights treaties is to supply a standard against which national law can be measured, the problem with the language of the Charter is apparent.

Must we conclude then that the protection afforded by the extensive provisions of the African Charter is largely illusory? Until the Commission begins to apply its provisions, this cannot be answered. However, a suggestion as to how some of the less satisfactory provisions of the Charter might be amplified, can be based on Article 60. This provides:

> The Commission shall draw inspiration from international law on human and peoples' rights, particularly from the provisions of various African instruments on human and peoples' rights, the Charter of the United Nations, the Charter of the Organization of African Unity, the Universal Declaration of Human Rights, other instruments adopted by the United Nations and by African countries in the field of human and peoples' rights as well as from the provisions of various instruments adopted within the Specialised Agencies of the United Nations of which the parties to the present Charter are members.

In relation to the problem under discussion, the wide range of source material which this article makes available suggests that if the Commission wishes to fill out the more enigmatic parts of the

Charter and keep its limiting provisions within sensible bounds, it may be able to derive valuable assistance from practice elsewhere.[19] For example, in determining what constitutes an 'arbitrary' deprivation of liberty, the African Commission could usefully refer to the detailed list of permissible actions set out in Article 5 of the European Convention. Similarly, the Strasbourg organs already have an extensive jurisprudence on the question of what is needed for an action to be in accordance with the law,[20] and the fact that Article 12 of the European Convention recognises the right to marry subject 'to the national laws governing the exercise of this right' has not prevented the Court and the Commission from ruling that such laws are acceptable only in so far as they do not interfere with the 'substance' of the Convention right.[21] How far the African Commission will be prepared to adopt this kind of approach remains to be seen, but if the Commission is prepared to look for it, material to support the dynamic interpretation which the Charter needs would not be hard to find.

(b) Economic, social and cultural rights The African Charter deals with these rights in Articles 17 and 18, but the two provisions cover a total of seven aspects of economic, social and cultural rights as follows:

1. The right to education.
2. The right to participate in the cultural life on one's community.
3. The duty of the State to promote and protect morals and traditional values.
4. The duty of the State to take care of the physical and moral health of the family.
5. The duty of the State to assist the family as the custodian of morals and traditional values.
6. The duty of the State to eliminate discrimination against women and ensure the protection of the internationally recognised rights of women and children.
7. The right of the aged and disabled to special measures of protection.

The right to education is guaranteed in the American Convention and in the First Protocol to the European Convention. The other rights are unique to the African Charter.[22] The place of economic, social and cultural rights in international law will be considered in the next chapter and so a detailed discussion of this part of the Charter would be inappropriate at this stage. However, since the inclusion of rights of this kind in a regional treaty is so unusual, it is worth briefly considering the way they are dealt with and the implications of their inclusion.

A comparison between the provisions of the African Charter and those of the Covenant on Economic, Social and Cultural Rights indicates that the latter is more comprehensive in the sense that it covers more rights. It is also more detailed, because rights which are merely stated in the Charter are usually elaborated in the Covenant. The right to education, for example, which appears in Article 7(1) of the Charter in the simple form 'Every individual shall have the right to education', is covered by Article 13 of the Covenant which runs to 400 words and is actually longer than the treatment of economic and social rights in the whole of the Charter. Comparison between the terms of the African Charter and those of the European Social Charter reveals a similar contrast.

The conclusion to be drawn from this is not that support for economic and social rights by the African States is lukewarm or a sham. Many, after all, are parties to the United Nations Covenant, while Article 17(3) of the Charter, which makes the promotion and protection of morals and traditional values a duty of the State, goes much further than any other treaty. Moreover, as we shall see shortly, in evaluating the Charter's treatment of economic and social rights, account must be taken of its later articles on duties. It remains true, however, that the Charter is not a detailed treatment of economic and social rights. The reason, it is suggested, is that the intention of the framers was simply to emphasise the importance of economic and social rights and especially their close relationship with civil and political rights, which could be done without a full elaboration. This conclusion, which is consistent with the background to the Charter considered earlier, is supported by the fact that since many African States were already parties to the Covenant on Economic, Social and Cultural Rights, an exhaustive treatment of these matters at the regional level was hardly necessary. Looked at in this way, as a symbolic affirmation of the place of economic and social rights in the thinking of the African States, the inclusion of a relatively small number of rights, set out in a broad and unparticularised way, becomes easier to understand and justify.

(c) **Peoples' rights** These rights are contained in Articles 19 to 24 of the Charter which cover the following collective rights:

1. The right to equality of peoples.
2. The right to self-determination.
3. The right to dispose of wealth and natural resources.
4. The right to economic, social and cultural development.
5. The right to national and international peace and security.
6. The right to 'a general satisfactory environment' favourable to development.

It is perhaps worth emphasising that although all the rights in this part of the Charter are collective rights, two appear elsewhere as individual rights. These are the right to equality, which is covered in Articles 2 and 3, and the right to cultural development, which, as we have just seen, is included in the articles on economic, social and cultural rights (Article 17(2)). What the later articles of the Charter are dealing with, however, is not the individual's rights to equality and cultural development, but the corresponding rights of peoples.

In our earlier discussion of the right of self-determination we saw that the impulse to use international law to further human rights came originally from the idea that rights inhere in individuals, and this is still the basis of modern thinking. It follows that the concept of collective rights introduces a quite new element into the law which may sometimes be hard to reconcile with the traditional approach.[23] Some of the difficulties were touched on earlier and will be further explored in Chapter 7. For the moment, therefore, we shall concentrate on the specific features of the African Charter.

The Charter is the first international agreement to list collective rights in such detail, but it is not the first to mention them. Moreover, as we shall see, some of the ideas which are presented here as collective rights are to be found in other instruments in a different form. Thus, as in the case of economic and social rights and the provisions we shall consider shortly on duties, the treatment of collective rights, though a new departure in one sense, is also an extension of current ideas.

Articles 19 and 20, which cover the rights to equality and self-determination, were clearly inspired by Article 1(1) of the two United Nations Covenants. In the light of their historical experience it is in no way surprising that the African States wished to include these provisions, nor that they chose to elaborate the right to self-determination by recognising the right of colonised or oppressed people to free themselves 'by resorting to any means recognised by the international community' (Article 22(2)) and proclaiming a peoples' right to assistance from other parties 'in their liberation struggle against foreign domination, be it political, economic or cultural' (Article 22(3)).

The Covenants also inspired Article 21 of the Charter, which deals with the right to dispose of wealth and natural resources. It will be recalled that this is covered in Article 1(2) of the Covenants, but the Charter is again more elaborate. Article 21(2) provides that 'In case of spoliation the dispossessed people shall have the right to lawful recovery of its property as well as to an adequate compensation'. Article 24(4) lays down that the parties shall exercise the right to dispose of wealth and natural resources 'with a view to strengthening African unity and solidarity'. And Article 24(5) contains an undertaking by the parties 'to eliminate all forms of foreign economic exploitation' in order to benefit their peoples. These details have no counterpart in the Covenants.

Article 23 deals with 'the right to national and international peace and security' and has a number of links with other instruments. Although no other instrument guarantees the right explicitly, the Universal Declaration comes close in its Article 28, which provides, 'Everyone is entitled to a social and international order in which the rights and freedoms set forth in this Declaration can be fully realised'. Moreover, both the Covenant on Civil and Political Rights and the American Convention contain an undertaking to prohibit propaganda for war, which is a means to the same end. In addition to the general statement of the right in Article 23(1), the Charter provides that States will ensure that an individual enjoying the right of asylum 'shall not engage in subversive activities against his country of origin or any other State party to the Charter' (Article 23(2)(a)) and also that 'their territories shall not be used as bases for subversive or terrorist activities against the people of any State party to the present Charter' (Article 23(2)(b)). Although these provisions have no equivalent in other human rights treaties, the first qualifies the right of asylum under Article 12 in a way which is easy to justify and could perhaps be implied, while the second is a statement in terms of peoples' rights of a duty of all States under general international law.

Two provisions which are unique to the African Charter and have no equivalent at all in other international instruments are

Article 22 on the right to development and Article 24, which states 'All peoples shall have the right to a general satisfactory environment favourable to their development'. These articles are typical third-generation rights which will be discussed later. It is worth noting that since both articles refer to 'development' they are related. However, because neither this concept nor the key terms of Article 24 are defined, establishing the scope of these rights will be difficult.

A problem which arises in relation to all the articles in this part of the Charter is to decide what constitutes a 'people'. The general issue here, which occurs whenever collective rights are being considered, has been discussed in our earlier review of the United Nations Covenants and need not be reiterated. In relation to the situation in Africa, however, several points are particularly worth bearing in mind.

The emphasis which the African States have given to the maintenance of stable frontiers in the continent, and their equally strong anxiety to maintain the integrity of existing States despite the fissiparous tendencies of tribalism, make it likely that for most, if not all, of the parties to the Charter the concept of 'a people' is identified with the African nation-State. It therefore seems probable that the main use of these provisions will be in the context of nation-building, with the result that, for example, claims to self-determination on behalf of tribal or regional groups will not be regarded as raising issues under the Charter. If, however, 'peoples' and States come to be thought of as identical in all respects the concept of peoples' rights will fail to achieve its potential. Because so many African States contain diverse indigenous groups the concept of peoples' rights, if treated as relevant to tribalism and similar problems, could mark a real advance in the promotion of human rights in Africa. Thus, while a desire to avoid its more destructive consequences is understandable, if used constructively the concept of human and peoples' rights could be an interesting and useful innovation.

(d) Duties The subject of duties is dealt with in Articles 27 to 29, which form Chapter II of the Charter. It begins with three general principles: every individual has duties towards his family and society, the State, 'other legally recognised communities', and the international community; rights and freedoms must be exercised with due regard to the rights of others, collective security, morality, and common interest; and every individual has a duty to respect and consider others without discrimination and to promote mutual respect and tolerance. We then find a list of eight specific duties which are set out in Article 29 as follows:

1. The duty to the family.
2. The duty to use one's physical and intellectual abilities for the benefit of the State.
3. The duty to avoid compromising the security of the State.
4. The duty to preserve and strengthen social and national solidarity.
5. The duty to preserve and strengthen the national independence and territorial integrity of one's country and to contribute to its defence.
6. The duty to work to the best of one's ability and to pay taxes.
7. The duty to preserve and strengthen 'positive African cultural values' and to promote the moral well-being of society.
8. The duty to do one's best to promote African unity.

Although the African Charter is the first human rights treaty to prescribe the individual's duties in such an elaborate way, the inspiration for some of these provisions can be traced back to earlier instruments. Thus, Article 27, which sets out the principle of duties towards others and the obligation to respect others' rights, is similar to Article 32 of the American Convention and Article 29(6), which makes work a duty as well as a right and also establishes the obligation to pay taxes, has a direct counterpart in Articles 36 and 37 of the American Declaration of the Rights and Duties of Man.

Certain other provisions in this part of the Charter, though lacking a precise equivalent elsewhere, can be seen as a sequel to some of the rights laid down in earlier articles. Thus, Article 28, which establishes the duty not to discriminate, is the corollary of Article 2, which establishes the right not to be discriminated against, whilst Article 29(1), laying down the individual's duty to his family, is complementary to Article 18, which ascribes a similar duty to the State. Although the Charter therefore is unusual in prescribing these duties expressly, the provisions concerned are in a sense implicit in its earlier content.

Where the Charter breaks entirely new ground is in its elaborate statement of the individual's political duties in Article 29. Since these, like the earlier references to peoples' rights, are something new in human rights law, it is worth pausing to consider why it was thought necessary to include such provisions and what their effect is likely to be.

We may dismiss at once the idea that the articles in question were included so that the Charter could be used to force the individual to do his duties, as well as to enable him to protect his rights. In other words, there seems no prospect of claims being brought against individuals on the basis of these provisions. As we shall see shortly, the institutional arrangements of the Charter are completely unsuitable for this purpose, and in any case a human rights treaty is not a criminal code.

What then is their purpose? The duties set out in Article 29 are collectively referred to in Article 10 as 'the obligation of solidarity' and this, perhaps, is a clue to the answer. The Charter includes a section on duties for the same reason as it includes a group of articles on economic and social rights and peoples' rights. It includes these articles because the States concerned wished to put forward a distinctive conception of human rights in which civil and political rights were seen to be counter-balanced by duties of social solidarity, just as they are complemented by economic and social rights and supplemented by peoples' rights. There is, it may be recalled, one other text which adopts the same approach, the American Declaration on the Rights and Duties of Man of 1948, which lists ten duties of the individual, though in rather different terms from those of the African Charter. When the American Convention was drawn up almost all the references to duties were omitted. The African States, on the other hand, needing a treaty which would perform the functions of both the Declaration and the Convention, included references to duties, economic and social rights and peoples' rights so that one document would contain the complete picture.

Although the articles on duties are unlikely to be enforced against individuals, they will have an effect. Indeed, if, as we have suggested and their content confirms, they reflect a distinctive attitude towards human rights in Africa, their effect is likely to be substantial. This, it is suggested, will be seen when the Commission begins to consider the scope of the rights protected. For the fact that the Charter contains such a categorical statement of the duties of the individual seems bound to colour the interpretation of its other provisions. Suppose, for example, someone objects to military service on religious or moral grounds and argues that Article 8, which guarantees freedom of conscience, requires that he should be recognised as a conscientious objector. Article 29(5) requires the individual to contribute to the defence of his country and must inevitably have an important bearing on his claim. Similarly, if a doctor is required to work in an unpopular part of the country and argues that this constitutes 'exploitation' contrary to Article 4, or an interference with his right to freedom of movement under Article 12, the contrary argument is very likely to rest on his duty to serve the national community 'by placing his physical and intellectual abilities at its service' according to Article 29(2).

The point is not that these cases would necessarily be decided against the individual. For there is no reason in principle why duties should be regarded as any more absolute than rights. It is rather that, in a treaty which places so much weight on duties, provisions dealing with rights cannot be interpreted as if they stood alone. It is worth noting here that the other regional conventions recognise the issue of social solidarity but deal with it by using a different drafting technique. First, they define the rights which they protect in some detail, then they employ both general and specific provisions to restrict their scope by reference to the interests of others. This largely avoids the need to refer in the text to the individual's duties, or the claims of community and society.[24] The African Charter, with its briefer treatment of rights and limitations, perhaps needs the concept of duties to make up for earlier omissions. It remains to be seen whether the distinctive approach of the African Charter is just a matter of technique – a different path leading to the same destination – or whether, as seems more likely, an emphasis on the individual's duties will lead to a narrower conception of his rights.

3. *The system of international control*

Implementation of the Charter is entrusted to a Commission of eleven members appointed by the Conference of Heads of State of the OAU.[25] They sit in a personal and independent capacity and, in conformity with the general practice, no two members of the Commission may be nationals of the same State.

The functions of the Commission fall into two parts. In accordance with the thinking which provided much of the inspiration for the Charter, the Commission has important promotional functions. However, it is not, as once seemed likely, only a promotional body. For the Commission also has the task of ensuring that the rights laid down by the Charter are protected, and for this purpose is equipped with powers comparable, though not identical, to those of the European and American Commissions.

The promotional role of the Commission is set out in Article 45(1) of the Charter, which requires it to collect documents, undertake studies and research on African problems in the field of human and peoples' rights, organise seminars, symposia and conferences, disseminate information, encourage national and local institutions concerned with human rights, and, where necessary, give its views or make recommendations to governments. As part of the same process the Commission is 'to formulate and lay down rules aimed at solving legal problems relating to human and peoples' rights', so as to provide a basis for national legislation. It is also to co-operate with other African and international institutions on human rights issues.

Turning now to the functions of the Commission in protecting human rights, we find that under Article 48 if one State claims that another is violating its obligations under the Charter, either may refer the matter to the Commission for investigation. The Charter makes it clear, however, that the primary objective in such situations is to secure a friendly settlement. Not only is this the first aim of the Commission when a case is referred to it, but under Article 47 a State with a complaint is encouraged to approach the other party directly, with a view to settling the matter without involving the Commission at all.[26] Arrangements for friendly settlement are, it will be recalled, a feature of both the European and American Conventions, but Article 47, which reflects the African States' preference for informal methods of dispute settlement, is unique to the African Charter.

A matter which is referred to the Commission can only be dealt with if all local remedies have been exhausted, unless it is obvious that this process would be unduly prolonged. For issues within its competence the Commission has wide powers of investigation. It can ask the States concerned to provide it with information and they are entitled to appear before it and submit oral or written representations. Article 52 provides that when the Commission has obtained from the States concerned 'and from other sources' all the information it deems necessary, and has attempted to reach an amicable solution, it must prepare a report containing the facts and its findings. The report is sent to the States concerned and to the Heads of State and Government, to whom the Commission may also make 'such recommendations as it deems useful'.[27] In addition to its reports on individual cases, the Commission, as might be expected, is required to submit a general report on its activities to each ordinary session of the Assembly of Heads of State and Government.

In our discussion of the machinery of the European Convention in Chapter 4 the point was made that permitting States to complain of human rights violations is a useful step, but that for a system of international protection to be fully effective, individuals as well as governments must be able to initiate proceedings. The African Charter, like the European and American Conventions, contains arrangements of this kind, but the provisions concerned, though not insignificant, fall short of the ideal in several respects.

Article 55 provides for the Secretary of the Commission to prepare 'a list of the communications other than those of States' and to transmit it to the Commission which decides by a simple majority if a communication is to be considered. The significant points about this provision are, first, that there seems to be no restriction as to who may file a communication. There is therefore nothing corresponding to the requirement in Article 25 of the European Convention that the applicant must claim to be the 'victim' of a violation. A second point of interest is that the powers of the Commission under Article 55 are mandatory. It will be recalled that acceptance of the right of individual petition under the European Convention is optional. In contrast, the African Commission's competence to deal with individual or other non-State communications is accepted automatically, as soon as a State ratifies the African Charter.

Before a communication can be investigated it must satisfy certain conditions of admissibility which are laid down in Article 56. In most respects these follow the usual pattern: a communication must not be anonymous or insulting, local remedies must have been exhausted, if available, and the communication must not be out of time. An unusual condition is that communications must not be 'based exclusively on news disseminated through the mass media'.[28] This is clearly designed to limit the opportunities for an *actio popularis* suggested by Article 55, a restriction which, if other evidence is hard to find, may be regrettable. On the other hand, the treatment of the problem of the applicant who tries to use several procedures simultaneously is unusually generous, as the Charter only prevents the Commission from considering cases which have actually been settled by the use of another procedure.

Prior to the Commission's consideration of a communication on the merits, it must be brought to the attention of the State concerned (Article 57). Then, if it appears to the Commission 'that one or more communications apparently relate to special cases which reveal the existence of a series of serious or massive violations of human and peoples' rights', the Commission must draw the matter to the attention of the Heads of State and Government. The Assembly may then request the Commission to undertake 'an in-depth study of these cases and make a factual report accompanied by its findings and recommendations' (Article 58(2)). In addition, under Article 58(3) the Chairman of the Assembly is authorised to request an in-depth study in all cases of emergency.

What, then, is the function of the Commission in relation to communications which are not special cases? Here, unfortunately, the Charter is vague and two views of its meaning are possible. One view is that the Commission has no function at all in such cases. In other words, its only job is to identify 'special cases' and refer them to the Assembly in the hope that they will be passed back for further investigation. Any case which does not fall into this category would thus be rather like a case which is declared inadmissible: the Commission would scan it but proceed no further. The other view is that for cases outside the special category the Commission has the same functions as under the inter-State procedure. In other words, it must conduct an investigation, attempt conciliation, and report its conclusions to the Assembly. It need hardly be pointed out that if the first view is correct the Commission's role in relation to individual communications will be insignificant by comparison with its European and American counterparts. As a body without independent authority, the Commission would scarcely be in a position to 'ensure the protection of human and peoples' rights' as Article 45 requires it to do. For these reasons, and because, as we have seen, individual rights are best protected by procedures which the individual can activate, it is a matter for satisfaction that when it met in 1988 to establish a procedure for receiving and considering communications, the Commission decided to interpret its powers in the wider way.[29]

As well as having the power to deal with communications from States and individuals, the Commission is authorised to issue what are in effect advisory opinions. For Article 45(3) permits it to 'interpret all the provisions of the present Charter at the request of a State party, an institution of the OAU or an African Organisation recognised by the OAU.' This power, which bears an obvious resemblance to that provided for in Article 65 of the American Convention, could be very important in practice. Straddling, as it does, the boundary between the Commission's promotional functions and its work in protecting human rights, Article 45(3) creates a possibility for cases to be referred to the Commission without the political problems which complicate and can sometimes inhibit inter-State complaints. As we saw in Chapter 5, the advisory jurisprudence of the Inter-American Court is making a major contribution to the elucidation of obligations under the American Convention, and there is no reason to suppose that the African Charter could not see a similar development.

Enough has been said to indicate that, despite certain limitations, the African Charter on Human and Peoples' Rights is a very significant step in international human rights law. Not only does the Charter itself contain many innovative provisions, but when the system as a whole comes into full operation it will be the largest regional human rights system in terms of the number of States concerned, as well as the only functioning arrangement in the Afro-Asian world. The first election of members of the African Commission took place in August 1987 and the first meeting in November, when the Commission elected its President and Vice-President. As already noted, at subsequent sessions the following year the Commission began its work on a positive note, though there is, as yet, no indication of what the members of the OAU will want, or will allow, it to do. The African Charter on Human and Peoples' Rights is nevertheless already a milestone in a continent where under-development and undemocratic government are endemic, and progress on human rights an urgent and a pressing need.[30]

III. Regionalism and universalism

The existence of three regional systems for the protection of human rights – the European, the American, and the African – and the possibility of a fourth regional system in the Arab world, lead inevitably to the question whether regional arrangements are compatible with the universal system of the United Nations, or whether they are likely to diminish the value of the human rights work of the UN and perhaps even undermine its effectiveness.

The issue has been much discussed. An early instance was the lively debate at the second International Colloquy on the European Convention, organised by the University of Vienna and the Council of Europe in 1965. The report on this subject presented by M. Jean-Flavien Lalive of Geneva argued in favour of the establishment of regional arrangements and regional Commissions, while the statement made by Mr Egon Schwelb, in the light of his long experience of the work of the United Nations Commission, took the contrary view.[31]

There is naturally a good deal to be said on both sides of the question. On the one hand, experience has shown that in Europe it was possible to conclude a Convention containing binding obligations and setting up new international machinery at a time when this was not possible in the world at large. Though the UN Covenants have now been widely ratified, the number of States which have accepted their optional provisions is still limited, so that for the foreseeable future the European system is likely to provide far more effective guarantees than the universal system. If a regional system can be justified in this way in one part of the world, logic requires the same view as regards regional systems elsewhere.

On the other hand, it can be argued that human rights belong to human beings by virtue of their humanity and should be guaranteed to everyone on a basis of equality and without distinction, wherever they may live. Discrimination on grounds of race, sex, religion, or nationality is forbidden both in the United Nations texts and in the regional Conventions. Equally, it might be said, there should be no distinction based on regionalism. The Arab and the Asian should have the same human rights as the European or the American.

This last principle is incontrovertible. How then are we to reconcile the two points of view?

A possible answer is as follows. Human rights should indeed be the same for all persons, everywhere, at all times. In other words, the normative content of different international instruments should in principle be the same. There may, of course, be variations in formulation, due to differences in drafting or legal traditions, but the basic rights and fundamental freedoms should be the same for all. Here the touchstone is the Universal Declaration, which sets out, as the Preamble puts it, 'a common standard of achievement for all peoples and all nations'. Hence, no regional system can be regarded as acceptable unless it is consistent with the norms and principles set out in the Universal Declaration.

When we come to measures of implementation, however, the position is different. While it is desirable that the most effective system possible should be established everywhere, it is a fact that the same system is not at present acceptable in all parts of the world. Even inside Europe this is the case, because not all members of the Council of Europe have accepted the optional provisions of the European Convention. If this is the case inside one regional organisation, how much more is it true of different regions of the world, two of which – Eastern Europe and Asia – have so far shown no signs of willingness to accept any form of international control at all.

It is therefore reasonable, on practical grounds, to set up regional arrangements for the protection of human rights which may differ from each other, provided that the rights to be protected are essentially the same and are substantially those established in the Universal Declaration. We saw in Chapter 4 that this is the approach adopted by the European Convention, in which the contracting parties expressed their determination '... to take the first steps for the collective enforcement of certain of the rights stated in the Universal Declaration'. Other regional systems are therefore equally legitimate if they also set up procedures which can be accepted by a group of States in a particular area, as a way of enforcing some or all of the rights proclaimed in the Universal Declaration.

This reasoning is supported by two other arguments. First, given the diversity of the modern State system, it is natural that regional systems of enforcement should be more readily accepted than universal arrangements. A State cannot be forced to submit itself to a system of international control and will do so only if it has confidence in it. It is much more likely to have such confidence if the international machinery has been set up by a group of like-minded countries, which are already its partners in a regional organisation, than if this is not the case. Moreover, it will be willing to give greater powers to a regional organ of restricted membership, in which the other members are its friends and neighbours, than to a world-wide organ in which it and its associates play a relatively smaller part.

The second supporting argument is the purely practical one of distance. To take Europe as an example, it is obviously easier and more convenient for all concerned when a complaint by one State against another, and *a fortiori* an individual application against a State, can be heard in Strasbourg rather than New York.[32] The same obviously applies to other regions of the world, in so far as their regional commissions have competence to consider inter-State complaints or individual applications.

A third point to be borne in mind is that the principle of regional settlement is perfectly consistent with the Charter of the United Nations. Articles 33 and 52 of the Charter expressly recognise the principle of regional settlement of disputes threatening international peace and security. The same principle can properly be extended to disputes about the violation of human rights. Indeed, this is explicitly recognised in Article 44 of the Covenant on Civil and Political Rights.

In principle, then, regional systems for the promotion and protection of human rights are not inconsistent with the world-wide system of the United Nations, provided that they constitute local arrangements to secure greater respect for the norms established by the United Nations in the Universal Declaration. However, it would be wrong to leave this topic without recalling that reconciling regional with universal schemes for human rights protection presents practical, as well as theoretical, problems.[33] The more regional systems are developed the more applicants will be in a position to try to pursue their claims at the universal and regional levels simultaneously. Whether this is possible and, if so, the conditions under which it may be done, will therefore become increasingly important issues. As we saw in Chapter 4, cases of this kind now crop up quite regularly and the organs concerned are in process of working out ways of dealing with them. But the issues here are difficult and will continue to demand attention as human rights systems are developed.

A different sort of problem arises from the application of the various human rights conventions. Here, the need is to find a way of ensuring that the guarantees which form the substance of human rights law are applied in different places in a broadly uniform way. The reason for this was put forward earlier. In principle human rights should be the same for all, and this is clearly a matter not just of texts, but also of interpretation. Notice, however, that the stipulation is for rights to be interpreted in a broadly uniform way, not identically. Since the texts themselves are often different, some differences in interpretation are inevitable. More significantly, since there is not in fact a uniform world culture, we have to recognise that differences in the way that rights are interpreted are a legitimate result of cultural diversity.[34] Which rights should be regarded as basic and immutable and which secondary and open to different interpretations is, of course, a matter for debate.

The fact that human rights are not viewed identically in different parts of the world is reflected in the language of the various instruments, as we have seen. This leads to our final point about the relation between the various systems, which is that the practical problems which stem from having two levels of protection would be significantly eased if there was more similarity between the different human rights treaties. Certainly the effect of cultural diversity must again be taken into account, and no one should underestimate the difficulty of securing even relatively minor additions to treaty obligations. If the will is there, however, the harmonisation of human rights provisions is by no means a fantasy, as the conclusion of recent protocols to the European Convention demonstrates. While some differences between human rights treaties will no doubt always exist, the goal of ensuring that regional and universal arrangements reflect a common standard makes efforts to bring them closer together well worth pursuing.

Notes

1 Further information on the history and structure of the Arab League was given in the first edition of this book at pp. 140–3. See also B. Boutros-Ghali, 'The Arab League (1945–1970)', *Revue Egyptienne de Droit International*, XXV, 1969, p. 67.

2 General Assembly Resolution 477 (V) of 1 November 1950.

3 ECOSOC Resolution 1159 (XLI) of 5 August 1966.

4 General Assembly Resolution 2081 (XX) of 20 December 1965.

5 Arab League Council Resolution 2304 (XLVII) of 18 March 1967.
6 Recommendation 6 (XXIII) of 23 March 1967.
7 See Arab League Council Resolution 2443 of 3 September 1968. The creation of the Commission and the decisions of the conference were reported to the UN Commission on Human Rights at its twenty-fifth session (doc. E/CN. 4/L1042 of 18 February 1969). For further discussion, see S. P. Marks, 'La Commission Permanente Arabe des Droits de l'Homme', *Human Rights Review*, III, 1970, p. 101.
8 See Council of Europe, *Human Rights Information Sheet*, No. 21. Strasbourg, 1988, p. 122. The text of the Draft Charter will be found *ibid.*, p. 243.
9 See J. G. Merrills, *International Dispute Settlement*, London, 1984, Chapter 6 and also T. O. Elias, 'The Commission of Mediation, Conciliation and Arbitration of the Organisation of African Unity', *British Year Book of International Law*, XL, 1964, p. 336 and H. A. Amankwah, 'International law, dispute settlement and regional organisations in an African setting', *Indian Journal of International Law*, XXI, 1981, p. 352. On the OAU in general, see T. O. Elias, 'The Charter of the Organisation of African Unity', *American Journal of International Law*, LIX, 1965, p. 243.
10 Document E/CN 4/L 940, draft Recommendation II, *Report of the Twenty-third Session* (E/4322) pp. 109–25.
11 The States concerned were the Congo, Dahomey, Nigeria, Senegal, and Tanzania.
12 Document E/CN. 4/966 and addendum (*Report of the UN ad hoc Study Group established under Resolution 6 (XXIII) of the Commission on Human Rights*).
13 The official report of the session is contained in UN doc. ST/TAO/HR/38, 1969. Part of this account was published in *Human Rights Law Journal*, II, 1969, pp. 696–702. A further account of the Cairo seminar was given in the first edition of this book at pp. 151–7.
14 Report in UN doc. ST/TAO/HR/48.
15 OAU doc. AHG/115 (XVI).
16 UN *Bulletin of Human Rights*, No. 25, (July–September 1979), pp. 23–5.
17 As of 1 January 1988. See J. –B. Marie, 'International instruments relating to human rights', *Human Rights Law Journal*, IX, 1988, p. 113. The text of the African Charter may be found in *International Legal Materials*, XXI, 1982, p. 58 and *Human Rights Law Journal*, VII, 1986, p. 403. For discussion of the Charter, see R. Gittleman, 'The African Charter on Human and Peoples' Rights: a legal analysis', *Virginia Journal of International Law*, XXII, 1981–82, p. 667; and U.O. Umozurike, 'The African Charter on Human and Peoples' Rights', *American Journal of International Law*, LXXVII, 1983, p. 902.
18 See, for example, B. O. Okere, 'The protection of human rights in Africa and the African Charter on Human and Peoples' Rights: A comparative analysis with the European and American systems', *Human Rights Quarterly*, VI, 1984, p. 141.
19 Also relevant in this connection is Article 61, which provides: 'The Commission shall also take into consideration, as subsidiary measures to determine the principles of law, other general or special international conventions, laying down rules expressly recognized by member states of the Organization of African Unity, African practices consistent with international norms on human and peoples' rights, customs generally accepted as law, general principles of law recognized by African states as well as legal precedents and doctrine.'

20 Thus, in the *Sunday Times case* the European Court held that the expression 'prescribed by law' in Article 10(2) of the European Convention must be interpreted as involving at least two requirements: 'Firstly the law must be adequately accessible: the citizen must be able to have an indication that is adequate in the circumstances of the legal rules applicable to a given case. Secondly, a norm cannot be regarded as a 'law' unless it is formulated with sufficient precision to enable the citizen to regulate his conduct: he must be able – if need be with appropriate advice – to foresee to a degree that is reasonable in the circumstances, the consequences which a given action may entail' (Series A, No. 30, para. 49). See further J. G. Merrills, *The Development of International Law by the European Court of Human Rights*, Melland Schill Monographs in International Law, Manchester University Press, 1988, pp. 117–20.

21 See the *Rees case*. Series A. No. 106, para. 50.

22 It will be recalled, however, that Article 26 of the American Convention contains a general undertaking to take measures to secure the rights generated by the economic, social and cultural standards set out in the OAS Charter.

23 For an interesting discussion of this question in the context of the African Charter, see S. C. Neff, 'Human rights in Africa: Thoughts on the African Charter on Human and Peoples' Rights in the light of case-law from Botswana, Lesotho and Swaziland', *International and Comparative Law Quarterly*, XXXIII, 1984, p. 331.

24 See P. Sieghart, *The International Law of Human Rights*, Oxford, 1983, p. 42.

25 For discussion of the Commission, see R. Gittleman, 'The African Commission on Human and Peoples' Rights', in H. Hannum (ed.) *Guide to International Human Rights Practice*, London, 1984, pp. 153–62.

26 It should be noted, however, that Under Article 49 a State which considers that another State has violated the Charter is entitled to refer the matter directly to the Commission by addressing a communication to the Chairman, to the Secretary-General of the OAU, and to the State concerned.

27 Article 53.

28 The UN Commission on Human Rights has a similar requirement when considering communications under the Resolution 1503 procedure (see Chapter 3), as does UNESCO when utilising the procedure for considering human rights complaints described in Chapter 7. See further Sieghart, *Human Rights*, pp. 426 and 435.

29 See *Rules of Procedure of the African Commission on Human and Peoples' Rights*, adopted on 13 Febuary 1988, Rules 101 to 118. Text in *Human Rights Law Journal*, IX, 1988, p. 333. On the other activities of the Commission in its first three sessions see the Commission's *Report* of 27 April 1988, *ibid*., p. 326.

30 For further discussion of human rights in Africa, with particular reference to the political context, see M. Haile, 'Human rights, stability and development in Africa', *Virginia Journal of International Law* XXIV, 1983–84, p. 575.

31 See A. H. Robertson (ed.) *Human Rights in National and International Law*, Manchester University Press, 1967, pp. 330–42 and 355–6.

32 In the case brought by the governments of Denmark, Norway, Sweden and the Netherlands against Greece in 1967, for example, the European Commission of Human Rights heard more than eighty witnesses and also visited the country concerned.

33 For discussion of this problem and related aspects of the same issue, see T. Meron, 'Norm Making and supervision in international human rights: reflections on institutional order', *American Journal of International Law*, LXVI, 1982, p. 754.

34 For illustration of this point in the context of the African Charter, see Neff, 'Human rights in Africa'.

CHAPTER 7

Economic, social and cultural rights

I. The International Covenant on Economic, Social and Cultural Rights

In 1950 the General Assembly of the United Nations decided that economic, social and cultural rights should be included in the single international Covenant which was then projected. Two years later, however, it changed its mind and decided that there should be separate Covenants dealing with the two categories of rights, but that they should be prepared simultaneously and contain as many similar provisions as possible. The Commission on Human Rights followed these instructions, with the result that the General Assembly was able to approve the International Covenant on Economic, Social and Cultural Rights on 16 December 1966, at the same time as the Covenant on Civil and Political Rights.[1]

1. The rights guaranteed

In the event, the wish that the two Covenants should contain as many similar provisions as possible could not be realised to any significant extent. Of course the rights protected are different, with the exception of the right of all peoples to self-determination, which forms Article 1 of both Covenants. In addition, however, the obligations assumed by the States parties and the two systems of international control are also very different in character, as we shall see.

Articles 2–5 of both Covenants set out the general provisions on the obligations of the States parties. But whereas the obligation assumed by contracting parties in the Covenant on Civil and Political Rights is intended to be of immediate application, the general obligation assumed by contracting parties in the Covenant on Economic, Social and Cultural Rights is not, and in this way reflects the nature of the rights secured. Paragraph 1 of Article 2 reads as follows:

> Each State Party to the present Covenant undertakes to take steps, individually and through international assistance and co-operation, especially economic and technical, to the maximum of its available resources, with a view to achieving progressively the full realization of the rights recognized in the present Covenant by all appropriate means, including particularly the adoption of legislative measures.

It is thus quite clear that this is what is known as a promotional convention, that is to say it does not set out rights which the parties are required to implement immediately, but rather lists standards which they undertake to promote and which they pledge themselves to secure progressively, to the greatest extent possible, having regard to their resources. As already indicated, this difference in the obligation results from the very nature of the rights recognised in this Covenant.

Of the remaining general provisions in the Covenant on Economic, Social and Cultural Rights, the non-discrimination clause (Article 2(2)) is similar to that in the other Covenant, as are also the proclamation of the equal rights of men and women (Article 3) and the provisions in Article 5 designed to prevent abuse of the rights secured, together with a general saving clause. Article 4 relates to limitations on the rights protected. Limitations are permissible only 'as determined by law ... and solely for the purpose of promoting the general welfare in a democratic society'. However, there is no provision for derogations in a state of emergency, as in the other Covenant. Finally, paragraph 3 of Article 2 contains the following unusual provision, designed to protect developing countries from economic exploitation by their more powerful neighbours: 'Developing countries, with due regard to human rights and their national economy, may determine to what extent they would guarantee the economic rights recognized in the present Covenant to non-nationals.' Plainly this paragraph reintroduces the principle of discrimination since it explicitly permits developing countries to discriminate against foreigners with regard to the enjoyment of certain economic rights. It was perhaps included to make the point that the Covenant cannot be used to protect foreign investments in developing countries. However, neither Covenant protects the right of property, and so this provision has little relevance to that problem.

When we come to the particular rights protected in the Covenant on Economic, Social and Cultural Rights, we find a longer list and more detailed definitions than those contained in the Universal Declaration. The latter included only six articles relating to these rights in 1948; by the time the Covenants were concluded in 1966 the number had increased to ten. This illustrates the tendency in the United Nations over the last forty years to pay increasing attention to economic and social rights. This tendency, which is due largely to the admission of so many developing countries as new members, has been accompanied by a corresponding reduction in emphasis on those rights of a civil and political character. It is perhaps indicative that in the General Assembly resolution approving the new Covenants the Covenant on Economic, Social and Cultural Rights was placed before the Covenant on Civil and Political Rights.

The economic, social and cultural rights protected by the Covenant are the following:

Article 6 The right to work.

7 The right to just and favourable conditions of work, including fair wages, equal pay for equal work and holidays with pay.

8 The right to form and join trade unions, including the right to strike.

9 The right to social security.

10 Protection of the family, including special assistance for mothers and children.

11 The right to an adequate standard of living, including adequate food, clothing and housing and the continuous improvement of living conditions.

12 The right to the highest attainable standard of physical and mental health.

13 The right to education, primary education being compulsory and free for all, and secondary and higher education generally accessible to all. (Article 14 permits the progressive implementation of this right.)

15 The right to participate in cultural life and enjoy the benefits of scientific progress.

There is a substantial amount of common ground between this list and that contained in the 1961 European Social Charter. As we shall see later, the Charter proclaims nineteen economic and social rights, but often formulates as two or three separate rights provisions which are grouped together in one article of the Covenant.

There is a major difference which is evident in the formulation of the economic, social and cultural rights as compared with the civil and political rights. The latter are stated in the classic form 'Everyone has the right to ...' or 'No one shall be subject to ...'. In the Economic and Social Covenant, on the other hand, the normative articles adopt a different formulation, usually 'The States Parties to the present Covenant recognise the right ...' [2] or 'The States Parties to the present Covenant undertake to ensure ...'[3] In other words, we find an undertaking or a recognition by States rather than the affirmation of a right inherent in the individual as such. When it is recalled that the undertaking of the contracting parties in Article 2 of the Covenant is '... to take steps ... with a view to achieving progressively the full realisation of the rights recognised in the present Covenant ...', the promotional character of the instrument is unmistakable.

2. *The system of international control*

For the implementation of the Covenant on Economic, Social and Cultural Rights, Articles 16–25 provide for a system of periodic reports by States detailing the measures adopted and the progress made in achieving the observance of the rights concerned. These reports are to be considered by the Economic and Social Council and furnished in accordance with a programme established by ECOSOC (Article 17). The Secretary-General is to send copies of all reports to ECOSOC (Article 16), which may make arrangements with the Specialised Agencies to obtain reports on the progress made in achieving the observance of those provisions of the Covenant falling within the scope of their activities (Article 18). ECOSOC may transmit the reports of States to the Commission on Human Rights for study and general recommendation (Article 19); and the States may then submit to the Council their comments on such general recommendations (Article 20). Finally, the Council may submit a summary of the information it has received, together with its reports and recommendations of a general nature, to the General Assembly (Article 21) and at the same time draw appropriate matters to the attention of other organs of the United Nations and the Specialised Agencies concerned (Article 22).[4]

It is therefore clear that the Economic and Social Council is the keystone in the system of implementation of this Covenant. This is really no surprise, given that the object is the implementation of economic and social rights. Nevertheless, two comments must be made. The principle that the organ responsible for supervision should be independent, which is respected in the other Covenant, is jettisoned here, since ECOSOC consists of representatives of governments and not individuals acting in a personal capacity. The other point is that the tasks conferred on ECOSOC by Articles 16–22 of the Covenant are very extensive, and the amount of paperwork involved in obtaining, receiving and analysing reports from more than ninety governments, consulting the Commission on Human Rights and appropriate Specialised Agencies, making and transmitting general recommendations to governments and obtaining their comments, and finally reporting on all this to the General Assembly, is formidable. In view of the length and complexity of the agenda of ECOSOC, and the difficulty which the Council experiences in coping with its numerous other tasks, it must be doubtful whether as a practical matter, it was the most appropriate choice to serve as the organ of implementation of the Covenant.

How its supervisory functions were to be reconciled with its other work was a question which ECOSOC considered as soon as the Covenant came into force in 1976. The solution adopted was to establish a Sessional Working Group to assist it in its new task. At the same time it established a programme for the periodic reports, requiring their presentation in biennial stages.

The Sessional Working Group, which was formally set up in 1978, consited of fifteen members of the Council which were also States parties to the Covenant. It will be noted that the members of the group were States, which delegated their representatives, and not individual experts. The principle of equitable geographical distribution was secured by having three members from each of the five regional groups: African, Asian, East European, Latin American, and Western and other States. Various others were invited as observers, including other parties to the Covenant and representatives of the relevant Specialised Agencies when matters within their competence were discussed.

From 1979 to 1986 the Sessional Working Group met annually for three weeks during the first regular session of ECOSOC. It was not a success. Not only were the sessions too short for it to give proper consideration to the reports which States submitted, but the composition of the group meant that much of the time available was wasted in wrangling over the scope of its supervisory role. Here, as so often, the root of the problem was that while many governments wished to see an effective system of supervision, a minority, including the Soviet Union and East Europeans, did not. With some members determined to prevent any questioning of parties' performance of their obligations, and a bitter controversy over the role of the Specialised Agencies, the Working Group's reports were merely a description of its activity without conclusions or recommendations.[5]

In 1985 ECOSOC, recognising the inadequacy of the Working Group procedure, decided to make a fresh start. To assist it in supervising the Covenant it set up a new committee, consisting of eighteen experts elected in their personal capacities and on the basis of equitable geographical distribution. The new body, which is known as the United Nations Committee on Economic, Social and Cultural Rights, held its first session in March 1987.[6]

As one would expect, a large part of the work of the Committee to date has been taken up with organisational matters, especially the vexed question of procedures on which its predecessor had foundered. Although the Committee consists of independent experts, many of the disagreements which blighted the Working Group still persist. Thus, the Committee has given consideration to proposals to provide States with more detailed guidelines for their reports. These would place reports on a more uniform basis, and make them more informative and easier to use. Suggestions for such changes were, however, initially opposed by the Soviet, Polish, and Bulgarian members of the Committee. Similarly, the issue of information from sources other than governments remains a controversial one, although here, despite a minority attempt to commend the restrictive practice of the Working Group, some progress has been made as regards the position of the Specialised Agencies and that of non-governmental organisations. On the same matter, to assist its examination of reports, the Committee has decided to follow the practice of the Committee on the Elimination of Discrimination against Women by requesting the Secretariat to provide it with a compilation from UN sources of statistical information relevant to the reports of States.

As well as defining and developing its methods of work, the Committee has made a start on its main substantive task, consideration of the reports of States as to how they are discharging their obligations under the Covenant. At its first session, in addition to the matters already described, it was able to consider a total of eleven reports from eight States parties. However, the time available was short and a number of States which were anxious to present reports were unable to do so. Those which were considered often left much to be desired in terms of substance and presentation. As a member of the Committee has recorded, 'One extreme consisted of excessively short and uninformative reports, the other of very lengthy ones containing all too little meaningful data'.[7] Most of the reports are presented by experts and the members of the Committee are able to put questions. In its report to ECOSOC the Committee's consideration of these reports was summarised and various recommendations of a general character were made.

It will be apparent that the arrangements for supervising the Covenant on Economic, Social and Cultural Rights, as they stand at present,[8] fall short of the conditions which were indicated in Chapter 2 as essential for an effective reporting system. It is true that States' reports are now examined by independent persons who are not government officials. On the other hand, the time available for this review, limited as it is to a single annual session of three weeks, is still too short to allow the job to be done properly. On the question of information from sources other than governments, things are improving, but there is a long way to go before the Committee can be assured of having at its disposal a regular and reliable way of testing the accuracy of governments' assertions. As for the co-operation of governments, again the record is mixed. If experience elsewhere is a reliable indicator, matters here will almost certainly improve if and when the Committee is able to develop improved reporting guidelines, but ultimately the adequacy of States' reports must always rest on their good will.

The final requirement, it will be recalled, is the right to make recommendations for improvements in the law and practice of individual States. Here, as also on the issue of independence, it is important to remember that the Committee on Economic, Social and Cultural Rights is not an autonomous body like the Human Rights Committee, but a subsidiary organ, set up by ECOSOC to assist it in carrying out its tasks under the Covenant. ECOSOC, however, has no right to address itself to governments which have defaulted on their obligations, since it can only make 'recommendations of a general nature' to the General Assembly. Whilst one may therefore be able to envisage a time in the future when the Economic and Social Committee may be prepared to make recommendations relating to specific parties, these, like the Committee's other recommendations, must then be passed on to the political organ. This would not make them meaningless, of course, but demonstrates the point made at the beginning: that the Covenant on Civil and Political Rights and the Covenant on Economic, Social and Cultural Rights have very different systems of implementation.

II. Economic and social rights: the ILO

The International Labour Organisation was established by the Treaty of Versailles in 1919. Its constitution, which forms Part XIII of the treaty, does not refer to human rights as such, but confers important functions on the Organisation in the field of what we now call economic and social rights. So, for example, such matters as the regulation of the hours of work, the prevention of unemployment, the provision of adequate wages, social security, equal pay for equal work, and freedom of association all come within its scope.[9]

The Declaration of Philadelphia of 1944, which was incorporated in the Constitution of the ILO two years later, made more specific references to freedom of expression and association and continued: 'All human beings, irrespective of race, creed or sex, have the right to pursue both their material well-being and their spiritual development in conditions of freedom and dignity, of economic security and equal opportunity.' Here then we have a direct link with the conception of human rights as generally understood today.

In discharging the functions for which it was established, the ILO has been a pioneer in the international protection of economic and social rights and has an impressive record of achievement in this field. As with other international organisations, there are two principal aspects of this work: standard-setting and measures of implementation or international control. Although the two aspects are intimately and necessarily linked, it is convenient, at least initially, to consider them separately.

As regards standard-setting, the ILO employs two principal methods: the conclusion of international Conventions and the adoption of recommendations. The Conventions, of course, are binding only on the States which ratify them, but under Article 19 of the ILO Constitution the member States are required to submit Conventions to the competent authority (normally the legislature) with a view to their ratification within a period of twelve or eighteen months. This provision is designed to avoid the situation which so often occurs elsewhere, when a text is approved in an international organisation but no action is taken at the national level. Recommendations of the ILO, on the other hand, do not create legal obligations for States. Their purpose is rather to set standards which are intended to provide guidance for governments in their national legislation or administrative practice.

In the seventy years of its existence the ILO has adopted more that 150 international Conventions, which constitutes an unparalleled body of 'international legislation'. The number of ratifications exceeds 5,000. Forty States have ratified more than forty Conventions and fifteen States more than sixty. The number of recommendations addressed to governments is even larger than the number of Conventions.

It is clearly impossible to list all the ILO Conventions here, but the following may be noted as among the most important from the point of view of human rights: the Convention on Freedom of Association and Protection of the Right to Organise (1948), the Convention on the Right to Organise and Collective Bargaining (1949), the Equal Remuneration Convention (1951), the Abolition of Forced Labour Convention (1957), and the Discrimination (Employment and Occupation) Convention (1958). Another instrument of particular importance is the Employment Policy Convention of 1964.[10] Other matters dealt with in ILO Conventions and Recommendations are social security, various aspects of the right to work (employment agencies, and vocational training, for example), conditions of work (minimum wages, reduction of hours of work, a weekly rest period, holidays with pay), the protection of migrants, children and young workers, and the rights of women as regards maternity leave, night work and other matters.

Of special interest from the standpoint of human rights is the system of international control operated by the ILO, for, as we shall see, this is considerably more effective than that provided in the United Nations Covenants.[11]

In the first place, there is the ILO reporting system. This system is not the product of a specific Convention, which would naturally apply only to States which had ratified that Convention. It is provided for in the ILO Constitution itself, and therefore automatically applies to all members of the Organisation. Under Articles 19 and 22 of the Constitution member States are required to report to the ILO on the measures they have taken to bring Conventions and Recommendations to the attention of the competent national authorities with a view to ratification or other suitable action. As regards Conventions which they have ratified, States report on their implementation. As regards Conventions which they have not ratified, they report on their intentions for giving them effect and any difficulties which impede ratification. About 3,000 reports a year are sent to the ILO in accordance with these provisions, which create a most effective form of supervision.

A particularly important stipulation is that governments must send copies of their reports to national organisations of employers and workers, who thus have the opportunity of commenting on them if they wish. Their observations must then be communicated by the governments to the ILO. It is clear, therefore, that one of the key features of an effective reporting system, the availability of critical information from other responsible sources, which is a weak point in the International Covenant on Economic, Social and Cultural Rights, is fully provided for in the procedures of the ILO.

Another important element is the examination of the governments' reports by an independent organ, made up of people who are not government officials. This is secured in the ILO system at two stages. First, there is the Committee of Experts on the Application of Conventions and Recommendations. This consists of eighteen members who are appointed, not by governments, but by the Governing Body of the ILO on the recommendation of the Director-General. They are persons who are experts in legal and social matters, such as judges and university professors, whose task is to examine in complete independence and objectivity whether the situation revealed in the national reports and the comments of the professional organisations, corresponds in all respects to the obligations which the State concerned has assumed. The Committee of Experts makes 'observations' on any situation which it regards as not in conformity with those obligations and these form part of its annual report to the International Labour Conference. The committee also makes 'requests' direct to governments, which permit the latter to explain or rectify certain discrepancies without the matter becoming public. Like the friendly settlement procedure under the European Convention on Human Rights, this discreet means of dealing with problems can be just as effective as more spectacular methods. Several hundred observations and requests are made each year.

The second stage of supervision takes place at the International Labour Conference, which each year appoints a Committee on the Application of Conventions and Recommendations. This body, being a committee of the conference, has the tripartite structure which is the distinctive feature of the ILO, and so consists of representatives of governments, employers and workers – over 100 members in all. It examines the reports of the Committee of Experts, particularly the observations about discrepancies between obligations and national practice, and asks the governments concerned for explanations. The presence of representatives of both sides of industry means that the discussions are well informed. They may, and often do, lead to vigorous criticism of governments whose record is defective. In due course the committee itself reports to the plenary conference.

This is therefore a system of international control which, with the scrutiny of independent experts and the participation of organisations with separate sources of information, is far more effective than if it were operated exclusively by governments. Research has demonstrated that over one fourteen-year period more than 1,000 improvements in national practice resulted from the use of these procedures, and in the sphere of freedom of association alone there were fifty-five cases in which discrepancies were eliminated.[12]

In addition to these reporting procedures, the ILO Constitution also provides for a complaints procedure, under which one State may bring a complaint against another if it considers that the latter is not complying with the obligations of a Convention by which both are bound.[13] In such a case the Governing Body of the ILO sets up a Commission of Enquiry to hear the evidence. The Commission, which consists of three members, follows a judicial procedure and can hear witnesses or make an on the spot investigation. This formal procedure has, however, rarely been used and the cases concerned have generally had political overtones. *Ghana* v. *Portugal*, for example, in 1961, concerned allegations of forced labour in the Portuguese colonies and *Portugal* v. *Liberia*, in the same year, raised similar issues. In 1968 complaints were made about freedom of association under the military regime in Greece and in 1974 about working conditions in Chile. In each case the Commission of Enquiry established the facts and made various recommendations which the governments concerned accepted.

One of the economic and social rights to which the ILO rightly attaches special importance is freedom of association, because this right is the basis of all trade union activities. Those who have followed events in Poland since 1980, and especially the treatment of the independent union 'Solidarity', will readily appreciate this point. Apart from the two Conventions on Freedom of Association (1948) and the Right to Organise and Collective Bargaining (1949), the ILO has set up special procedures to protect freedom of association which apply not only to the parties to those Conventions, but, by virtue of the Constitution, to all members of the Organisation. The procedures in question were established in 1950 and have been formally recognised by the Economic and Social Council of the United Nations.[14]

First, there is the Committee on Freedom of Association, which consists of nine members of the Governing Body, three from each group in the tripartite membership. A complaint may be referred to the committee either by a government or by one of the professional organisations. Naturally it is the workers' organisations which most frequently start proceedings. The examination of a complaint is normally conducted on the basis of documents alone, but an on the spot investigation is sometimes undertaken on the committee's behalf. Detailed reports containing proposed recommendations to the governments concerned are then submitted to the Governing Body, which has almost invariably approved them.

More than 1,000 cases have been handled by this procedure, relating to many aspects of freedom of association, including dissolution of trade unions, the arrest of union leaders, and interference by governments in trade union affairs. An assessment of the results indicates that in a number of cases governments have acted on the committee's recommendations, though regrettably this is not always so. However, a substantial body of case-law has been built up, the principle of accountability is being progressively developed, and other organs of the ILO can now be brought into play when appropriate.

The second organ concerned with freedom of association is the Fact-finding and Conciliation Commission, which consists of independent persons appointed by the Governing Body on the proposal of the Director-General. As its name implies, the Commission has the primary task of establishing the facts concerning a particular situation and attempting to achieve an amicable solution. But it can examine a problem only with the consent of the government concerned. As a result it has dealt with far fewer cases than the Committee on Freedom of Association, although in several cases it did important work, including those involving Japan (1964), Greece (1965), and Chile (1974).[15]

We are therefore justified in concluding that in the particular field of economic and social rights the International Labour Organisation has established a number of different methods, some based on reporting by governments, others on complaints procedures, which taken together constitute a highly developed system of international control over the performance of human rights obligations. This system, impressive and effective though it is, is unfortunately too little known outside a limited group of specialists. It is a pity that more account was not taken of the ILO system when the measures of implementation of the Covenant on Economic, Social and Cultural Rights were worked out. Quite possibly a number of governments were unwilling to see measures as effective as the ILO system included in the Covenant precisely because they would have involved a greater measure of international control. It would be appropriate, however, if ECOSOC, acting in accordance with Article 18 of the Covenant, could arrange to profit from the experience of the ILO and so render more effective the protection of the economic and social rights which it enshrines.

III. Cultural Rights: UNESCO

Several of the Specialised Agencies of the United Nations are concerned with the promotion, in a broad sense, of economic and social rights. For example, the Food and Agriculture Organisation (FAO) does important work in helping governments to improve and increase food supplies, so helping to combat undernourishment and starvation. These activities were carried on long before – and quite independently of – the adoption of the UN Covenants in 1966, but nevertheless are directly relevant to the obligations assumed by States in Article 11 of the Covenant on Economic, Social and Cultural Rights, which recognises the right of everyone to an adequate standard of living, including adequate food, clothing and housing, and the fundamental right of everyone to be free from hunger.

Similarly, the work of the World Health Organisation is directly relevant to the right of everyone to the enjoyment of the highest attainable standard of physical and mental health, recognised in Article 12 of the same Covenant. The World Bank is likewise concerned, though less directly, with the right of all peoples freely to pursue their economic development, which is recognised in Article 1 on the right of self-determination. However, the FAO, WHO, and the World Bank have not, and almost certainly could not, establish international systems for the protection of these rights, which is the subject matter of this book. It is therefore sufficient for our purpose to note in passing that their work is both relevant to, and designed to promote, the rights we have mentioned, without going into details of their respective programmes. This relevance is indeed recognised in Article 18 of the Covenant on Economic, Social and Cultural Rights, which, it will be recalled, provides that ECOSOC may make arrangements for the Specialised Agencies to report on progress in achieving implementation of those provisions of the Covenant falling within their scope.

Of more immediate interest is the work of UNESCO in the promotion and protection of cultural rights. Article 1 of the Constitution of UNESCO states that the purpose of the Organisation is:

> to contribute to peace and security by promoting collaboration among the nations through education, science and culture in order to further universal respect for justice, for the rule of law and for the human rights and fundamental freedoms which are affirmed for the peoples of the world, without distinction of race, sex, language or religion, by the Charter of the United Nations.

The promotion of human rights and fundamental freedoms is thus expressly affirmed as one of UNESCO's aims when undertaking activities in the fields of education, science and culture.

As in the case of FAO and WHO, these activities began and were developed for twenty years before the General Assembly approved the two Covenants; but the fact that the first Covenant is concerned with economic, social *and cultural* rights plainly demonstrates a field of common interest. Article 13 of this Covenant, it will be recalled, establishes the right of everyone to education, and continues by providing that primary education shall be compulsory and free for all, while secondary education, including technical and vocational training, and higher education shall be made generally accessible, through the progressive introduction of free education. Article 15, moreover, relates to the right to take part in cultural life and to enjoy the benefits of scientific progress and its applications. It is therefore evident that UNESCO should be able, in accordance with Article 18 of the Covenant, to make a significant contribution to the work of ECOSOC in supervising its implementation.

While the Covenants were still being negotiated, UNESCO produced the Convention against Discrimination in Education, adopted by the General Conference in December 1960.[16] This Convention, which is comparatively short and simple, contains undertakings to eliminate and prevent discrimination in education based on race, colour, sex, language, religion, and other grounds. It provides that primary education shall be free and compulsory and secondary and higher education generally available and accessible. These provisions correspond closely to Article 13 of the Covenant on Economic, Social and Cultural Rights, which already existed in draft form. The Convention itself does not provide for measures of implementation in the generally accepted sense, although there is a provision for information to be communicated to UNESCO in periodic reports and for disputes about its interpretation or application to be referred to the International Court of Justice. To supervise the reporting procedure a Special Committee to examine the Reports of Member States, consisting of twelve members, was established in 1965.

Two years after the conclusion of the Convention, a Protocol was approved and opened for signature in December 1962. This provides for a Conciliation and Good Offices Commission, to which any State party can refer a dispute if it considers that another

State party is not respecting its obligations. The Commission, which consists of eleven members serving in their personal capacity, has the task of ascertaining the facts, offering its good offices, and seeking a friendly settlement of the matter. It may make recommendations, although it has no judicial function. The Commission has been set up, but has not yet been called on to deal with a dispute.

UNESCO, like the United Nations though on a smaller scale, receives complaints about the violation of human rights in the educational and cultural fields. Initially, again like the United Nations, it considered that it had no competence to deal with such communications. However, as UN practice changed, and after the Optional Protocol had been approved by the General Assembly in 1966, UNESCO's policy changed too. In April 1978, after various preliminary decisions of the Executive Board and consideration of a detailed study by the UNESCO Secretariat, the Executive Board took a decision on the procedures which should be followed in the examination of cases and questions which might be submitted to UNESCO concerning the exercise of human rights within its spheres of competence.[17] This decision recognised that UNESCO may be called upon to examine two types of communications: those concerning individual and specific cases and those concerning massive, systematic or flagrant violations forming a consistent pattern. The main feature of the new procedure is that communications of both types are referred to the committee which was originally established to consider the reports of States on the implementation of the Convention and Recommendation against Discrimination in Education. The name of this body had been changed in 1971 to 'Committee on Conventions and Recommendations in Education' and its membership increased to fourteen. In 1978 it was given the revised title of 'Committee on Conventions and Recommendations', and in the following year the number of members was increased to twenty.

The resolution of the Executive Board requires that provided the author agrees, communications should be transmitted to the government concerned and to the Committee which will examine them in private sessions, which representatives of the government concerned may attend. The Committee must first decide whether the communication is admissible. Here the usual rules apply: the matter must be within the competence of UNESCO, the applicant must indicate whether he has attempted to exhaust domestic remedies, and so on. The task of the Committee is then to try to bring about a friendly solution of the matter. It is required to submit confidential reports on these activities to the Executive Board which considers them in private session and decides what further action is necessary. But questions of massive, systematic or flagrant violations, which include the consequences of aggression, colonialism, genocide, and apartheid, must be considered by the Executive Board and the General Conference in public meetings.

Because individual complaints are dealt with on a confidential basis, the value and effectiveness of this aspect of UNESCO's work is not easy to assess.[18] It appears that about fifty communications are examined at each session. Some, naturally, are rejected as inadmissible and consideration of others may be deferred. The remainder are examined on the merits, when the Committee may decide to request further information from the author, the relevant government or both, or recommend other action. The Committee may, for example, request the Executive Board to invite the Director-General to address an appeal to the government concerned for clemency or the release of a detained person. It is clear that as a way of dealing with individual complaints, this is a procedure which emphasises informality and conciliation, which may sometimes be more effective than more spectacular methods. It is also worth remembering that the basis of the procedure is a progressive interpretation of UNESCO's constitutional responsibilities and not a human rights treaty in the normal sense. As such, the activity of the Committee on Conventions and Recommendations, already a striking example of the relevance of human rights to the work of a Specialised Agency, suggests interesting possibilities for the future.

IV. The European Social Charter

As we saw in Chapter 4, the Council of Europe, when drafting the European Convention on Human Rights, chose to concentrate on the protection of civil and political rights and to leave the question of economic and social rights for later consideration. Once the Convention had entered into force in 1953, closely followed by its First Protocol in 1954, the Council turned its attention to the second category.

The issues here were far more difficult. One reason was the wide difference in the economic and social circumstances of the member States. It is only necessary to compare the economy and social services of Britain and the Scandinavian countries, on the one hand, with those of Greece and Turkey, on the other, to appreciate the problem of securing agreement on common standards. Another difficulty arose from the very nature of the rights to be protected. The civil and political rights of the citizen can be enforced by a court of law. If someone is wrongfully imprisoned, he can apply for a writ of habeas corpus. If he is not given a fair trial, he can appeal to a superior court, and so on. With economic and social rights, however, it is different. The realisation of the right to work depends on the economic situation, and if the job centre is unable to find a person employment, the writ of a court of law will not change matters. Similarly, a reasonable standard of living for everyone is a proper objective of social policy, but depends much more on a flourishing economy than on legislation. This does not mean that there cannot be legally enforceable measures designed to give effect to economic and social rights, but it did mean that the whole approach to the protection of those rights had to be different from that of the European Convention, and this was also true of the two United Nations Covenants.

The first step was the political decision that a new legal instrument should be prepared. During the winter of 1953–54 the Committee of Ministers was engaged in preparing 'a well-defined programme of work for the Council of Europe'.[19] When it transmitted this to the Assembly in May 1954, the Committee recorded the following decision as part of the social programme:

> Our Committee will endeavour to elaborate a European Social Charter which would define the social objectives aimed at by Members and would guide the policy of the Council in the social field, in which it would be complementary to the European Convention on Human Rights and Fundamental Freedoms.[20]

The task of preparing this Social Charter was to be the responsibility of the new Social Committee, whose constitution was decided at the same time and which was set up as a permanent organ of co-operation between the member States in social matters, under the authority of the Committee of Ministers.[21]

The Assembly welcomed this new development and instructed its

Committee on Social Questions to prepare a draft setting out its views.[22] By October 1955 the Committee had done this and submitted a complete draft Charter, containing far-reaching provisions for the protection of various economic and social rights.[23] It also proposed the creation of a European Economic and Social Council as an organ for its implementation. But these proposals received a mixed reception in the Assembly and so a revised draft was produced in the following April. This provided for rather less extensive rights than the earlier version and was therefore considered retrograde by some and more realistic by others. It also proposed the convening of an Economic and Social Conference on an *ad hoc* basis, that is as and when required, instead of a permanent institution established by treaty.[24] This draft was acceptable to the Economic Committee and the majority of the Social Committee, but a dissident minority succeeded in getting the whole matter referred to the Political Committee for further study. This resulted in the preparation of a third draft, which was discussed by the Assembly in the following October.[25] It was clear, however, that there were irreconcilable differences of opinion on many points. The Assembly refrained from endorsing the latest draft to be submitted, but recommended that the Committee of Ministers should 'establish a European Convention on Social and Economic Rights, taking into consideration the present draft and the observations and suggestions during the debates in public session . . .'.[26]

It was now the turn of the governmental Social Committee to see what provisions were acceptable to the member governments. In December 1958 the Committee of Ministers published a draft Charter which its experts had produced.[27] Taking advantage of a provision in the agreement concluded between the Council of Europe and the ILO in 1951, it invited the latter to convene a tripartite conference with delegations representing governments, employers and workers to examine this text. The conference was held in Strasbourg in December 1958. It did not produce any formal conclusions, but published a report which contained the record of its proceedings, including the views of the participants and the various groups on the provisions contained in the draft Social Charter.[28]

After receiving a further opinion from the Assembly in January 1960,[29] the experts then worked out the final draft of the Charter, which was duly signed at a ceremony held in Turin on 18 October 1961.[30] These long negotiations, extending over seven years, have been described here because they show the complexity of this type of law-making, how the different organs of the Council of Europe, parliamentary and governmental, each played their part, and how, as a happy illustration of co-operation between international organisations, the ILO also made a contribution. In its final form the Charter has a character which is intended to correspond to the needs of contemporary free Europe and which might well be unacceptable to governments in other parts of the world. Its ideal is security in freedom. By proposing a system of guarantees for what have been called 'the bread-and-butter rights of the working man', it is intended to bring him the practical benefits of European social ideals.

Certain basic features of the Social Charter are worth pointing out before we study its provisions in detail. The first is the fact that a number of 'rights' which it asserts are really objects of social policy rather than rights which are legally enforceable. The difficulty here was that if these 'rights' were merely proclaimed as objectives, the Charter would have little value as an effective guarantee of economic and social standards. On the other hand, if its provisions were limited to the legal obligations which member governments could reasonably be expected to assume, its scope would be rather restricted and the results of so much work disappointing. The solution was to divide the Charter into several distinct parts. In the first part are set out nineteen separate rights, the realisation of which the contracting parties accept as the aim of their policy. This permits general affirmations of a far-reaching character, but as statements of policy without precise legal commitments. Part II then contains the legal obligations which the parties undertake so as to ensure the effective exercise of the rights proclaimed in Part I. With this double formulation it is thus possible to combine the general statement of long-term objectives with particular and more limited commitments of immediate application.[31]

The second basic characteristic of the Charter is its approach to the problem raised by variations in the economic and social development of the different member States. It was clearly unrealistic to expect that the less developed countries in Europe could assume the same obligations as their more fortunate partners.

Equally, it would have been contrary to the general policy of the Council of Europe to draft an instrument to which only the more developed countries could subscribe. It was therefore provided that a member State would not be obliged to accept all the provisions of the Charter before ratifying it, but that it could initially be bound only by a stated minimum, in the expectation that it would find itself able to accept additional obligations with the passage of time. In this way it was hoped to achieve the progressive implementation of a Charter which, when fully applied, would guarantee a high standard of economic and social rights for everyone in Western Europe.

The third basic feature of the Charter is the attention given to the question of supervising its implementation. As we have seen, the Assembly had suggested an Economic and Social Council which would have had representatives of employers, workers, and consumers. The governments did not favour this approach, but agreed to an elaborate system of control based on reports by governments as to how they are implementing the Charter. This system, which makes supervision a task for the various committees and organs of the Council of Europe, will be described later in this chapter.

1. The rights protected

Part I of the Charter begins by providing that 'the Contracting Parties accept as the aim of their policy, to be pursued by all appropriate means, both national and international in character, the attainment of conditions in which the following rights and principles may be effectively realised ...'. These 'rights and principles' are then listed:

1 The right to work, which is formulated as: 'Everyone shall have the opportunity to earn his living in an occupation freely entered upon'.
2 The right to just conditions of work.
3 The right to safe and healthy working conditions.
4 The right to a fair remuneration.
5 The right to organise.
6 The right to bargain collectively.
7 The right of children and young persons to protection against 'physical and moral hazards'.
8 The right of employed women to special protection in case of maternity, and in other situations as appropriate.

9 The right to vocational guidance.
10 The right to vocational training.
11 The right to protection of health.
12 The right to social security.
13 The right to social and medical assistance.
14 The right to benefit from social welfare services.
15 The right of the disabled to special facilities.
16 The right of the family to social, legal and economic protection.
17 The right of mothers and children to social and economic protection.
18 The right to earn one's living on a footing of equality in the territory of another Contracting Party.
19 The right of migrant workers who are nationals of a Contracting Party and their families to protection and assistance.

Part II of the Charter, as already noted, then contains more precise commitments which the contracting parties assume with a view to ensuring the effective exercise of these rights. The provisions vary considerably, according to the nature of the right to be protected. The right to just conditions of work, for example, involves, among other things, limitation of working hours, public holidays with pay, two weeks' annual holiday with pay, and a weekly rest period. Similarly, the right to a fair remuneration includes additional pay for overtime, equal pay for men and women, and so on. The right of children and young persons to protection includes ten separate provisions for their benefit. The undertakings designed to secure the right to protection of the family and of mothers and children, on the other hand, are rather more general and imprecise.

A number of the rights covered in the Social Charter were already the subject of the other conventions and agreements concluded earlier by the members of the Council of Europe. Though cross-references are, understandably, not given in the Charter, it is clear that its authors had these other instruments in mind. The right to organise, for example, is already guaranteed by Article 11 of the Convention on Human Rights. The right to social security in its international aspects forms the subject of two Interim Agreements on Social Security signed in Paris in December 1953,[32] and standards of social security are dealt with in the European Code of Social Security, concluded in April 1964.[33] Moreover, the right to social and medical assistance, also in its international aspects, forms the subject of the European Convention on Social and

Medical Assistance of December 1953,[34] and the right to earn one's living in another country is one of the matters covered in the European Convention on Establishment of December 1955.[35]

Part III of the Charter contains the provisions which permit progressive implementation. They are rather complicated, but their key element is as follows. Seven rights were regarded as particularly important:

The right to work.
The right to organise
The right to bargain collectively.
The right to social security.
The right to social and medical assistance.
The right of the family to special protection.
The right of migrant workers and their families to protection and assistance.

Under the provisions of Article 20 any contracting party must agree to be bound by the Articles of Part II of the Charter relating to at least five of these rights. In addition, it must agree to be bound by the provisions relating to at least five other rights as set out in Part II. It is possible, however, instead of accepting ten articles in their entirety, to accept a larger number in part.[36]

2. *Measures of implementation*

Part IV of the Charter contains the provisions concerned with the control of its implementation. The Committee of Ministers, though rejecting the idea of a new European Economic and Social Council, agreed to the appointment of an independent Committee of Experts 'of the highest integrity and of recognised competence in international social questions', who would be joined by a representative of the International Labour Organisation in a consultative capacity.[37] Every two years this Committee of Experts receives and examines reports by the contracting parties on the way in which they are applying the Charter. Moreover, copies of the reports are sent to national organisations of employers and trade unions, whose comments the governments are obliged to transmit to the Council of Europe. This provides an opportunity to obtain information from independent sources, which, as we have explained earlier, is essential if a reporting system is to be effective. The governments' reports, and the comments of the Committee of Experts, are then examined by a Governmental Committee on the Social Charter, which represents the contracting parties and is assisted by selected organisations of employers and trade unions. The conclusions of the experts are also sent to the Consultative Assembly, which communicates its views to the Committee of Ministers. Finally, the latter examines the results of these consultations and, by a two-thirds majority, may make appropriate recommendations to each contracting party.[38]

This machinery is certainly complicated, but provides a system of regular monitoring to ensure that the Charter is being applied. Because of the way the supervision operates, undue reticence by any government is exposed to the light of publicity and brought to the attention of both the governmental and the parliamentary organs of the Council of Europe.

Other points of interest in the final clauses (Part V) of the Charter are an article similar to Article 15 of the Convention on Human Rights, permitting derogations 'in time of war or other public emergency threatening the life of the nation'; Article 32 of the Charter, which, like Article 60 of the Convention, preserves any more favourable treatment that may already be provided for under domestic law or other international treaties; and Article 33, which deals with the implementation of certain obligations through collective agreements.

The Charter was signed on 18 October 1961 on behalf of thirteen members of the Council of Europe. Article 35 provides for its entry into force after the deposit of the fifth instrument of ratification; this occurred on 26 February 1965. It has now been ratified by fourteen States: Austria, Cyprus, Denmark, France, the Federal Republic of Germany, Greece, Iceland, Ireland, Italy, the Netherlands, Norway, Spain, Sweden, and the United Kingdom.[39]

3. *The application of the Charter*

Article 20 of the Charter, as we have mentioned, requires that a contracting party should agree to be bound by at least ten out of the nineteen articles in Part II, including at least five out of the seven more important articles. Alternatively, it may agree to be bound by at least forty-five out of the seventy-two separate paragraphs in those nineteen articles.

In fact, nearly all States which have ratified the Charter have accepted considerably more than the minimum number of obligations, with the result that ten countries out of fourteen are bound by more than eighty per cent of its provisions.[40]

The reporting system has now been in operation for more than twenty years. Each supervision cycle covers a period of two years, and the governments of the contracting parties, in accordance with Article 21 of the Charter, regularly send the Council of Europe reports on the application of those provisions of the Charter which they have accepted. As might be expected, the independent experts have been more critical of the governments' reports than the Governmental Committee on the Social Charter. Similarly, the Parliamentary Assembly has been more diligent in detecting shortcomings than the Committee of Ministers. The professional organisations of employers and workers, on the other hand, have been less active than might have been anticipated. On the whole, however, the system has functioned reasonably well, and a certain number of discrepancies between obligations and performance have been detected. In the course of the first five supervision cycles, covering the first ten years of the Charter's application, the Committee of Ministers preferred to transmit the reports of the various organs of control to the governments concerned, drawing their attention to the contents of the reports, instead of using its power to make recommendations under Article 29. This is no doubt more diplomatic, and was perhaps natural in the early years, but the Committee of Ministers cannot afford to let Article 29 become a dead letter or the system instituted by the Charter will not be fully effective.

What practical results have been achieved? A number of discrepancies have been corrected as a result of the control system and, perhaps more important, various changes have been made in national legislation and practice in accordance with the spirit of the Charter, sometimes as a requirement of ratification. Cyprus, for example, introduced a new scheme of social security in 1973 in accordance with the requirements of Article 12 of the Charter. Various other examples of its effect may for convenience be illustrated under four headings:

(a) The right to work and related rights Austria amended two laws which were incompatible with the guarantee of freedom of choice of occupation (Article 1 of the Charter). The Federal Republic granted additional holidays with pay to miners working underground (Article 2) and limited the working hours of young persons of school age (Article 7). Ireland took similar measures in relation to the working hours of young persons under sixteen (Article 7) and introduced legislation requiring adequate notice in the event of dismissal (Article 4). The United Kingdom also limited the working hours of young persons (Article 7), and Sweden has forbidden the employment of children of school age in agriculture (Article 7).

(b) Special provisions concerning women Both Ireland and Italy have substantially increased the amount of maternity benefits (Article 8). Ireland also abolished the prohibition of the employment of married women in the public service (Article 1), and Sweden has extended the length of maternity leave (Article 8).

(c) Migrant workers Article 19 of the Charter contains ten separate provisions for the protection of migrant workers. In order to comply with their obligations, Cyprus and Italy changed their laws on the expulsion of foreigners; Denmark and Sweden have done so as regards residence permits for foreign workers, while France now grants maternity benefits for the children of foreign workers on the same basis as for French children. France also changed the age limit for the children of foreign workers seeking to rejoin their families and has abolished the *cautio judicatum solvi* which was a financial deposit previously required of foreigners before they could start legal proceedings.

(d) Seamen Until recently the law of many countries made it illegal for a seaman to leave his ship during the period for which he had accepted an engagement. Though the reason for this rule can be appreciated, it violated the principle of freedom of choice of one's occupation (Article 1 of the Charter). Consequently Cyprus, Denmark, the Federal Republic, Norway, Sweden, and the United Kingdom have all amended their laws in this respect.

The impact of the European Social Charter has been less spectacular and certainly less dramatic than that of the European Convention on Human Rights. Nevertheless, the Charter has been useful and provides an apt illustration of the distinctive measures of implementation which are appropriate for rights of an economic and social character. The effect of the Charter will, of course, be greater if more of the contracting parties agree to be bound by all of its provisions, and if those members of the Council of Europe which have not yet ratified it can be persuaded to do so. That is one direction in which more intensive efforts are required. The other, no less important, is to ensure that where the obligations of the Charter have been accepted, governments are not allowed to resile from their commitments for reasons of ideology or political convenience. Thus, while the Charter occupies an important place in the development of international protection for economic and social rights, there is no room for complacency if, as its drafters intended, it is to be an effective guarantee of 'the bread and butter rights of the working man'.

V. Some other proposals: 'new human rights'

In recent years a good deal of thought has been given to the question of extending the scope of human rights beyond those to be found in the Universal Declaration and the two international Covenants. An early indication of this tendency was the proclamation of a 'right to development', which was mentioned in Chapter 1. The thinking here is that, quite apart from moral considerations, the economic development of the poorer countries of the world is essential to their social well being and political stability and that without it they are in no position to guarantee the civil, political, economic, social and cultural rights prescribed in the major international texts. As a consequence, the 'right to development' is asserted as a human right.[41]

In a similar way, the concern felt in many countries and international organisations about the need for the protection of the environment, particularly against the pollution generated by modern industrial societies, has led some to the conclusion that there is a human right to a clean and healthy environment.

Then there are those who go further and consider that there is a human right to peace and a human right to share in the 'common heritage of mankind', that is the natural resources of the deep sea bed and other areas not subject to territorial sovereignty. Indeed, some have suggested that the so-called 'new human rights', including the four just mentioned, constitute the 'third generation of human rights' which should receive international recognition after the two first 'generations' or categories protected by the UN Covenants of 1966.

A distinct but related question, which has been much discussed in the United Nations in recent years, is the establishment of a new international economic order. The developing countries constitute seventy per cent of the world's population but possess only thirty per cent of the world's income. On achieving their independence all became members of the United Nations, with a consequent increase in their political influence, especially when they act together. The group of non-aligned developing countries established at Bandung in 1955 with seventy-seven members now comprises more than 110, and so constitutes two-thirds of the total membership of the General Assembly. It has been pressing vigorously for concerted new measures to redress the existing inequalities between the richer and poorer nations, and for this purpose adopted as its slogan the concept of a 'new international economic order'.

Everyone agrees on the desirability of helping the less developed countries to develop their economies in order to achieve an adequate standard of living and, for example, to be able to implement the right to work, as proclaimed in the Universal Declaration and Covenant on Economic, Social and Cultural Rights. The difficulty is to find a way of achieving this objective, particularly at a time when many of the developed countries are themselves suffering from inflation, unemployment, and other economic problems.

The United Nations has held a series of special sessions largely devoted to these issues and has announced successive 'development decades'. In May 1974 the Sixth Special Session of the General Assembly adopted a Declaration and Programme of Action on the Establishment of a New International Economic Order (NIEO),[42] which was followed in December that year by the Charter of Economic Rights and Duties of States.[43] Detailed examination of these important texts is not possible here, but in any study of human rights they cannot be ignored. They proclaim twenty principles on which the new economic order should be founded. These include the broadest co-operation of all States in fighting inequality, better prices for raw materials and primary commodities, active assistance to developing countries by the whole international community free of political conditions, the use of a reformed international monetary system for the better promotion of development, and many others. If this ambitious programme could be carried out, it would make an important contribution to the realisation of economic and social rights in the Third World. It has even been claimed that the establishment of the new economic order is a pre-condition of respect for human rights in many countries. The General Assembly has gone further still, because its 1977 Resolution on the future work of the United Nations with respect to human rights states that the realisation of the new economic order is 'an essential element for the effective promotion of human rights and fundamental freedoms'.[44] Although this is obviously an exaggeration, because there are many countries which respect human rights without waiting for a new international economic order, it reflects the thinking of the majority in the General Assembly and exemplifies the tendency to link human rights and economic development.

The tendency just mentioned contains some truth but is also dangerous. It is evident that many economic and social rights, including freedom from hunger, the right to an adequate standard of living and to the enjoyment of physical and mental health, cannot be secured in countries where the majority of the population are living on or below the poverty line. It is also right that the developed countries should be frequently reminded of this. The danger, however, is that this may be used as an excuse for the non-observance of other rights which have little or nothing to do with underdevelopment. Economic circumstances are never a justification for arbitrary arrest, State-sponsored murder, or detention without trial. Without waiting for the achievement of a new international economic order, we can acknowledge that better economic conditions are often essential for the realisation of economic and social rights, yet insist that their absence is no justification for the abuse of civil and political rights.

This brings us back to the so-called 'new rights': the right to development, the right to the environment, the right to share in the common heritage of mankind, the right to peace, and so on. Are these concepts human rights in any meaningful sense of that term? In trying to answer this question, there are several factors to be borne in mind.

In the first place, the word 'human' in the expression 'human rights' has a specific meaning. It indicates that the rights under consideration are rights pertaining to human beings by virtue of their humanity. As stated in both the UN Covenants, 'these rights derive from the inherent dignity of the human person'. In our view this means that the rights which can properly be called 'human rights' are rights of individual human beings stemming from their nature as human beings, and not rights of groups, associations, or other collectivities. This is borne out by the wording repeatedly used in the Universal Declaration and in the Covenant on Civil and Political Rights, 'Everyone has the right . . .'; while the Covenant on Economic, Social and Cultural Rights repeatedly stipulates that 'the States Parties . . . recognise the right of everyone to . . .' the different rights protected. It is quite clear from this language that what the Universal Declaration and the Covenants are concerned with is the rights of individual human beings. True, there is an exception in Article 1 of both Covenants, which states, 'All peoples have the right of self-determination'. But it is clear from the *travaux* that this was regarded as a special provision,[45] and its exceptional character is underlined by the fact that is placed in a distinct chapter of each Covenant, and separated from the articles relating to individual human rights.

This being so, is it accurate to designate as 'human-rights' so-called rights which pertain not to individuals but to groups or collectivities? Usage, of course, is a matter of convention and there is room for more than one view as to what is appropriate here. In our view, however, language and thinking will be clearer if we use the expression 'human rights' to designate individual rights and 'collective rights' to designate the rights of groups and collectivities, a distinction which also has the advantage of being consistent with much generally accepted practice.

The second consideration relates to the use of the word 'rights' in the expression 'new human rights.' Economic development, the protection of the environment, the common heritage of mankind and peace: are these concepts 'rights' in any meaningful sense? They can, and should, be objectives of social policy. They may be items in a political programme. However, they are certainly not legally enforceable claims. Most people no doubt prefer peace. But if one's country is at war, it is certain that there is no legally enforceable 'right to peace'. Naturally it would be possible to define 'rights' in such a way as to include all desirable objectives of social policy, and in that event, the 'new human rights' would become 'rights' by virtue of the definition. But this would be to distort the ordinary meaning given to the term 'human rights' and, more seriously, would run together goals which enlightened humanity ought to pursue with claims which are already protected by international law. The trouble arises, then, because advocates of the 'new human rights' are confusing objectives of social policy with rights in the lawyers' sense. If one wishes to see some objective achieved – a clean and healthy environment, for example – it is tempting to say that this is a right to which we are all entitled. But it is not a good idea to take wishes for reality.

The last point to be borne in mind is that there is a crucial distinction between legal rights and moral rights. We may consider that we have a moral right to something – consideration from others, perhaps – when we have no legal right to it at all. Countless examples could be given. If advocates of the 'new human rights' assert that we have a moral right to peace, to the environment, and so on, then many will be inclined to agree. But there is all the difference in the world between these and other moral rights, on the one hand, and, on the other, rights, whether civil and political or economic and social, which have been incorporated in international treaties. While it is true that moral ideas provide both an incentive to create new law and a yardstick for its interpretation, until the process of law-making has taken place, 'new human rights' must remain in the realm of speculation.[46]

Notes

1 For the text of the Covenant, see I. Brownlie, *Basic Documents in Human Rights*, second edition, Oxford, 1981, p. 118.
2 See Articles 6, 7, 9, 10, 11, 12, 13 and 15.
3 See Article 8.
4 For discussion of these provisions, see E. Schwelb, 'Some aspects of the measures of implementation of the Covenant on Economic, Social and Cultural Rights', *Human Rights Journal*, I, 1968, p. 363.
5 See H. Hannum (ed.), *Guide to International Human Rights Practice*, London, 1984, pp. 173–76 (D. D. Fischer).
6 See P. Alston and B. Simma, 'First session of the U.N. Committee on Economic, Social and Cultural Rights', *American Journal of International Law*, LXXXI, 1987, p. 747.
7 *Ibid.*, p. 753.
8 On the progress which was made at the meeting of the Committee in March 1988, see P. Alston and B. Simma, 'Second session of the U.N. Committee on

Economic Social and Cultural Rights', *American Journal of International Law*, LXXXII, 1988, p. 603.

9 A great deal has been written about the work of the ILO in protecting the social rights with which it is especially concerned. The following are particularly useful: C. W. Jenks, *Human Rights and International Labour Standards*, London, 1960; *idem*, *Social Justice in the Law of Nations*, Oxford University Press, 1970; *idem*, 'Economic and social change in the law of nations', 138 *Hague Recueil des Cours*, 1973, p. 455; F. Wolf, 'Human rights and the ILO', in T. Meron (ed.) *Human Rights in International Law*, Oxford, 1984, pp. 273–306.

10 For the texts of these and other ILO conventions, see Brownlie, *Basic Documents*, pp. 176–231.

11 See N. M. Poulantzas, 'International protection of human rights: implementation procedures within the framework of the ILO', *Revue Hellenique de Droit International*, XXV, 1972, p. 110 and F. Wolf, 'ILO experience in the implementation of human rights', *Journal of International Law and Economics*, X, 1975, p. 599. For the particular merits of ILO procedures in relation to fact-finding, see T. M. Franck and H. S. Fairley, 'Procedural due process in human rights: fact-finding by international agencies', *American Journal of International Law*, LXXIV, 1980, p. 308.

12 See N. Valticos in K. Vasak (ed.), *Les Dimensions Internationales des Droits de l'Homme*, UNESCO, 1978, p. 457.

13 See L. Swepston, 'Human rights complaint procedures of the International Labor Organisation', in Hannum, *Guide*, 74–93.

14 See ECOSOC Resolution 277(X). For discussion of this aspect of the work of the ILO, see K. Yokota, 'International standards of freedom of association for trade union purposes', 144 *Hague Recueil des Cours*, 1975, p. 309.

15 For discussion of these cases and the 1975 case involving Lesotho, see Franck and Fairley, 'Procedural due process', pp. 340–4.

16 The text of this treaty can be found in the UN publication *Human Rights: a Compilation of International Instruments* (ST/HR/1/Rev. 1), 1978, p. 35 and Brownlie, *Basic Documents*, p. 234. By 1 January 1988 seventy-seven States had ratified this Convention.

17 Decision of the Executive Board 104 Ex/Decision 3.3 of 28 April 1978. The relevant part of this text is set out in P. Sieghart, *The International Law of Human Rights*, Oxford, 1983, pp. 434–6. See also P. Alston, 'UNESCO's procedure for dealing with human rights violations', *Santa Clara Law Review*, XX, 1980, p. 665.

18 For a useful discussion of the recent activity of the Committee, see S. Marks, 'The complaint procedure of the United Nations Educational, Scientific and Cultural Organisation (UNESCO)', in Hannum, *Guide*, pp. 94–107.

19 Special Message of the Committee of Ministers transmitting to the Consultative Assembly the Programme of Work of the Council of Europe, *Documents of the Assembly*, 1954, doc. 238, para. 1.

20 *Ibid.*, para. 45.

21 *Ibid.*, paras. 42–4.

22 Opinion No. 9, *Texts adopted by the Assembly*, May 1954.

23 *Documents of the Assembly*, 1955, doc. 403. The discussions in the Assembly and its various committees are described more fully in A. H. Robertson, *Human Rights in Europe*, first edition, Manchester University Press, 1963, Chapter VIII.
24 *Documents*, 1956, doc. 488.
25 *Ibid.*, doc. 536.
26 Recommendation 104, *Texts adopted*, October 1956.
27 *Documents*, 1959, doc. 927.
28 ILO, *Record of the Proceedings of the Tripartite Conference convened by the I.L.O. at the request of the Council of Europe*, Geneva, 1959.
29 Opinion No. 32, *Texts adopted*, January 1960.
30 The text of the Charter may be found in various publications including the Council of Europe's, *Human Rights in International Law: Basic Texts*, Strasbourg, 1979, p. 41 and I. Brownlie, *Basic Documents*, p. 301. For an excellent analysis of the Charter, see D. J. Harris, *The European Social Charter*, University of Virginia Press, 1984.
31 See F. Tennfjord, 'The European Social Charter – an instrument of social collaboration in Europe', *European Yearbook*, IX, 1961, p. 71.
32 *European Treaty Series* Nos. 12 and 13.
33 *Ibid.*, No. 48.
34 *Ibid.*, No. 14.
35 *Ibid.*, No. 19. These five Conventions and Agreements may be found in the collection published by the Council of Europe, *European Conventions and Agreements*, I (1949–61) and II (1961–70).
36 The nineteen articles in Part II of the Charter contain seventy–two numbered paragraphs. A State may ratify the Charter if it agrees to be bound by no fewer than forty–five numbered paragraphs, provided that it accepts no fewer than five of Articles 1, 5, 6, 12, 13, 16, and 19.
37 Articles 25 and 26 of the Charter.
38 Articles 27–9 of the Charter.
39 As of 1 January 1988.
40 For discussion of the application of the Charter, see Harris, *The European Social Charter*; and for the earlier history F. Sur, 'La Charte Social Européenne: dix années d'application', *European Yearbook*, XXII, 1974, p. 88 and H. Wiebringhaus, 'La Charte Sociale Européenne et la Convention Européenne des Droits de l'homme', *Human Rights Journal*, VIII, 1975, p. 527.
41 In addition to the references in Chapter 1, see S. Marks, 'Development and human rights', *Bulletin of Peace Proposals*, VIII, 1977, p. 236; O. C. Eze, 'Les Droits de l'Homme et le sous–developpement', *Human Rights Journal*, XII, 1979, p. 5; P. Alston, 'Human rights and basic needs: a critical assessment', *ibid.*, p. 19; R. Y. Rich, 'The right to development as an emerging human right', *Virginia Journal of International Law*, XXIII, 1982–83, p. 287 and R. J. Vincent, *Human Rights and International Relations*, Cambridge University Press, 1986, Chapter 5.
42 Resolutions 3201 (S–VI) and 3202 (S–VI). See also Resolution 3362 (S–VII) of the Seventh Special Session.
43 Resolution 3281 (XXIX).

44 Resolution 32/130, para. 1(f).

45 This is evident from the *travaux préparatoires*, see UN doc. A/2929 of 1 July 1955, Chapter IV, paras 2–7.

46 For an excellent discussion of the questions raised by the issue of new human rights, see P. Alston. 'Conjuring up new human rights: a proposal for quality control'. *American Journal of International Law*, LXXVIII, 1984, p. 607.

CHAPTER 8

Humanitarian law

I. Introduction

The origins of humanitarian law[1] were outlined in Chapter 1, where we noted various developments during the nineteenth century relating to the first matters of concern to the Red Cross: the condition of the sick and wounded in the field, the condition of the sick and wounded and shipwrecked at sea, and the care and exchange of prisoners of war. These early measures culminated in the international recognition given to the Red Cross in 1919 by Article 25 of the Covenant of the League of Nations. During the decade which followed various steps were taken to establish a constitutional structure for the Red Cross. The League of Red Cross Societies was founded in 1919 as the 'parent body' of the various national societies. And not long afterwards the eighteenth international conference of the Red Cross, meeting at The Hague in 1928, approved statutes which established the following structure: the International Committee of the Red Cross (ICRC) in Geneva, the League of Red Cross Societies, originally in Paris, but transferred to Geneva during the Second World War, and the national societies themselves. The latter took the title of the Red Crescent in Moslem countries, and the Red Lion in Iran.[2]

A further strand in the development of humanitarian law concerns the rules which regulate the weapons which may be used in warfare. At the Hague Peace Conference in 1899, a Declaration concerning Asphyxiating Gases was adopted which contained an undertaking not to use projectiles for the diffusion of such substances. The Hague Convention of 1907 went further and contained a general prohibition on the use of poison or poisonous weapons in land warfare. This, however, did not prevent the extensive use of poisonous gases on the western front during the war of 1914–18. Matters were taken a stage further by the Geneva Protocol of 1925, which prohibited the use in war of asphyxiating, poisonous or other gases and also extended the prohibition to the use of bacteriological methods of warfare, prohibitions which were respected during the Second World War.

How far is it possible to employ humanitarian law to limit the use of weapons in a situation which is itself in flat contradiction of the basic concepts of humanity? Or, as Professor Draper has put it, how is an essentially inhumane activity to be conducted, even in part, in a humane manner?[3] The problem which arose earlier this century in relation to poisonous gases and bacteria became much more acute in 1940 with the indiscriminate bombing of cities, in 1945 with the atomic bomb and, in the second half of the century, with the threat of thermo-nuclear weapons. These developments show how the horizons of humanitarian law have widened during the course of this century. A hundred years ago humanitarian law was concerned with combatants who, through sickness or injury, could no longer take part in the combat. It was extended to prisoners of war, that is, combatants who, on account of their capture, can no longer fight. It is now concerned with whole sectors of the population consisting of persons, including women, children and the aged, who are not and cannot be combatants, but whose very existence is imperilled by the methods of warfare now available.

This leads us to another concern of humanitarian law; the protection of the civilian population. Until recent times a clear distinction could be, and usually was, made between the armed forces and the civilian population, although the latter was often the victim of appalling atrocities, as in the religious wars of the sixteenth and seventeeth centuries. But the distinction was easy to make, even if the proper conclusion was not always drawn. Consequently, in the eighteenth century it was not unknown for civilians to travel without difficulty in countries with which their own State was at war because, being civilians, they were not concerned with the hostilities and their status as non-combatants was respected.

In the twentieth century things have changed for the worse. Quite apart from the question of weapons of mass destruction, the concept of total war involves the fate of the civilian population as never before. This applies with particular force in occupied territories. The taking of hostages, reprisals on the civilian population, the treatment of resistance groups ('patriots' to one side, 'terrorists' to the other), the conscription of labour, and many other problems arise. These matters were largely outside the treaty framework of humanitarian law in its early years, but formed the subject of one of the Geneva Conventions in 1949.

The cataclysm of the Second World War led to a fundamental reappraisal of humanitarian law. The War had produced suffering and desolation on a scale never before even imagined. It is estimated that the First World War was responsible for 10 million deaths, but the Second for 50 million. This included 26 million combatants and 24 million civilians, of whom 1½ million were civilians killed in air raids.[4] Appalled by this calamity, the League of Red Cross Societies, the International Committee and the national governments agreed to undertake a revision of humanitarian law. The result was the four Geneva Conventions of 1949, which amount to a codification of existing law, plus a marked development in the light of recent history.

The Geneva Conventions of 1949 relate to:

1 The amelioration of the condition of the sick and wounded in the field.
2 The amelioration of the condition of the wounded, sick and shipwrecked members of armed forces at sea.
3 The treatment of prisoners of war.
4 The protection of the civilian population in time of war.

The first three Conventions deal with what might be called the traditional functions of the Red Cross. The fourth was quite new and represents the first attempt to draw up a treaty to deal with the problems mentioned earlier. The question of chemical and bacteriological warfare remained regulated by the Geneva Protocol of 1925.

At the time of writing the Geneva Conventions of 1949 have been ratified by 165 States.[5] While it is beyond the scope of this chapter to analyse them in detail, particular topics will be discussed in the following section. The following general points may also be noted. Article 1, common to all four Conventions, provides that the parties 'undertake to respect and to ensure respect for the present Convention in all circumstances'. In other words, the obligation is general and absolute and does not depend upon reciprocal respect for its obligations by the other party or parties to the conflict. Article 1, in addition, requires States to use their best endeavours to secure respect for the Conventions by non-governmental organisations under their control and also, significantly, by other contracting States.

Article 2 of all four Conventions lays down that they shall apply to 'all cases of declared war or of any other armed conflict ...', so that a legal state of war is no longer essential for the application of humanitarian rules.

Article 7 of the first three Conventions, and Article 8 of the fourth, provide that a beneficiary of their provisions may in no circumstances renounce his or her rights. In other words, the rules established by the humanitarian conventions are rules of *ordre public*. Offenders who violate their provisions incur obligations under international law, although the obligations concerned must be enforced by the national courts to whose jurisdiction the offenders are subject. Should there also be an international organ before which they are responsible? Likewise, should the individual beneficiary have an international remedy if his rights are violated? As yet there is no international body to enforce the conventions and no corresponding remedy for the individual. These are, however, issues which are increasingly discussed and which suggest that humanitarian law may have something to learn from human rights law.

II. Current problems and recent developments: the Protocols of 1977

The two major problems under discussion in recent years concern the situation which arises in cases of undeclared war or civil strife and the problem of the use of weapons of mass destruction.

1. Undeclared war or civil strife

The typical situation which gave rise to the application of the rules of humanitarian law in the past was a war as generally understood, that is an international conflict between two or more States. Traditionally this occurred after a declaration of war, although, especially today, international conflicts can and do take place without such a declaration. Usually, however, there is no difficulty in ascertaining the existence of a conflict of an international character. Article 2 of the Conventions of 1949, as we have seen, makes it clear that they apply to 'all cases of declared war or of any other armed conflict'.

In the twentieth century there has been an increasing number of conflicts of a very different nature. Do the rules of humanitarian law apply when the conflict is national rather than international? How is such a situation to be defined? There are marked differences between a full-scale civil war, such as those in Spain between 1936 and 1939, in the Congo in the early 1960s, in the Yemen in 1965, or in Nigeria in 1968–69, on the one hand, and, on the other, various situations of rebellion or civil strife in which an established government maintains that it is simply suppressing a local insurrection, but other States give support to the insurgents on the ground that they are a national liberation movement. Such situations, moreover, arouse particularly strong feelings and so can lead to appalling atrocities. While most soldiers will respect the integrity, and therefore the human rights, of a member of the armed forces of an enemy State, they may feel and behave very differently to one whom they consider a traitor or murderous criminal. Thus, the application of humanitarian law becomes particularly difficult in situations of civil strife, especially when insurgents receive assistance from a sympathetic foreign power, with the result that the conflict is in some respects international, even though the armed forces of two countries are not directly involved.

Article 3 of the four Conventions of 1949 represented the first attempt to deal with this problem.[6] It sets out rules which apply to 'armed conflict not of an international character occurring in the territory of one of the High Contracting Parties'. In such cases 'persons taking no part in the hostilities, including members of armed forces who have laid down their arms and those placed *hors de combat* by sickness, wounds or any other means ... are, in all circumstances, to be treated humanely, without any distinction founded on race, colour, religion or faith, sex, birth or wealth, or any other similar criteria ...'. Article 3 also prohibits specifically:

(a) Violence to life and person, in particular, murder of all kinds, mutilation, cruel treatment and torture.

(b) The taking of hostages.
(c) Outrages upon personal dignity, in particular, humiliating and degrading treatment.
(d) The passing of sentences and the carrying out of executions without previous judgement pronounced by a regularly constituted court, affording all the judicial guarantees which are recognised as indispensable by civilised peoples.

This provision marked an important advance in international humanitarian law and has been described as 'an audacious and paradoxical provision which aims at applying international law to a national phenomenon'.[7] Nevertheless, there has been considerable difficulty in securing its application. This is largely because States are reluctant to admit the existence of 'an armed conflict not of an international character', perhaps through fear of the construction that may be put on such an admission, in spite of the fact that the same article states that 'the application of the preceding provisions shall not affect the legal status of the parties to the conflict'.

An illustration of the problem is provided by the Algerian war, in which France had about 400,000 troops engaged and the insurgent FLN had a well developed organisation of its own. It was, however, only at a late stage in the fighting that the French government admitted that Article 3 was applicable. Moreover, the applicability of Article 3 has been recognised in only a few of the cases of internal conflict which have occurred since 1949. The need for further international action on this subject was therefore plain.

2. *Weapons of mass destruction*

The problem raised by modern methods of mass destruction, whether bombing with conventional weapons, as in the Second World War, or by atomic and thermo-nuclear devices, is obvious. Whereas humanitarian law as it has developed over the last hundred years has sought to distinguish between combatants and non-combatants, such methods of warfare by their very nature do not, and cannot, make such a distinction.

In 1965 the twentieth Red Cross Conference at Vienna attempted to tackle this problem, and adopted its Resolution XXVIII, which contained the following declaration:

> The Conference,
> ... solemnly declares that all Governments and other authorities responsible for action in armed conflicts should conform at least to the following principles:
> that the right of the parties to a conflict to adopt means of injuring the the enemy is not unlimited;
> that it is prohibited to launch attacks against the civilian populations as such;
> that distinction must be made at all times between persons taking part in the hostilities and members of the civilian population to the effect that the latter be spared as much as possible;
> that the general principles of the law of war apply to nuclear and similar weapons.

The same matter was discussed, together with other aspects of humanitarian law, by the International Conference on Human Rights at Tehran in 1968. In its Resolution XXIII the conference noted that the provisions of the Geneva Protocol of 1925 had not been universally accepted or applied and might need revision in the light of modern developments. Then, in the operative part of the Resolution, the conference requested the General Assembly of the United Nations to invite the Secretary-General to study:

> (a) Steps which could be taken to secure the better application of existing humanitarian international conventions and rules in all armed conflicts.
> (b) The need for additional humanitarian international Conventions or for possible revision of existing Conventions to ensure the better protection of civilians, prisoners and combatants in all armed conflicts and the prohibition and limitation of the use of certain methods and means of warfare.

The conference also requested the Secretary-General, in consultation with the International Committee of the Red Cross, to take steps to bring the subject to the attention of all members of the United Nations.

There was a great deal of discussion of these problems during the next few years, both in the General Assembly of the United Nations[8] and at the twenty-first International Conference of the Red Cross at Istanbul in 1969. Resolution XIV of the Istanbul conference related to weapons of mass destruction, and read in part as follows:

> The twenty-first International Conference of the Red Cross, Considering that the first and basic aim of the Red Cross is to protect mankind

> from the terrible suffering caused by armed conflicts, Taking into account the danger threatening mankind in the form of new techniques of warfare, particularly weapons of mass destruction, ... Requests the United Nations to pursue its efforts in this field, Requests the International Committee of the Red Cross to continue to devote great attention to this question, consistent with its work for the reaffirmation and development of humanitarian law and to take every step it deems possible,
> Renews its appeal to the Governments of States which have not yet done so to accede to the 1925 Geneva Protocol and to comply strictly with its provisions,
> Urges Governments to conclude as rapidly as possible an agreement banning the production and stock-piling of chemical and bacteriological weapons.

In addition, the conference, in its Resolution XIII, encouraged the ICRC to maintain and develop its co-operation with the United Nations and to pursue its efforts with a view to proposing rules to supplement existing humanitarian law and arranging a diplomatic conference for the purpose.

As a result of these and other developments the Swiss government convened the Diplomatic Conference on the Reaffirmation and Development of International Humanitarian Law applicable in Armed Conflicts. This held four sessions in Geneva from 1974 to 1977, which were attended by the representatives of more than a hundred governments, and produced two Protocols to the Geneva Conventions of 1949. The success of international conferences often depends on proper preparation, and the groundwork for this conference was laid by two sessions of a Conference of Government Experts in 1971 and 1972. Thus, when the Protocols finally emerged, they were the result of seven years' work by some of the world's leading specialists on the subject of humanitarian law.

3. The Protocols of 1977

The First Protocol relates to the protection of victims of international armed conflicts and was intended to bring the provisions of the 1949 Conventions up to date, especially as regards the use of weapons of mass destruction and the protection of the civilian population. The Second Protocol relates to the protection of victims of non-international armed conflicts and develops the rules in

Article 3 of the four Geneva Conventions which has already been quoted.[9]

Before agreement was reached on the Protocols there was a sharp difference of opinion as to whether humanitarian law can properly equate what is essentially an internal, national conflict with an international conflict. As already noted, since 1945 there has been an increasing number of conflicts which involve national liberation movements but which are not wars in the traditional sense. In discussion of these conflicts at the United Nations many Third World countries advocate the recognition of what they see as struggles against colonial and alien domination and racist regimes, in pursuit of the right to self-determination and independence. In December 1973, on the eve of the Diplomatic Conference, the General Assembly adopted a resolution in which it declared that such conflicts should be regarded as international armed conflicts in the sense of the Geneva Conventions of 1949 and that the participants in such conflicts should be accorded the same legal status as that granted to participants in international conflicts by the Conventions of 1949.[10] Whether the Protocols should reflect this policy was then fervently debated by the Diplomatic Conference in 1974. There, as in the UN General Assembly, there was a majority in favour, and as a result paragraph 4 of Article 1 of the First Protocol states explicitly that it applies to 'armed conflicts in which peoples are fighting against colonial domination and alien occupation and against racist régimes in the exercise of their right to self-determination ...'. The principle is thus expressly recognised in the text, but it raises many problems,[11] and may account for the fact that many governments have still to ratify this Protocol.

Other important provisions of the First Protocol are to be found in Part III, section 1 (Articles 35–42), concerning 'Methods and Means of Warfare', and Part IV (Articles 48–79), relating to the civilian population. Both concern the problems raised by modern weapons of mass destruction. Article 35 sets out three basic rules:

1. In any armed conflict, the right of the parties to the conflict to choose methods or means of warfare is not unlimited.
2. It is prohibited to employ weapons, projectiles and material and methods of warfare of a nature to cause superfluous injury or unnecessary suffering.
3. It is prohibited to employ methods or means of warfare which are

> intended, or may be expected, to cause widespread, long-term and severe damage to the natural environment.[12]

The next article relates to the development of new weapons and provides that in developing or acquiring them contracting parties are under an obligation to determine whether their use would violate the Protocol or any other rule of international law. The remaining articles of this section deal with other rules of general application, including the prohibition of killing, injuring or capturing an adversary by resort to perfidy; the prohibition of the improper use of the emblems of the Red Cross and the United Nations, the prohibition of giving no quarter, and the prohibition of attacking a person *hors de combat*. Section 2 of Part III then sets out a number of rules on combatant and prisoner-of-war status.

Part IV of the First Protocol contains more than thirty articles on the protection of the civilian population during hostilities, which are designed to develop and bring up to date the principles established in the Fourth Convention of 1949. Article 48 sets out the basic rule requiring that the parties to a conflict 'shall at all times distinguish between the civilian population and combatants and between civilian objects and military objectives and accordingly shall direct their operations only against military objectives'. Article 51 takes this further by providing that 'the civilian population as such, as well as individual civilians, shall not be the object of the attack' and by prohibiting indiscriminate attacks, including indiscriminate bombardment on a city, town or village, even if it contains a military objective. Many other prohibitions are set out in the following articles, including prohibitions of attacks on civilian objects, on historic monuments and works of art; the prohibition of the starvation of civilians or destruction of their food supplies; and of attacks on the natural environment. Reprisals against the civilian population are also prohibited. There are also separate and detailed provisions (Articles 61–7) about respect for civil defence organisations and services and about humanitarian relief measures (Articles 68–71). It is evident that these provisions are based on humane considerations and, to the extent that they are observed in practice, will do much to mitigate the effect of hostilities on the non-combatant population.

The Second Protocol of 1977 relates to the protection of victims of non-international armed conflicts.[13] It must be remembered, however, that wars of national liberation and armed struggle against racist regimes, as already explained, have been promoted by Protocol I to the status of international conflicts. Protocol II is therefore concerned with other forms of internal conflict, that is to say, with civil wars as generally understood.

The main object of this Protocol is to secure the humane treatment of those threatened by, but not directly involved in, such conflicts. This is stated in Article 4, of Part II, which is devoted to 'Humane Treatment':

> 1. All persons who do not take a direct part or who have ceased to take part in hostilities, whether or not their liberty has been restricted, are entitled to respect for their person, honour and convictions and religious practices. They shall in all circumstances be treated humanely, without any adverse distinction. It is prohibited to order that there shall be no survivors.
> 2. Without prejudice to the generality of the foregoing, the following acts against the persons referred to in paragraph 1 are and shall remain prohibited at any time and in any place whatsoever:
>   (a) violence to the life, health and physical or mental well-being of persons, in particular murder as well as cruel treatment such as torture, mutilation or any form of corporal punishment;
>   (b) collective punishments;
>   (c) taking hostages;
>   (d) acts of terrorism;
>   (e) outrages upon personal dignity, in particular humiliating and degrading treatment, rape, enforced prostitution and any form of indecent assault;
>   (f) slavery and the slave trade in all their forms;
>   (g) pillage;
>   (h) threats to commit any of the foregoing acts.

Protocol II, with twenty-eight articles, is much shorter than Protocol I (102 articles). Part III contains five articles on the treatment of the wounded, sick and shipwrecked, which recall the first two Conventions of 1949. Part IV then sets out in Articles 13–18 provisions concerning the protection of the civilian population. These rules are broadly similar to, though less detailed than, the corresponding provisions of the First Protocol. They prohibit attacks on the civilian population, starvation and destruction of food stocks, attacks on historic monuments and works of art, and the displacement of the civilian population, and also contain rules protecting the personnel of relief organisations. The last ten articles are Final Provisions of a technical nature.

The two Protocols of 1977 represent the culmination of many years' work by the representatives of more than a hundred governments.[14] It was especially significant that many States from the Third World, which were not independent when the Conventions of 1949 were drafted, were able to play their part in the development of humanitarian law nearly thirty years later. There is no doubt that the substantive provisions of the Protocols were conceived in a liberal and humanitarian spirit which is to be encouraged. The Protocols, which were opened for signature in June 1977, both came into force in December 1978. At the present time Protocol I has received seventy-one ratifications and Protocol II sixty-four ratifications.[15]

4. *The protecting power*

Another issue with a direct bearing on human rights, and which has been the subject of a great deal of discussion in recent years, is the institution of the 'protecting power'.[16]

The utilisation of protecting powers can be traced back to the Franco-Prussian War of 1870 and the system was widely adopted during the First World War. It was first established on a conventional basis in the Geneva Convention on the Treatment of Prisoners of War of 1929. It involves a triangular arrangement between the two belligerents and a third, neutral power. Each of the belligerents accepts that a third power should be charged with the protection of its interests in the other belligerent State. During the Second World War the scope of the conflict was such that the number of neutral States which could act as protecting powers was very small. As a result Switzerland represented thirty-five belligerents, and Switzerland and Sweden together represented practically all of them.

All four Geneva Conventions of 1949 recognised the system of the protecting power. They also provide that 'the High Contracting Parties may at any time agree to entrust to an organisation which offers all guarantees of impartiality and efficacy, the duties incumbent upon the protecting powers by virtue of the present Convention'. When there is no agreed protecting power or organisation so appointed, then humanitarian organisations, such as the International Committee of the Red Cross, may request or be requested to assume the humanitarian functions provided for in the Convention.

Thus, in the words of the UN report, the system of the Geneva Conventions may be summed up by saying that while the primary responsibility for the application of the Conventions rests with the parties themselves, a protecting power or a substitute humanitarian organisation should be available in all cases to co-operate with the parties and to supervise the application of the Conventions.[17]

In practice, however, this system has not functioned well in the many armed conflicts which have broken out since the Second World War. Indeed, over the last forty years advantage has rarely been taken of the institution of protecting powers. It is estimated that the services of the International Committee of the Red Cross have been accepted in approximately half the armed conflicts which have occurred during this period. A further point is that today the functions of the protecting power or agency should not be, as in the original conception, to look after the interests of the belligerent State. What is required, in the context of modern humanitarian law, is a system to look after the interests and secure the humane treatment of the sick, the wounded, prisoners and other victims of armed conflict.

These considerations led the UN Secretary-General to conclude that:

> While the International Committee of the Red Cross and certain organisations play a most useful role, there would be pressing need for measures to improve and strengthen the present system of international supervision and assistance to parties to armed conflicts in their observance of humanitarian norms of international law. These measures, based on what already exists, should be regarded as complementary rather than competitive.[18]

The need for strengthening and improving the existing system led him to put forward the suggestion that an international agency of an independent character, possibly within the framework of the United Nations system, should be set up in order to exercise the necessary functions.[19] Reference was made to a proposal by the French delegation at the Geneva conference of 1949 for the creation of a 'High International Committee' consisting of thirty members, who would be eminent personalities known for their independence and services to humanity, such as religious leaders, eminent scientists, and Nobel Prizewinners. This proposal was not adopted in 1949, but the report suggested that it might be revived in a modified form. The usefulness of a UN organ to discharge humanitarian functions is illustrated by the record of service of the International Refugee Organisation, UNRWA, UNICEF and the Office of the High Commissioner for Refugees.

This suggestion was not meant to be a criticism of the International Committee of the Red Cross, but was put forward in the belief that an inter-governmental organisation, financed by governments, might have possibilities of action and financial resources greater than those of the ICRC. A variant of the same idea would be to entrust the proposed functions to the ICRC, if this would be acceptable, at the same time enlarging its competence and increasing its budget by international agreement, in order to enable it to carry out these additional tasks.

Ideas of this sort, however, did not find favour with the diplomatic conference. Instead, Article 5 of the First Protocol retains and strengthens the existing system of the protecting power. Paragraph 3 of this article provides that if a protecting power is not appointed, the ICRC 'shall offer its good offices to the Parties to the conflict', with a view to the designation of a protecting power; and that if this attempt is unsuccessful, 'the Parties to the conflict shall accept without delay an offer which may be made by the ICRC ...'. There is thus a definite obligation on them to admit the good offices of the ICRC and, if necessary, to accept it as a substitute. There is, however, no corresponding provision in the Second Protocol relating to internal conflicts.[20]

III. Human rights and humanitarian law

This brief survey of the recent evolution of humanitarian law and some of its current problems brings us to what for the human rights lawyer is the heart of the matter: the relationship between human rights and humanitarian law.[21]

M. Jean Pictet has written: 'Humanitarian law comprises two branches: the law of war and the law of human rights.'[22] While recognising the force of this view, the approach we have adopted is quite different. The contention of this book is that humanitarian law is one branch of the law of human rights, and that human rights provide the basis for humanitarian law.

It is not difficult to see why the opposite view is held. The emergence of humanitarian law antedates that of human rights law: the former has developed over more than a hundred years, while the latter has been the concern of international law for less than half a century. The United Nations Charter in 1945 contained brief, if numerous, references to human rights and it was only in 1948 that the Universal Declaration was adopted in Paris, just a year before humanitarian law, already highly developed, was codified in the Geneva Conventions of 1949.

When we look at the substance of the two disciplines, however, it is apparent that human rights law is the genus of which humanitarian law is a species. Human rights law relates to the basic rights of all human beings everywhere, at all times. Humanitarian law relates to the rights of particular categories of human beings, principally, the sick, the wounded and prisoners of war, in particular circumstances, that is during periods of armed conflict.

When seen in this perspective, it is clear that the basic texts relating to human rights, notably the Universal Declaration and the United Nations Covenants, lay down standards of general application to all human beings, by reason of their humanity. Those standards ideally should apply at all times and in all circumstances. Unfortunately, some of them are suspended in time of war, which is in many ways a contradiction of the whole idea of human rights. But even in time of war certain rights must be respected by combatants towards their enemies and, precisely because war is a time when many rights are suspended, it becomes all the more necessary to define and protect those rights which must still be respected. They constitute what might be called 'core human rights', from which no derogation is permitted, even in times of armed conflict.

As we saw in Chapter 2, the United Nations Covenant on Civil and Political Rights recognises this principle in Article 4. This permits derogations from the obligations resulting from the Covenant 'in time of public emergency which threatens the life of the nation and the existence of which is officially proclaimed'. But paragraph 2 of Article 4 lists seven 'core' rights with regard to which no derogation may be made. These are:

1. The right to life.
2. The prohibition of torture or inhuman treatment.
3. The prohibition of slavery and servitude.
4. The prohibition of imprisonment for debt.
5. The prohibition of retroactivity of the criminal law.
6. The right to recognition as a person before the law.
7. The right to freedom of thought, conscience and religion.

The same approach is found in Article 15 of the European Convention on Human Rights, which permits derogation 'in time of war or other public emergency threatening the life of the nation', but permits no derogation as regards four rights: the right to life,[23] the prohibition of torture and inhuman treatment, the prohibition of slavery or servitude, and the prohibition of retrospective criminal law.

There are similar provisions in the American Convention on Human Rights,[24] while neither the African Charter on Human and Peoples' Rights, nor the Covenant on Economic Social and Cultural Rights has any provision permitting derogation.

It is therefore clear that the major human rights treaties are all based on the principle that some human rights are so fundamental that they must be respected at all times, even in periods of armed conflict. This, of course, is one of the foundations of humanitarian law. But it is not sufficient. The effective protection of the victims of armed conflict requires not only that they should enjoy certain of the basic rights which belong to everyone, but also that they should benefit from certain supplementary rights which are necessary precisely because they are victims of armed conflict, such as medical care, the right of prisoners to correspond with their families, the right of repatriation in certain circumstances, and so on. These are the matters on which the provisions of humanitarian law for the particular situation of armed conflict go beyond the requirements of human rights law, which are of general application.

Thus, it is evident that a number of the rights which humanitarian law attempts to ensure to the victims of armed conflict have been included in human rights treaties as rights which should be guaranteed to everyone. To see this interaction more clearly, it is necessary to look at these texts in a little more detail. Which humanitarian rights are secured by the UN Covenant on Civil and Political Rights even in times of war?

The first of the rights from which no derogation may be made is the right to life (Article 6). The text permitting derogations (Article 4) does not indicate that they are permissible in time of war, no doubt on account of the reluctance of the General Assembly to admit that war can ever be lawful, but the phrase 'in time of public emergency which threatens the life of the nation' is clearly wide enough to include a time of war. It should be observed, however, that in order for a derogation to be lawful, the public emergency must be 'officially proclaimed'. This means that in situations of undeclared war or civil strife no derogation is permissible in the absence of an official proclamation of a state of emergency, with the result that in this kind of situation all the rights proclaimed in the Covenant must continue to be respected.

The special protection of the right to life means that even in time of armed conflict acts such as the killing of prisoners and the execution of hostages are unlawful. Article 15 of the European Convention also treats the right to life as sacrosanct, but adds the limitation 'except in respect of deaths resulting from lawful acts of war'. However, such acts as the killing of prisoners and the execution of hostages are never 'lawful acts of war', so the result is the same. Does this article also prohibit the killing of civilians by weapons of mass destruction? It would seem difficult to maintain that it does not.

The second sacrosanct article in the UN Covenant is of supreme importance: 'No one shall be subjected to torture or to cruel, inhuman or degrading treatment or punishment. In particular, no one shall be subjected without his free consent to medical or scientific experimentation' (Article 7). This prohibition of inhuman treatment is far-reaching and covers many of the rights protected by humanitarian law. Admittedly, it would be better to have a positive formulation, such as 'all persons shall be treated with humanity and with respect for the inherent dignity of the human person'. Such a positive formulation is to be found in Article 10 of the Covenant, where it relates to 'all persons deprived of their liberty', which would, of course, include prisoners of war. But this is a less effective guarantee, because Article 10 is not one of the articles from which no derogation may be made.

Article 8 is also important in the present context. Its first two paragraphs prohibit slavery and servitude and are not subject to derogation. Unfortunately, paragraph 3, containing the prohibition of forced or compulsory labour is subject to derogation, with the result that this guarantee does not necessarily apply at a time of public emergency which is officially proclaimed. Nevertheless, the right of derogation is not absolute. Article 4 permits States to take measures derogating from their obligations under the Covenant only 'to the extent strictly required by the exigencies of the situation' and 'provided that such measures are not inconsistent with their other obligations under international law and do not involve discrimination ...'. Consequently, there are many circumstances in which the prohibition of forced or compulsory labour will still apply, and so it seems fair to regard this also as a humanitarian right which is, as a general rule, protected by Article 8, paragraph 3.

Four other rights protected by the Covenant are specially protected and not subject to derogation. As indicated in the list given earlier, these are: freedom from imprisonment for debt, prohibition of retrospective criminal law, the right to recognition as a person before the law, and freedom of thought, conscience and religion. However, these are perhaps less relevant to our present investigation of the relationship between humanitarian law and the law of human rights.

Drawing attention to the fact that a number of important humanitarian rights are protected by the UN Covenant, and *a fortiori* by the European Convention on Human Rights, is not meant in any way to disparage or to undervalue the humanitarian Conventions. Our object is simply to show that the two disciplines share a number of areas of common concern and that, though humanitarian law was developed earlier in time, human rights law is coming to cover some of the same ground and is likely to continue to expand. This has consquences we shall consider in a moment.

That there is now a growing measure of convergence between the two subjects has been amply demonstrated at international conferences. The Tehran conference in 1968 was an 'International Conference on Human Rights' and the major event of International Human Rights Year. It is generally agreed that one of the more important texts adopted by the conference was its Resolution XXIII, which carried the title 'Human rights in armed conflict'. This was based on the fundamental precept that 'peace is the underlying condition for the full observance of human rights and war is their negation'. Resolution 2444 (XXIII) of the General Assembly, adopted later in the same year, is a resolution 'on respect for human rights in armed conflicts', and the same title was given to the report prepared by the Secretary-General following the adoption of this resolution. It is therefore abundantly clear that humanitarian law is coming to be recognised as the particular branch of human rights law which relates to human rights in times of armed conflict.

The convergence – one may even say interpenetration – of the two disciplines was underlined by the 'Istanbul Declaration' of the twenty-first International Conference of the Red Cross in 1969. This read, in part, as follows:

> The twenty-first International Conference of the Red Cross,
> Aware of the unity and indivisibility of the human family,
> Declares:
> That man has the right to enjoy lasting peace,
> That it is essential for him to be able to live a full and satisfactory life founded on respect of his rights and of his fundamental liberty,
> That this aim can be achieved only if human rights as set forth and defined in the Universal Declaration of Human Rights and the Humanitarian Conventions are respected and observed.
> That it is a human right to be free from all fears, acts of violence and brutality, threats and anxieties likely to injure man in his person, his honour and his dignity,
> ...
> That the universally recognised general principles of law demand that the rule of law be effectively guaranteed everywhere ... .

The Red Cross, therefore, is concerned with human rights, fundamental freedoms, non-discrimination and the rule of law, just as the United Nations, for its part, is concerned with humanitarian law and respect for human rights in times of armed conflict.

What is the practical effect of this convergence and interpenetration of the two disciplines? The UN Covenant on Civil and Political Rights, as we have seen, affords a new legal basis for the protection of several humanitarian rights. Moreover, it will have a number of other important consequences. The entry into force of the Covenant means that the contracting parties are under an obligation to report to the United Nations on the measures they have adopted to give effect to the rights which the Covenant guarantees. Under the provisions of Article 40 the procedure involves examination by the Human Rights Committee of the reports of governments, possible consideration of them by the Economic and Social Council and by the appropriate Specialised Agencies and, under Article 45, an annual report by the Human Rights Committee to the General Assembly, via ECOSOC, on the work it has accomplished. This therefore constitutes the basis of a modest system of international supervision as regards certain humanitarian rights.

Another possible consequence is that if the States concerned have accepted the optional procedure for inter-State complaints under Article 41 of the Covenant, other States may bring a violation before the UN Committee. Moreover, it will be recalled that if they are parties to the Optional Protocol to the Covenant, they accept that the UN Human Rights Committee can 'receive and consider communications from individuals subject to its jurisdiction who claim to be victims of a violation ... of any of the rights set forth in the Covenant'. This clearly amounts to a further step in the direction of international supervision.

A final consequence is that acceptance of the Covenant, with or without the optional arrangements, involves accepting that respect for its provisions is a matter of concern to international law and the international community. It follows that a party to the Covenant cannot properly object that the question of respect for the rights protected is a matter 'essentially within the domestic jurisdiction of the State' within the meaning of Article 2(7) of the Charter. It can therefore be seen that the inclusion of certain humanitarian rights in the UN Covenant is of major significance because as part of the Covenant they are subject to a greater measure of international control than under existing humanitarian Conventions.

Notes

1 This chapter is based in part on a report presented by Professor A. H. Robertson to a conference organised by the International Institute of Humanitarian Law at San Remo in 1970 and published under the title *Human Rights as the basis of International Humanitarian Law*, Lugano, 1971. From the many works dealing with humanitarian law and the Red Cross the following merit particular attention: H. Coursier, 'L'evolution du droit international humanitaire', 99 *Hague Recueil des Cours*, 1960, p. 357; G. I. A. D. Draper, 'The Geneva Conventions of 1949', 114 *Hague Recueil des Cours*, 1965, p. 63; G. Schwarzenberger, *International Law as applied by International Courts and*

Tribunals. Vol. II The Law of Armed Conflict, London, 1968; R. I. Miller (ed.), *The Law of War*, Lexington, 1975; S. E. Nahlik and others, 'Changing rules for changing forms of warfare', *Law and Contemporary Problems*, XLIV, 1978, p. 1; M. Walzer, *Just and Unjust Wars*, London, 1978; G. I. A. D. Draper, 'The implementation and enforcement of the Geneva Conventions of 1949 and of the two additional Protocols of 1978', 164 *Hague Recueil des Cours*, 1979, p. 1; T. Meron, 'On the inadequate reach of humanitarian and human rights law and the need for a new instrument', *American Journal of International Law*, LXXVII, 1983, p. 589 and Y. Dinstein, 'Human rights in armed conflict: international humanitarian law', in T. Meron (ed.), *Human Rights in International Law*, Oxford, 1984, pp. 345–68. An extensive bibliography is *International Humanitarian Law: Basic Bibliography*, compiled by Jiri Toman and Huynh Thi Huong, Henry Dunant Institute, Geneva, 1979.

2 For a good account of the Red Cross and the various national movements, see S. Rosenne, 'The Red Cross, Red Crescent, Red Lion and Sun and the Red Shield of David', *Israel Yearbook of Human Rights*, V, 1975, p. 9.

3 G. I. A. D. Draper, 114 *Hague Recueil des Cours*, 1965, p. 66.

4 The figures are from J. S. Pictet, 'Armed conflicts – laws and customs', *I.C.J. Review*, 1969, p. 30.

5 As of 1 January 1988. See J.-B. Marie, 'International instruments relating to human rights', *Human Rights Law Journal*, IX, 1988, p. 113. For discussion of the effects of such widespread adherence, see T. Meron, 'The Geneva Conventions as customary international law', *American Journal of International Law*, LXXXI, 1987, p. 348.

6 See particularly G. I. A. D. Draper, *op. cit.* n. 3, pp. 82–100.

7 J. S. Pictet, 'The twentieth International Conference of the Red Cross', *I.C.J. Journal*, VII, 1966, p. 15.

8 See particularly Resolution 2444 (XXIII) of 1968, reaffirming that it is prohibited to launch attacks against the civilian population as such; the Secretary-General's report on *Respect for Human Rights in Armed Conflict* (UN doc. A/7720, 1969); Resolution 2597 (XXIV) of 1969, requesting the Secretary-General to consult the International Committee of the Red Cross about further action; Resolution 2603 (XXIV) of 1969, declaring the use of chemical and bacteriological weapons contrary to international law; and the discussions in the Commission on Human Rights in 1970, doc. E/CN. 4/1039, pp. 24–6.

9 The text of the two Protocols may be found in various collections and are published as a separate booklet, *Protocols additional to the Geneva Convention of 1949*, by the International Committee of the Red Cross, Geneva, 1977. For discussion, in addition to the later references in n. 1, see: L. C. Green, 'The new law of armed conflict', *Canadian Yearbook of International Law*, XV, 1977, p. 3; Y. Dinstein, 'The new Geneva Protocols', *Yearbook of World Affairs*, XXXIII, 1979, p. 265; G. H. Aldrich, 'New life for the laws of war', *American Journal of International Law*, LXXV, 1981, p. 764 and B. A. Wortley, 'Observations on the revision of the 1949 Geneva "Red Cross" Conventions', *British Year Book of International Law*, LIV, 1983, p. 143.

10 The General Assembly was divided on this issue. The Resolution was adopted by eighty-three votes in favour, thirteen against and nineteen abstentions.

11 Two of the problems which arise are the following. In any international conflict there are two (or more) governments which are parties to the conflict and can assume the obligations resulting from the Geneva Conventions. In struggles against colonial domination, etc., there is a government, on the one side, and the insurgents, on the other. Are the insurgents legally capable of assuming international obligations and materially capable of enforcing respect for them? Article 96(3) of Protocol I attempts to deal with this problem by stating that 'the authority representing a people' engaged in such a conflict may make a declaration undertaking to apply the Conventions. But will this work in practice? Who decides whether the 'authority' is capable of assuming international obligations and whether the government represents 'colonial domination, alien occupation or a racist regime'? Secondly, what happens when there are several different liberation movements (as in Angola before independence) which do not constitute or recognise any single 'authority'? For discussion of these and other problems relating to internal conflict, see W. V. O'Brien, 'The *jus in bello* in revolutionary war and counterinsurgency', *Virginia Journal of International Law*, XVIII 1977–78, p. 193; D. Schindler, 'The different types of armed conflicts according to the Geneva Conventions and Protocols', 163 *Hague Recueil des Cours*, 1979, p. 117; and G. Abi-Saab, 'Wars of national liberation in the Geneva Conventions and Protocols', *ibid.*, vol. 165, 1979, p. 353.

12 When signing the Protocols the United Kingdom and the United States declared that they interpreted the First Protocol as not relating to the prohibition or use of nuclear weapons. Their view was (and is) that such questions should be settled at other meetings and not in the framework of humanitarian law. For discussion of the status of other weapons, see W. J. Fenrick, 'New developments in the law concerning the use of conventional weapons in armed conflict', *Canadian Yearbook of International Law*, XIX, 1981, p. 229.

13 For discussion of this Protocol, see D. P. Forsythe, 'Legal management of internal war: the 1977 Protocol on Non-International Armed Conflict', *American Journal of International Law*, LXXII, 1978, p. 272; A. Cassese, 'The status of rebels under the 1977 Geneva Protocol on Non-International Armed Conflicts', *International and Comparative Law Quarterly*, XXX, 1981, p. 416 and D. P. Forsythe, 'Human rights and internal conflicts: trends and recent developments', *California Western Journal of International Law*, XII, 1982, p. 287.

14 110 governments were represented at the Diplomatic Conference, 1974–77.

15 As of 1 January 1988. For a list of the parties to the Protocols, see Marie, 'International instruments'.

16 On the operation of the system of the protecting power and of the International Red Cross, see H. S. Levie, 'Prisoners of war and the protecting power', *American Journal of International Law*, LV, 1961, p. 374; D. P. Forsythe, 'Who guards the guardians: third parties and the law of armed conflict', *ibid.*, LXX, 1976, p. 41; and A. B. Pierce, 'Humanitarian protection for the victims of war: the system of protecting powers and the role of the ICRC', *Military Law Review*, LXXXX, 1980, p. 89. See also UN doc. A/7720, paras 202–27. This document is a report by the Secretary-General to the General Assembly in 1969 which examines many of the problems discussed in this chapter.

17 *Ibid.*, para. 212.
18 *Ibid.*, para. 215.
19 *Ibid.*, paras. 221–7.
20 For further suggestions aimed at strengthening the measures of implementation of humanitarian law, see the first edition of this book at pp. 181–4.
21 On this subject in addition to the references in n. 1, see Pictet, 'Conference of the Red Cross', and M. Mushkat, 'The development of international humanitarian law and the law of human rights', *German Yearbook of International Law*, XXI, 1978, p. 150.
22 Pictet, 'Conference of the Red Cross', p. 22.
23 Except in relation to deaths resulting from lawful acts of war.
24 Article 27(2) of the American Convention, in which there are eleven rights which are not subject to derogation.

CHAPTER 9

International human rights law today and tomorrow

Having reviewed the position in human rights law by examining the various instruments and procedures individually, we are now in a position to stand back a little and consider what this extensive and varied range of material can tell us about the present state of human rights law and the factors which will determine its future.

1. The growth of human rights law

No one reading the material set out in the preceding chapters can fail to be struck by the dramatic development of this part of international law over the last forty years. As we have seen, the Universal Declaration of 1948 was the first international text to list human rights as such, although the United Nations Charter, three years earlier, had already indicated that these were likely to be a prominent issue in the post-war world. From such early beginnings developed the elaborate network of treaties which form the basis of the modern law.

Among these treaties it is not difficult to identify some which can be considered as of key significance. Of the regional instruments pride of place must be granted to the European Convention of 1950, the first, and in terms of effectiveness still the most important, of the regional instruments, and the instrument which, by demonstrating the feasibility and value of regional arrangements, set the pattern for the subsequent American Convention of 1969 and the African Charter of 1981. At the universal level the most significant treaties are, of course, the two United Nations Covenants of 1966. The outcome of a long period of gestation, the Covenant on Civil and Political Rights enables any State which wishes to do so to assume obligations not unlike those of the

European Convention, while the Covenant on Economic, Social and Cultural Rights reflects the desire of many members of the United Nations to broaden the human rights agenda to include matters of social and economic policy.

The instruments just mentioned are rightly regarded as landmarks in the evolution of the modern law. However, the contribution of agreements dealing with more specific aspects of human rights should not be forgotten. Although it has not been possible to discuss these in detail, we have tried to show that the general obligations created by the regional conventions and the Covenants have not only been refined by a more detailed treatment in other treaties, but in many cases have been supplemented by the creation of entirely new obligations and procedures. It will be recalled, for example, that the 1966 Convention on the Elimination of All Forms of Racial Discrimination and the 1979 Convention on the Elimination of All Forms of Discrimination against Women have each made an important contribution to the developing law on discrimination, and in the field of economic and social rights, the treaties and recommendations emanating from the ILO have generated an enormous and effective code of international labour law.

Treaties dealing with individual issues are especially important where their subject matter falls outside the mainstream of human rights law. In this respect the various agreements relating to humanitarian law are particularly noteworthy. While torture and a number of other issues which arise in this field are already covered by other treaties, humanitarian law is a subject which is sufficiently specialised to have acquired its own set of rules and principles. As we saw in the previous chapter, after this need was recognised at the end of the last century, such a system soon began to evolve and, following one major revision in the four Geneva Conventions of 1949, has been further developed in the two Protocols of 1977.

The latest additions to humanitarian law are a reminder that the treaties which form the basis of the modern law are constantly being modified and added to. New law may take the form of more or less elaborate arrangements to supplement existing conventions, as with the Geneva Protocols and the various protocols to the European Convention, or entirely new agreements, as with the recent UN, European and American Conventions on torture. The form depends largely on the subject matter and is of secondary importance.[1] The vital point is that the number of human rights treaties is not static, but is constantly being increased.

The conclusion of a treaty is usually a sign of progress, but to create new obligations the products of so much diplomatic effort must be accepted by States. The real test of legal progress is therefore not the number of new agreements, but the extent to which human rights treaties are being ratified. To put the point in a slightly different way, even if no new human rights treaties were to be concluded, we could still speak of human rights law developing if those already agreed were being more widely accepted.

Applying the test of ratification, we find that the present position gives considerable cause for the satisfaction. There is, naturally, often an interval of several years between the conclusion of a treaty and its entry into force, but some recent conventions have been ratified very quickly – the European Convention on Torture, for example –, others have come into force sooner than expected – the African Charter, for example –, while agreements such as the UN Covenants, which have been in force for some time, continue to attract a steady stream of adherents. This is encouraging because it shows that the network of obligations is continuing to develop. It is worth remembering, however, that a great many members of the United Nations have yet to accept either of the Covenants.

As these and other conventions receive progressively wider adherence, the absence of this or that State will become less important since the obligations concerned can become binding on all States by virtue of customary international law. However, this cannot happen in relation to instruments such as the Optional Protocol, which deal with important procedural matters, and in any case States are more likely to respect a commitment which has been accepted specifically rather than one which arises by virtue of customary law. The wider ratification of human rights treaties must therefore be regarded as an objective at least as important as the conclusion of new treaties.[2]

If the growing network of treaty obligations is one measure of the growth of human rights law, the development of means of implementation is perhaps even more significant. An international lawyer from the pre-United Nations era would no doubt be surprised at the range of obligations which States have assumed in the field of human rights. However, he would be astounded by the range and number of international bodies which have been given the competence to supervise the performance of those obligations and whose powers of investigation may extend into every corner of domestic jurisdiction. As we have seen, these range from independent bodies such as the United Nations Committee on Human Rights, to groups of governmental representatives such as the UN Commission; from courts, like the European and Inter-American Courts of Human Rights, to quasi-judicial and non-judicial bodies like the various regional commissions and the two UN bodies; and from bodies with a rather broad remit like all of those just mentioned, to those with a very specific function such as the UN Committee on the Elimination of Discrimination against Women and the European Committee for the Prevention of Torture. These are clearly very different kinds of organs. Yet they are all concerned in some sense with the implementation of human rights. As it is now rather unusual for a human rights treaty to be concluded without some form of supervisory machinery, the proliferation of such bodies and the corresponding recognition that means of implementation are an essential complement to substantive obligations, must be regarded as a second element in the growth of human rights law.

No review of the developments which have taken place in recent years would be complete without reference to a third element which has contributed to the growth of the law and which seems likely to be even more important in the future. We refer to the practice of the bodies which have just been mentioned. Human rights law is more than the substantive and procedural obligations to be found in treaties or general international law; it is the process whereby the procedures are used to interpret and apply the substantive principles, the process, in short, through which law on paper becomes law in action.

It is easy to see that it is at the level of application that human rights law is at present least satisfactory. Although, as we have noted, the creation of means of implementation is in itself highly significant, the deficiencies of many of our current arrangements are all too obvious. The incompleteness, which is evident when we study the substantive law, is even more apparent when we consider the means of implementation. For where implementation procedures are optional, States often decline to accept them. Encouraging States to accept the competence of the Human Rights Committee, or the optional provisions of the regional conventions, is therefore a primary goal.

Similarly, the machinery itself is often not as good as it might be. In addition to the problems of possible conflicts of jurisdiction, many institutions need more powers than States have so far been prepared to give them, if they are to work effectively. Then there is the crucial issue of enforcement. Even an organ with the jurisdiction and powers to handle cases properly requires some form of institutional support to implement its decisions. However, such support is rarely available. Greece, as we have seen in Chapter 4, was effectively expelled from the Council of Europe for violating its undertakings, but in most situations, even when violations of human rights are gross and persistent, sanctions of this kind are simply not available.

But there is also another side to the picture. Institutions to supervise the application of human rights conventions exist and are used. Individuals are released from detention, claimants are compensated, laws and administrative practices are exposed and changed, all as a result of proceedings before international bodies. Moreover, although the primary purpose of such proceedings is to vindicate the rights of the individual, in many cases the decisions which are handed down also develop the law. Much of the work we have described has had this effect and, as the institutions set up by the various treaties continue their work, this source of law is likely to grow.

How this process occurs is a subject we have discussed elsewhere and which need not be considered here.[3] That it occurs, and sometimes in ways that might not be expected, is sufficiently demonstrated by the work of the European Court of Justice, which has held that fundamental rights and general principles of law analogous to fundamental rights are part of Community Law.[4] In reaching this conclusion the Court relied on the European Convention which, as we have seen, has itself already generated a substantial jurisprudence. Now it would be wrong to equate the work of the Court of Justice, which is mainly concerned with other matters, with that of the Strasbourg institutions, which are wholly concerned with human rights. It would similarly be wrong to suggest that all bodies concerned with human rights questions have made, or are likely to make, equally important contributions to legal development. Together, however, they make a contribution which is too important to ignore, giving life to each human rights text and materiality to its ideals.

2. The reality of human rights law

What has been said so far is enough to demonstrate that at the United Nations, through the work of the Specialised Agencies and in the various regional systems, there have come into being a number of schemes of human rights protection, all of which are being both developed and added to. The question which must now be considered is whether, as a result of this activity, it is correct to speak of a developing international law of human rights. We must first consider what this question means. If we are content to regard 'the international law of human rights' as simply the sum total of the various treaties, procedures, principles of customary law and case-law, the answer is obviously 'yes'. If, on the other hand, what we mean is whether in the light of current practice the different human rights schemes now exhibit a degree of convergence which makes it inappropriate to think of them as entirely separate phenomena, then our question is more interesting, and the answer more complex.

There is, of course, no doubt that historically the law of human rights grew up in a number of separate compartments. We saw in Chapter 1 that international concern for human rights can be traced to the movement to abolish slavery in the early years of the nineteenth century and the beginnings of the movement to humanise warfare later in the century. Though both sprang from a similar humanitarian impulse, as legal developments they had little in common, and this was also true of the next step, the attempt to provide minorities with protection through the League of Nations. As this was another quite separate issue, it was dealt with through its own treaties and procedures.

The signing of the United Nations Charter brought about a fundamental change. For the first time 'human rights' were referred to in the constitution of an international organisation. It is true that the reference was in general terms, but the very mention was significant because it suggested that here was a concept of universal application. As we have seen, the Universal Declaration in 1948 then sought to define what was meant. The process of defining human rights was carried further by the United Nations Covenants and the various regional and other instruments.

Now although each new development was influenced by what had gone before, and in turn influenced its successors, this process did not produce a series of identical conventions. For, as we have noted, the various regional conventions differ to a considerable extent in the ground they cover, and even when they are concerned with the same right – the right to a fair trial, for example – they are frequently couched in different terms. In the same way, although there are important areas of overlap between the various regional conventions and the United Nations Covenants, there are again many important differences between them.

The result is a complex pattern of obligations, so that while it is certainly possible to think in terms of what the Inter-American Court of Human Rights has called 'the common core of basic human rights standards',[5] generalisation is difficult and each right or concept should be considered separately. It is obviously beyond the scope of the present work to undertake this kind of investigation.[6] However, a glance at some of the recent case-law of human rights tribunals will perhaps be enough to show how treaty provisions can have a significance beyond their immediate context, and how human rights law is being progressively developed.

Human rights conventions often divide their articles into two parts. First a statement of the right concerned, then a qualifying provision defining the circumstances under which a derogation, or limitation, of the right is permitted. Probably the best known is the phrase to be found in several articles of the European Convention that any limitations on a right shall be 'prescribed by law' and 'necessary in a democratic society' for the attainment of certain objectives. The meaning of these words has been an issue in a number of cases in the European Court. In the *Malone case*,[7] for example, the Court emphasised that to be 'in accordance with law' an interference must not only have some basis in the domestic law, but the law in question must also be accessible and formulated with sufficient precision to enable the citizen to regulate his conduct. This interpretation has also been adopted in other cases.

Other human rights instruments, as one would expect, contain some very similar qualifications. For example, Article 15 of the American Convention provides for the right of peaceful assembly subject only to restrictions which are 'imposed in conforming with the law and necessary in a democratic society ...'[8] and Article 16 deals with freedom of association in similar terms. Likewise, Article 8 of the African Charter on freedom of conscience and religion and Article 9 on freedom of assembly,[9] and in the same vein Article 4 of the United Nations Covenant on Economic, Social and Cultural Rights, which provides that:

> ... in the enjoyment of those rights provided by the State in conformity with the present Covenant, the State may subject such rights only to such limitations *as are determined by law only in so far as this may be compatible with the nature of these rights and solely for the purpose of promoting the general welfare in a democratic society.*[10]

In view of this very similar terminology it would seem that we are justified in speaking here of an international law of human rights and in suggesting that the approach which is adopted towards these common provisions in one system is likely to be important generally. If that is correct, then in view of the extensive practice which is now on record under the European Convention and which has already influenced the Inter-American Court,[11] we already have a significant jurisprudence in which the scope and meaning of some key concepts in human rights law have been considered.

The point just made about the transferability, so to speak, of interpretations of general concepts applies with equal force to many substantive provisions. Again, the essential requirement is that the right is dealt with in substantially similar terms.

In the provisions concerning a fair trial, for instance, there is an important difference in the treatment of civil rights and obligations, but the reference to a 'criminal charge' is substantially similar in the European Convention, the American Convention and the International Covenant on Civil and Political Rights.[12] The question of what constitutes a 'criminal charge' has generated almost as much case-law for the European Court as the meaning of civil rights and obligations. The Court has had to consider, for instance, how far disciplinary proceedings in prison involve criminal charges,[13] how the article applies to military discipline,[14] and whether it is open to a State to avoid Article 6 by classifying road traffice offences as 'administrative offences'.[15] The reasoning of the European Court in these cases should prove very helpful when similar questions arise, as no doubt they will, in other international bodies. Here, then, because we are dealing with a right couched in broadly similar terms in the various conventions, we can certainly speak of the development of a truly international human rights law.

The meaning of 'criminal charge' is just one example and there are many others. For example, the meaning of 'discrimination' was considered by the European Court in the *Belgian Linguistics case*[16] in a judgement which was referred to by the Inter-American Court in the *Proposed Amendments case.*[17] The meaning of 'forced labour' in Article 4 of the European Convention is another instructive example. When interpreting this term in the *Van der Mussele case*,[18] the Court treated the concept of forced labour as a general one by making use of an ILO Convention on the subject.[19] Likewise, there is the requirement in Article 6 of the European Convention that the tribunal hearing a case be 'independent and impartial' and that its judgement and proceedings shall be public. These requirements have all been subject to extensive interpretation in cases raising issues which will certainly arise in other tribunals. Finally, it is interesting to note that when considering the requirement of publicity for a domestic court's judgement, the European Court referred to the corresponding provision of the International Covenant on Civil and Political Rights.[20] Although the Covenant is in slightly different terms, the Court's decision in this case had the effect of assimilating the two provisions.

Before leaving this topic there is one important qualification which should be made. This relates to the way in which human rights law is applied in various sytems. There is, as we have seen, already a good deal of overlap among the various human rights instruments as regards both general concepts and the rights which are to be protected. As a consequence, even if there is no further harmonisation, it seems reasonable to speak here of 'international human rights law' and to expect that where a particular right is common to, say, the European Convention and the American Convention, the interpretation and application of a provision by the European institutions will influence the decisions of the American institutions and vice-versa. This influence is, however, something which will vary a good deal from case to case, not just because there is no formal obligation to follow the rulings under another Convention, but also because, as we pointed out when discussing the merits of regionalism, in some situations it would be unreasonable to do so.

An example which springs to mind is the right to a hearing 'within a reasonable time'. This is common to all three regional conventions. However, it is very unlikely that this requirement will be applied in exactly the same way in Europe, in Latin America, and in Africa, and in view of the very different conditions in which the legal systems function in those regions, such uniformity would hardly be appropriate.

Another example might be the prohibition on inhuman or degrading treatment or punishment which is common to all three of the regional conventions, as well as to the International Covenant on Civil and Political Rights. In a case in 1978, as noted earlier, the European Court held that this prohibition (which is in Article 3 of the European Convention) was contravened by the birching of a juvenile in the Isle of Man.[21] The decision was somewhat controversial in the European context and there is no reason to suppose that it would necessarily be followed elsewhere. Torture, which is also prohibited by Article 3, is a concept on which there is likely to be a large measure of agreement.[22] Inhuman or degrading treatment or punishment, on the other hand, particularly in the field of penal policy, is a matter on which one can expect to see greater differences of view.

So the qualification is that while interpretation of human rights obligations under one set of institutional arrangements may be significant and influential, it will not always be enough to produce this effect for provisions to be couched in similar terms, because the cultural or other factors which determine the interpretation and application of human rights in one setting may have no relevant counter-part elsewhere.

3. *The politics of human rights*

When asked about their attitudes towards human rights, individuals, and for that matter government spokesmen, will normally say that they are in favour. Conversely, it is very difficult to find anyone who will deny that human rights law is a good thing, or that the degree of protection available to those under threat is excessive and ought to be reduced. With so much apparent agreement about the importance of human rights, it is easy to think of this aspect of international law as somehow outside, or more accurately above, politics and to imagine it continuing to develop in a similar apolitical way. This would, however, be a serious mistake. Human rights issues are unavoidably political, and unless this is appreciated, neither the development of the law to date, nor the possibilities for growth in the future can be properly understood.

The political aspect of human rights can clearly be seen in the historic formulations of civil and political rights on which so many of the texts we have been considering are based. When Locke wrote his *Second Treatise of Civil Government*, and Rousseau his *Social Contract*, they were well aware that they were not just discussing the moral relationship between ruler and ruled, but dealing with issues of the utmost political importance. In a similar way, when governments subscribe to human rights treaties, they know that they are endorsing a certain set of political values and will be expected to implement them. Ratifying a human rights treaty is therefore more than a moral gesture. It is a recognition of the special status of certain ideals, with the political expectations which that creates.

Since the acceptance of legal obligations in this, as in other fields, changes the contours of the political landscape, it is not surprising that governments approach the negotiation of a human rights treaty with these considerations firmly in mind. When dealing with the background to the various conventions, we have described, at what may have seemed tedious length, some intricate and extended processes of drafting and negotiation. No apology is made for this because understanding that human rights texts do not spring into existence overnight, but are the outcome of political assessment and bargaining, is a major step to appreciating their real significance.

The political importance of the decision to treat a matter as an issue of human rights is something we have encountered throughout this book. The inclusion in the United Nations Covenants of the right to self-determination and the right to dispose of natural wealth and resources was part of the campaign which the developing States had been pursuing on these issues for many years. Likewise, the omission from the Covenant on Civil and Political Rights of any mention of a right to property stemmed from the unwillingness of many of the same States to see this right guaranteed. The European Convention, on the other hand, does protect the right to property in its First Protocol, but contains no guarantees as regards the right to divorce, or the right of access to the civil service. As in the case of the Covenant, these omissions are deliberate.[23]

The political content of human rights is also apparent in the way particular rights are defined. Although the European Convention recognises the right of property, it does so in terms which provide the State with a far greater measure of control than Locke would have thought acceptable. This is because in the 300 years since Locke ideas about the role of the State and the sanctity of property have changed. This change is reflected in the Convention, which permits States to make compulsory purchase orders, establish programmes of nationalisation, or restrict property rights in other ways, so long as certain safeguards are observed.

So far we have been indicating the political content of the substantive guarantees to be found in human rights treaties. If we turn to another feature of such instruments, their means of implementation, the political aspect of human rights is even more conspicuous. Providing a treaty with means of implementation acknowledges that human rights are a matter on which the State is accountable to an outside body. As such, the decision is one with major political implications, as is apparent in the way governments have often resisted the creation of implementation machinery by invoking the concepts of domestic jurisdiction and national sovereignty.

Assuming means of implementation are acceptable in principle, the next question is the form which they should take. Here the political issue is the extent to which governments are prepared to have their laws and practices subjected to independent scrutiny. The variety of means of implementation which we have encountered demonstrates the range of attitudes on this question. It is significant, for example, that none of the many human rights treaties sponsored by the United Nations provides for the independent judicial supervision which we find in both the European and Inter-American Conventions. To be sure, judicial supervision is not always appropriate, but another feature of United Nations procedures is a marked preference for entrusting supervision to bodies such as the Commission on Human Rights, composed of the representatives of States and consequently lacking independence. This is not an invariable practice of course. The Human Rights Committee, the Committee on the Elimination of Discrimination against Women, and the newly formed Committee on Economic, Social and Cultural Rights are, it will be recalled, all independent bodies. We have seen, however, that their powers are severely circumscribed, which confirms States' reluctance to submit themselves to independent scrutiny.

The contrast, it should be emphasised, is not between arrangements for supervision which have been influenced by political considerations and those which have not. For all arrangements for implementing human rights are, like the rights themselves, the reflection of political decisions. Rather, the contrast is between means of implementation which are structured in a way calculated to further the protection of human rights and those which are not. The European Convention, with its optional provisions relating to individual petitions and the jurisdiction of the Court, its filtering of applications by the Commission and its provisions for friendly settlement, points very clearly to the political factors which governments have in mind when devising implementation machinery. Unlike most States, however, the members of the Council of Europe were fully committed to protecting rights and therefore prepared to set up an effective system.

If politics is a prominent consideration when rights are being formulated and procedures for implementation being devised, it might also be expected to be relevant at the level of practice. This is so, and in a wider way than might be anticipated. The influence of politics on the application and interpretation of human rights by organs made up of the representatives of States scarcely needs reiteration. As we saw in Chapter 3, the work of the Commission on Human Rights, whether under the Resolution 1503 procedure, or in its other activities, is to a large extent conditioned by political considerations. States with political influence, or with powerful friends, can use this to avoid investigation or, if this has already started, can try to bring it to a halt before anything has been achieved. By the same token States which are politically isolated can be the object of both investigation and political pressure. Although in this second case the effect is to promote human rights, and is therefore to be encouraged, no one would pretend that a forum in which some States are more equal than others is anything other than a political body.

What is perhaps not so obvious is that there is a sense in which organs like the European Court of Human Rights and the Human Rights Committee, though independent, also act politically. We do not, of course, mean that the individuals who sit on these bodies take instructions from governments, or are influenced in their decisions by the identity of the respondent. Nor do we mean simply that they act politically in the sense that everyone who is part of a legal order can be said to act politically in carrying out his or her official functions. While that is certainly true, there is a more specific sense in which human rights organs act politically which derives from the functions they are required to perform.

Becoming a party to a treaty like the European Convention is rather like adopting a written constitution with judicial supervision. The effect is to give judges, or their equivalent, the final word on many highly political issues. It is no longer enough, therefore, for the legislature or executive to believe that a certain measure is desirable or necessary. If it can be challenged as an invasion of rights, it is for the judges to rule on whether it is permitted. This, it need hardly be pointed out, is to transfer political power from one set of institutions to another. As such, it invests the courts with a role very different from that which they have under a system of parliamentary sovereignty and, as controversies over appointments to the Supreme Court of the United States regularly remind us, places them very firmly on the political stage.

The relevance of all this to the work of human rights tribunals can readily be demonstrated by considering some of their more controversial cases. Issues such as telephone tapping, the control of immigration, the detention of suspected terrorists, and the regulation of homosexuality pose sensitive and highly controversial questions. In entrusting the final decision on these matters to international bodies, the parties to instruments like the European Convention are relinquishing an important part of their political sovereignty.

Appreciating the political role which bodies such as the European Court of Human Rights are required to play not only helps us to understand why States are often reluctant to entrust international bodies with such powers, but also enables us to see what they are doing in better perspective. One example must suffice. Consider the scope of the margin of appreciation doctrine under the European Convention on Human Rights. Here the issue is often debated in terms of a wider or a narrower interpretation of the individual's rights. Since most commentators are in favour of extending individual rights, decisions are praised or condemned according to whether they grant the respondent a narrow or a broad margin of appreciation. This, however, overlooks what is also at stake in these cases, namely the question of how much power the Strasbourg organs should have vis-à-vis the member States. This is a political issue which must be registered before the margin of appreciation question can be properly evaluated. There is actually no contradiction between believing, on the one hand, that individual rights are important, and on the other, that national parliaments enjoy a legitimate area of political authority which international institutions should respect. There can, of course, be differences of opinion about what the precise roles of national and international bodies are, but to see this as the question, rather than the scope of individual rights, one first needs to recognise the political significance of the European Court.[24]

A final word about the political dimension of human rights may be useful to avoid misunderstanding. Nothing which has been said here is intended to suggest that the moral dimension of human rights is unimportant. Similarly, we are not suggesting that because human rights have a political aspect, they do not also have a distinct legal aspect. Our point is simply that in studying human rights the legal, the moral, and the political aspect are all important. Like an apprentice steeple-jack, we shall not get far if we concentrate on the first and second, and ignore the third dimension.

4. *The theory of human rights*

In our discussion so far we have seen how international action relating to human rights has grown and is continuing to develop, how one result of these processes has been the emergence of something which can truly be described as international human rights law, and how all of this has been shaped by, and at the same time influences, international and domestic politics. The point which must now be considered, and the question with which it is perhaps appropriate to conclude this survey, is the role of theory in relation to this part of international law.

Is theory important? Some will say that it is, because until we have a proper theory there can be no plan and until we have a plan there can be no action, or at least no rational action. On this view a coherent theory is an indispensable prerequisite of measures to protect human rights internationally or, for that matter, at the domestic level. Others, however, will maintain that action comes first and theory later. On this view theory is not important because its function is merely to rationalise what is already happening. Needless to say, those who adopt this approach are not much interested in theory and, viewing the subject as of minor importance, may regard it as wholly academic, or a waste of time.

If it were necessary to choose between these two ways of thinking about theory, or more accurately between a way of thinking about theory and a way of not thinking about it, our choice would be impossible. For though neither is wholly correct, each is making a point about the relation between action and its justification which is important generally and has a direct bearing on the development and future of the law.

The idea that human rights law should develop in accordance with a theoretical plan, from which presumably it follows that nothing should be done until such a plan has been formulated, in present circumstances is clearly a prescription for total inaction. There are, as we have seen, different ways of thinking about human rights in theoretical terms which reflect different historical traditions, different cultural perspectives, and different political priorities.[25] If it had been necessary to accommodate these differences within a grand theoretical framework as a precondition of formulating legal texts, then the instruments described in earlier chapters would never have appeared. In this sense it is true that action can, and does, precede theoretical explanation and that to a degree theory stems from practice and not the other way round.

It is, however, one thing to say that theory is shaped by practice and another matter entirely to imagine that practice occurs in a theoretical vacuum. On the contrary, since the actions of governments, committees, commissions and courts are shaped by beliefs, the theories which people hold on human rights have a major effect on the way the law develops. Sometimes this will be obvious as when, for instance, a text emerges from a clash of opposing views. Sometimes, on the other hand, the significance of beliefs will be hidden because they are so widely shared as to be taken for granted. In the second case, however, the beliefs are still important and can usually be exposed with an appropriate strategy. Thus, the theoretical assumptions behind the European Convention on Human Rights stand out sharply when we compare it with an instrument such as the African Charter which reflects a different theory. The theory behind the European Convention is, of course, that of the Western democratic tradition. In fact, however, all human rights texts reflect theoretical assumptions of some description. Just as individuals who profess themselves uninterested in theory nevertheless have a set of beliefs which influence their behaviour, so human rights texts may not always have as clear and coherent a theoretical base as the European Convention, but could not have been devised without theoretical assumptions of some kind in the minds of the negotiators.

In studying human rights law, then, we are necessarily studying legal theory. While we can describe what has been done without having first developed a comprehensive theoretical framework, we can certainly not claim to understand it unless we appreciate that at each stage of its development the law of human rights has reflected ideas about what should be done, which rest either explicitly or implicitly on theories about human rights.

Although this book is primarily concerned with the practice of human rights, many theoretical issues have been touched on in the previous pages. Thus, we have considered the relation between civil and political rights on the one hand, and economic, social and cultural rights on the other. At various points we have also discussed the relation between individual rights, which are where the theory of human rights began, and the idea of collective rights, which originated with the concept of self-determination and has now been extended in the African Charter to include a number of other peoples' rights. It will be recalled that the African Charter also introduces the concept of duties, an idea which is, of course, a familiar one in political and moral philosophy, but which had not hitherto been prominent in a human rights text. The questions posed by the concept of duties are a reminder that even in a field where the theoretical ground is well trodden, there can be room for a fresh analysis.

The development of the law poses further theoretical problems. As we have explained, recognising rights of one type may not be compatible with recognising rights of another type. Thus, steps to eliminate discrimination based on sex may transgress religious or cultural precepts, respect for which is also guaranteed. Since it is impossible to ensure both, which is to be preferred? Is the answer here the concept of a hierarchy of human rights,[26] a concept which besides resolving the conflict between different rights, might also explain why some rights cannot be limited, even in a public emergency, while others can?

Finally, there is the issue touched on in Chapter 7, namely the question of when a matter of international concern can appropriately be treated as an issue of human rights. Rights are a vital concept, but even when supplemented by the concept of duties, are not a suitable vehicle for handling every issue. If we insist on translating all issues into the language of human rights, we not only trivialise this language, but also fail to use the resources of the law to their full potential. While there is therefore no reason to regard the scope of human rights law as fixed for all time in its present configuration, before adding new rights we should be clear about what we are doing because the price of failure to do so – of failure, that is, to think clearly about theoretical issues – is likely to be high. For here, as elsewhere, although the issues are theoretical, they must not be thought of as academic or inconsequential. On the contrary, because ideas about human rights influence the way the law develops, theoretical assumptions have immediate and practical consequences and are a critical influence on its future.

5. Conclusion

As we said at the beginning of this book, our aim has been, while recognising the lamentable state of human rights in many parts of the world, to show that more and more people are aware of this situation and are endeavouring to do something about it. The period over which this new edition was in preparation has provided ample confirmation of both assertions. Reports presented to the Commission on Human Rights and the General Assembly of the United Nations, the investigations of the Inter-American Commission on Human Rights into the situation in certain countries of Latin America, evidence produced to the Conference on Security and Co-operation in Europe about the treatment of ethnic and national minorities in Eastern Europe, and the reports of Amnesty International, all confirm the picture of systematic and repeated violations in many countries. On the other hand, the fact that these reports are made and widely publicised, the debates and discussions which follow their publication, and the number of people concerned with these problems in international organisations, national and international parliamentary bodies and non-governmental organisations demonstrate that people do care about human rights. The mounting pressure of public opinion in the years to come will continue to have an effect in persuading or shaming governments which systematically violate human rights to improve their behaviour. In this struggle international organisations and international lawyers have a particularly important role to play, one might say a special responsibility. The Universal Declaration called on every individual and every organ of society to 'strive by teaching and education to promote respect for these rights and freedoms and ... to secure their universal and effective recognition and observance'. If this book can make a modest contribution in helping them to do so, by explaining the international arrangements which exist, the factors which influence the development of human rights law and the deficiencies which should be remedied, then it will have achieved its object.

Notes

1 However, it is important that as regards both substantive and procedural issues the negotiation of new treaties takes place with sufficient attention to existing arrangements. Since the United Nations is the major source of new human rights instruments, its approach to international law-making is particularly critical. For an incisive appraisal of current practice in this regard, see T. Meron, *Human Rights Law-Making in the United Nations*, Oxford, 1986 and *idem*, 'Reform of lawmaking in the United Nations: the human rights instance', *American Journal of International Law*, LXXIX, 1985, p. 664.

2 For some valuable suggestions on this issue, see D. Weissbrodt, 'A new United Nations mechanism for encouraging the ratification of human rights treaties', *American Journal of International Law*, LXXVI, 1982, p. 418.

3 See J. G. Merrills, *The Development of International Law by the European Court of Human Rights*, Melland Schill Monographs in International Law, Manchester University Press, 1988.

4 See P. Pescatore, 'The content and significance of fundamental rights in the law of the European Communities', *Human Rights Law Journal*, II, 1981, p. 295; M. H. Mendelson, 'The European Court of Justice and human rights', *Yearbook of European Law*, I, 1982, p. 125; M. B. Akehurst, 'The application of general principles of law by the Court of Justice of the European Communities', *British Year Book of International Law*, LII, 1981, p. 29 and L. Marcoux, 'The concept of fundamental rights in European Economic Community Law', *Georgia Journal of International and Comparative Law*, XIII, 1983, p. 667.

5 See the *Other Treaties case*, Series A, No. 1, para. 40. Text in *Human Rights Law Journal*, III, 1982, p. 140.

6 For comparison of the various texts, see P. Sieghart, *The International Law of Human Rights*, Oxford, 1983; for discussion of the judicial contribution to the process, see Merrills, *Development of International Law*, *passim*.

7 Series A, No. 82.

8 The provision continues, '... in the interest of national security, public safety or public order, or to protect public health or morals or the rights or freedoms of others'.

9 These provide respectively that 'No one may, subject to law and order, be submitted to measures restricting the exercise of these freedoms' and that 'The exercise of this right shall be subject only to necessary restrictions provided for by law . . .'. It will be recalled, however, that the restrictions permitted by certain other articles of the Charter appear to be more far-reaching, see Chapter 6, section II, 2.
10 Emphasis added.
11 See the *Licensing of Journalism case*, Series A, No. 5, para. 46 (the European Court's interpretation of 'necessary' is 'equally applicable' to the American Convention, though note the qualification in para. 50 concerning the scope of the right to freedom of expression under the two conventions). Text in *Human Rights Law Journal*, VII, 1986, p. 74. See also the *Proposed Amendments case*, Series A, No. 4, para. 62, where the Court recognised the concept of the margin of appreciation. For text see *ibid.*, V, 1984, p. 161. For further discussion of these cases, see Chapter 5.
12 See Article 8(1) and Article 14(1) respectively.
13 *Campbell and Fell case*, Series A, No. 80.
14 *Engel case*, Series A, No. 22.
15 *Oztürk case*, Series A, No. 73.
16 Series A, No. 6.
17 Series A, No. 4, para. 56. Note also the points made about some of the decisions of the Human Rights Committee in Chapter 2.
18 Series A, No. 70.
19 See Merrills, *Development of International Law*, pp. 198–9.
20 *Pretto case*, Series A, No. 71. See Merrills, *ibid.*, pp. 201–2. The corresponding provision of the Covenant is Article 14(1).
21 *Tyrer case*, Series A, No. 26.
22 There was some disagreement on this concept in the European Court in the *Irish case*, Series A, No. 25. However, as torture has since been defined in both the United Nations and Inter-American conventions, albeit in slightly different terms, there is now less chance of this occurring.
23 See the Court's comment on these omissions in, respectively the *Johnston case*, Series A, No. 112, para. 52 and the *Kosiek case*, Series A, No. 105, para. 34.
24 See further Merrills, *Development of International Law*, Chapter 7.
25 For further discussion of this issue, see J. J. Shestack, 'The jurisprudence of human rights', in T. Meron (ed.), *Human Rights in International Law*, Oxford, 1984, pp. 69–114 and E. Kamenka and A. E.-S. Tay, *Human Rights*, London, 1978.
26 See T. Meron, 'On a hierarchy of international human rights', *American Journal of International Law*, LXXX, 1986, p. 1.

Index